# TAKING STOCK

## Scottish social welfare after devolution

John Stewart

First published in Great Britain in September 2004 by

The Policy Press
University of Bristol
Fourth Floor
Beacon House
Queen's Road
Bristol BS8 1QU
UK

Tel +44 (0)117 331 4054
Fax +44 (0)117 331 4093
e-mail tpp-info@bristol.ac.uk
www.policypress.org.uk

British Library Cataloguing in Publication Data
A catalogue record for this book is available from the British Library.

Library of Congress Cataloging-in-Publication Data
A catalog record for this book has been requested.

ISBN 1 86134 523 2 paperback

**John Stewart** is Principal Lecturer in History in the Centre for Health, Medicine and Society: Past and Present, Oxford Brookes University, UK.

Cover design by Qube Design Associates, Bristol.
*Front cover:* photograph supplied by kind permission of *The Scotsman.*
Printed and bound in Great Britain by Hobbs the Printers Ltd, Southampton.

# Contents

# Acknowledgements

Steven King, Martin Powell and David Williams constructively criticised earlier drafts of various chapters. Two anonymous referees for The Policy Press gave invaluable advice which I hope I have, at least in part, been able to incorporate. The response to a paper I gave at the University of Bath in November 2003 was helpful in clarifying, in particular, my overall conclusions about Scottish social welfare since devolution. Margaret Curran MSP, Scottish Minister for Communities, agreed to meet with me in October 2003, and I am grateful to her for putting aside time in this way. Dawn Rushen and her colleagues at The Policy Press have been models of professionalism. The History Department at Oxford Brookes University afforded me sabbatical leave to put together this work. Finally, my long-suffering family – Sue, Neil and Jim – have patiently put up with my repeated bouts of anxiety during the origin and creation of this book.

# ONE

# Introduction: welfare and devolution

In May 1999, for the first time in 300 years, elections were held for a Scottish Parliament. This body, to be located at Holyrood in Edinburgh, had a remit that consisted largely of powers in the area of social welfare. As we shall see, much of the argument for political devolution had revolved around social policy concerns. Elections to the Scottish Parliament, in 1999 and again in 2003, have resulted in the return of a Labour–Liberal Democrat coalition. Both these parties had been, and continue to be, leading advocates of devolution. Their declared aim in government was to reform and improve public services, if necessary by following a rather different path from that of the London government, and thereby to show that devolution could and would make a difference in real terms to the lives of the Scottish people. Devolution could thus bring, in a much-used phrase, Scottish solutions to Scottish problems. The implicit and explicit contrast here was with the alleged neglect, and indeed undermining, of social welfare in Scotland by the UK's Conservative administrations of the 1980s and 1990s.

This book examines the specifically Scottish aspects of social welfare since devolution, focusing primarily on the role of the Scottish Executive – put crudely, Scotland's government. Much fine work has been done on both the historical and the contemporary dimensions of social policy in Scotland, and this is extensively drawn upon. Nonetheless, there have been few attempts to paint a larger picture, a surprising situation given the long-standing significance of social welfare to a large number of Scots. The former is partly explicable by the understandable historical and sociological attention given to questions of nationhood, identity and class[1]. Equally, many works of social science, social policy, and the history of social welfare that purport to deal with Great Britain in fact focus almost exclusively on England (see, for example, Stewart, 1999)[2]! This work addresses this absence and in so doing focuses on two broad areas that have had, and continue to have, identifiably Scottish characteristics: children, education and lifelong learning (Chapter Four) and health policy (Chapter Five). Context is provided by this introduction, which describes the historical and contemporary environment in which Scottish social welfare policy is formulated and implemented. Chapter Two focuses on funding and expenditure priorities, while Chapter Three deals with poverty, inequality and social disadvantage. Chapter Six draws some broad conclusions about the recent development, and future trajectory, of the Scottish welfare state.

Given the areas covered in Chapters Four and Five, it will be evident that this work is consciously partial in its approach Social work, in general a much under-researched area of social policy, Scottish or otherwise, is dealt with tangentially by way of policies directed at children and at old people (for a brief general discussion of post-devolution policies, see Waterhouse and McGhee, 2002). Furthermore, this volume does not deal with social housing. At first sight, this might seem especially surprising given the qualitative and quantitative impact of local authority housing on 20th-century Scotland, an impact that crucially shaped people's lives, the urban landscape and local politics. State intervention in the housing market was in itself a reaction to the country's notorious housing problems. The Scottish Executive has certainly not been inactive in the housing field. Scottish Homes, the housing development body, has been reconstituted in the form of Communities Scotland as an Executive agency and with a wider brief, most notably in regeneration to be carried out through by a partnership between pubic and private sectors. The 2001 Housing (Scotland) Act dealt, among other issues, with homelessness and the right to buy. The present omission of housing is partly for reasons of space but also, more importantly and much more fundamentally, because of the change in patterns of home occupation that have taken place in Scotland over the past quarter of a century, changes that predate devolution. Homeowners are now in the majority and local authority house building is insignificant when compared with its post-war scale and peak. Executive policy thus encourages local authorities, for example, to move social housing to other providers, especially housing associations (Kearns and Parkes, 2003, pp 49-52). What is taking place is a form of devolution within devolution, with the overall effect of a fundamental shift away from the state – local or central – as a large-scale landlord.

Welfare policy determined by the British, rather than the Scottish, Parliament is likewise omitted from this book. Three important points need to be made. First, the absence of any direct discussion of, especially, social security and macro-economic policy does not imply their irrelevance to social welfare in Scotland – far from it. Nonetheless, it is the case that these areas are determined by the London Parliament operating on a UK-wide basis. Second, the broad areas of education and health are, I contend, at the heart of the Executive's programme and take up a significant proportion of its budget. They are also the principal concerns of the Scottish electorate, as polling evidence shows. Moreover, given the all-embracing nature of the Scottish social welfare strategy, we shall see that the terms 'education' and 'health' do not of themselves adequately describe the Executive's welfare ambitions. Third, while an emphasis on Scottish particularity is consciously and primarily at the core of this book, there is nonetheless no intention that this be seen in isolation. At various points, the extent of policy divergence is addressed, which of itself raises important issues, for instance, about the tension between social citizenship and federalism. The former emphasises uniformity of welfare provision, the latter diversity. As we shall see in Chapter Five, free personal care to the elderly in Scotland has become a case in point. This in turn raises the question, dealt with more fully in Chapter Six, of whether devolved administrations are now defenders of the welfare state, or at least of the classic welfare state of the post-war era.

Underpinning this work is the contention that contemporary Scottish social welfare must be placed in a longer historical context. We need an understanding of:

- Scottish particularities in social policy;
- what political devolution involved;
- how, if at all, politics differed and differ north of the border from the situation in, especially, England;
- how, broadly speaking, this has impacted on social welfare;
- and thus where devolution and welfare reform stand at the point of writing (late 2003/early 2004).

These considerations constitute the remainder of this chapter.

## Scotland and social welfare: from Union to devolution

As Timmins (2001, p 589) comments, even prior to devolution there had always existed some "subtle and not-so-subtle differences ... in welfare state services between Scotland and England". To understand why, we have to go back to the 1707 Union of the English and Scottish Parliaments. Under the terms of the Union, Scotland lost her parliament while retaining control over key areas of civil society: religion, local government, the law, education and social welfare. It was here that what Paterson has famously described as the "autonomy of modern Scotland" was to be found – hence his comment that:

> Scottish autonomy and the Scottish welfare state have been inseparable, each inconceivable in its present form without the other. (Paterson, 1994, passim; Paterson, 1997, p 55)

The recognition of this autonomy increasingly led historians and political scientists to question whether the UK had ever been, even prior to 1997, a unitary state (Kellas, 1989, p 1).

The setting up of the Scottish Office in 1885 further enhanced Scottish autonomy. This was a territorial rather than functional body (unlike, therefore, most other British government departments), with omnibus powers (that is, powers that in England are dispersed among several departments), and with historically a strong propensity to centralisation and intervention. Around the same time, the post of Scottish Secretary was revived. Although this body and this post have been superseded by the Scottish Executive and its First Minister, historically their very existence helped maintain a distinctively Scottish form of governance, largely concerned with social welfare. The significance of the long-standing autonomy of key social welfare provision, and of a significant degree of administrative autonomy, are evident enough in themselves; however, the other parts of civil society left in Scottish hands also impacted upon social policy formation and implementation. Scots law, for example, is historically and philosophically different form the Anglo-American model and has been more inclined to social interventionism than its English, common-law counterpart (Meston et al, 1991). More prosaically, the existence of a separate and distinctive body of law has often necessitated separate legislation.

Welfare autonomy – more accurately, *relative* autonomy (as we shall see, the Treasury and the London Parliament were never fully going to relinquish control) – persisted into the 20th century, reinforced by further administrative autonomy. All this should be placed in the context of a distinctively corporatist, consensual and centralising political culture (or, as critics would have it, cosy and complacent). Finlay (1994, pp 110-11) alerts us to the Scottish establishment's "close knitted interconnectedness" and how the Scottish Office's accumulation of power fitted well with "the established pattern of government by committee". It is worth emphasising that this approach was widely shared: one of its architects was Walter Elliot, an influential Conservative Scottish Secretary of State in the 1930s.

Paterson similarly finds, under the Union, a "pluralistic policy process and unified approach to social policy" which could be characterised as "Scottish social democratic unionism" (2000b, p 51). He also suggests that "civic republicanism" has been an influential part of Scottish political thought since the Enlightenment. One outcome of this has been, from the middle of the 20th century, "a quite uncritical faith in the state – not the UK state straightforwardly, but the Scottish quasi-state as embodied in and around the Scottish Office". The Scottish Parliament, he continues, "may simply reinforce these tendencies by giving that state greater legitimacy, coherence and power" (2000a, p 73). This, of course, can be seen as both positive and negative. Humes (1999, p 80), writing on the eve of the new parliament, argued that, despite the Scots' rather aggressive self-image, in education at least the "natural tendency" had always been to look to the centre for leadership, in the process showing "remarkable passivity in the face of professional and bureaucratic authority". This notion of a particularly Scottish view of governance and society recurs throughout this volume, with its more general implications being discussed in Chapter Six.

To give one instance of a distinctively Scottish policy development pre-devolution, the National Health Service (NHS) was introduced to Scotland under separate legislation passed in 1947 rather than 1946, as was the case for the rest of Great Britain, so illustrating both legislative requirements and differing historical paths. From the outset, the Scottish NHS was run separately and on more centralised lines than its southern counterpart, while at the same time often managing to gain a disproportionately high level of resources (Stewart, 2003). As we shall see in Chapter Five, this has had long-term implications. Cases such as this have been seen as deriving from a set of historical circumstances where, as Paterson puts it, the "setting up of the British welfare state from the 1920s to the 1940s (provoked) suspicion in Scotland that powers would be centralised in London". This may be rather overstated, although it is undoubtedly true that Scottish autonomy was jealously guarded where possible, but there was certainly a legacy of what Paterson again describes as a "more autonomous Scottish welfare state" (2000b, p 48) than might otherwise have been the case. In summary, in key areas of social welfare Scottish autonomy continued after the Union supported by legal, political, and administrative cultures that were, to varying degrees, distinctive.

On the other hand, what we also see in the course of the 20th century is a centralising tendency in British social welfare – an important constituent of the broader centralising tendency of the British state. Even the autonomy that Scotland enjoyed in certain welfare matters was double-edged: the Scottish NHS may indeed have had its own legislation and a significant level of self-governance, but in the last resort it relied on Treasury funding. While, as noted, the Scots tended to do disproportionately well in this area, Scottish politicians and officials were also aware that they could not press the particularist case too hard (Stewart, 2003). And of course, the NHS, whether in Scotland or elsewhere in the UK, had as its overarching aims the reduction of health inequities and inequalities and the provision of universal, comprehensive coverage paid for by general taxation. Even in a sphere where Scottish autonomy appeared traditionally strong – that is, education – commentators were by the 1990s pointing to convergence ('Englishing', as it was put by one authority) between Scotland and her southern neighbours (Littlewood, 1998, p 141). Scottish welfare autonomy, therefore, was not unqualified, nor was it immune to trends in the rest of the UK or, indeed, elsewhere.

## New Labour's welfare strategy

The 1997 General Election saw the installation of a New Labour administration. Scotland, however, had never fully bought into the Thatcherite project, remaining electorally loyal to the Labour Party throughout the 1980s and 1990s (Hutchison, 2001, epilogue, appendices I, II); and, in addition, was often portrayed as a bastion of Old Labour (an issue engaged with further in Chapter Six of this book). A brief discussion of New Labour is important for three reasons:

- its emphasis on welfare reform;
- its enactment of devolution;
- to provide the context for possible policy divergences between Labour in power in London and Labour in power in Edinburgh.

In 1997, Tony Blair's New Labour gained just over 44% of votes cast in Great Britain as a whole, a proportion that declined slightly to 42% in the 2001 General Election. For Scotland, the respective proportions were 45.6% and 44%. In Scotland the election issues were much as elsewhere. Parry (1998, p 198) claimed shortly afterwards that there was a pre-devolution paradox: that while social policy underpinning Scottish civil society, was the principal concern of the Scottish Office, and was the main area of debate in Scottish politics, nonetheless the "all-British political context and positions on the national question" were dominant at both national and local levels (Parry, 1998, pp 194-200; but see also Mooney and Johnstone, 2000, p 161).

The new government had a clear popular mandate and the benefit of, as Lowe points out, a "revived economy, with a growth rate higher than all Britain's major competitors" (Lowe, 1999, p 308). It had, furthermore, "inherited a radically restructured range of (welfare) services and the popular support they still continued to command" (Lowe, 1999, p 341). It was in these circumstances that New Labour began its welfare reforms, formulated in the party's long period in opposition. Modernisers such as Blair had sought to create a new form of politics that would, famously and in the event successfully, appeal to Middle England. New Labour would thus move away from what were seen as outdated and inflexible ideologies, hence the famous Third Way, a term also used by other European social democratic parties that, like Labour, had been out of office for some time (Clasen, 2002, p 67). This new strategy can be summarised as follows.

First, the days of the "classic welfare state" (Digby, 1989), built on the twin foundations of Keynes and Beveridge, were gone and thus, implicitly, the kind of universalism associated with the post-1945 social settlement. As Blair rather brutally put it in 1997, the "Keynsian post war consensus is over" (quoted in Wickham-Jones, 2003, p 36). Welfare reform – 'reform' is a key word and concept for New Labour – was of itself "one of the fundamental objectives" of the New Labour project. This was a view held not least by Gordon Brown, who saw himself as "the overlord of welfare reform", the essence of which was "means-testing by any other name" (Rawnsley, 2001, pp 110, 111). Brown's views were particularly important in that his early relinquishing of the day-to-day control of interest rates meant a fundamental shift in the Treasury's functions – from macro-economic management to domestic policy, and especially welfare. In turn, this was part of a broader New Labour approach that "large chunks of social policy were in fact an integral part of economic policy" (Timmins, 2001, p 611).

There has been much debate over the precise extent to which New Labour has succumbed in welfare policy to some or most of Thatcherism and rejected its own ideological roots. For Wickham-Jones, by 1997 New Labour had "retreated from any broad commitment to universal benefits provided as rights of citizenship". Its approach was now characterised by "remedialism and resignation" in the face of the allegedly inevitable processes of globalisation and an acceptance of the capitalist free market (Wickham-Jones, 2003, p 30 and passim). Timmins (2001, p 602), reviewing New Labour's first term, suggests that in welfare there were significant elements of continuity with the previous Conservative administrations, especially in social security where "Beveridge's argument for universality had finally been lost". The issue is almost certainly more problematic than this, but there can be little doubt that since the early 1990s welfare reform has been, as Driver and Martell (2002, p 182) put it, "at the heart of the Centre-Left's search for a new middle way between post-war social democracy and Thatcherite Conservatism".

For New Labour, an important component of welfare strategy had been the enhancment of human capital – in Esping-Andersen's phrase, "welfare as investment" (Esping-Andersen et al, 2002, p 9). In seeking to improve human capital, the "key force", according to Third Way proponent Anthony Giddens (2000, p 73), "obviously has to be education" (see also Chapter Four of this book). Another important Third Way characteristic is paid employment (as opposed to state benefits) as the best way out of poverty and, related to this, an acknowledgement of the rights of welfare consumers coupled with an emphasis on their duties and responsibilities. The family too receives considerable emphasis in Blairite welfare rhetoric, as do other non-state mechanisms, most importantly the market and private enterprise. What is important is what works, not ideology (although as Chapter Four of this book notes, this pragmatic approach is not as value-free as it purports to be). The operations of the market more generally are to be encouraged rather than constrained. A further end of welfare reform was to combat social exclusion, a phenomenon that embraced more than simply income poverty. Key to achieving this was unified and coordinated activity across government departments. Given the rejection of universalism, what this further implied was the targeting for attention of particular groups and individuals. Indeed 'target', both in the sense of things to be achieved and of objects of focused government attention, was to be another key word in the New Labour welfare lexicon.

Later chapters of this book examine the extent to which these objectives have been addressed in specific areas of post-devolution Scottish welfare policy. From the outset, however, we need to acknowledge welfare reform's significance for New Labour and its attempts to break with what it saw as a dirigiste welfare system. Such a system, for Blairite critics, entailed high levels of public expenditure; overly centralised control; the precedence of the producers of welfare, and unconditional rights; and demand-side economic management techniques. Prudence, Gordon Brown's famous friend, was put in charge of economic thought and deed, most famously in the commitment to stick in the first instance to the public expenditure plans of his Conservative predecessors. This was a strategy that had profound implications for social welfare and precipitated the government's first serious revolt, in late 1997, over benefits to single mothers, in itself a serious questioning of the place of universality in New Labour's plans (Rawnsley, 2001, p 111ff).

The rejection of the Keynes/Beveridge paradigm is part of a wider, post-industrial questioning of post-war social welfare regimes (Esping-Andersen, 1999). Related to this has been the phenomenon of social democracy examining its fundamental principles, resulting in turn in welfare restructuring being most systematically undertaken by parties purportedly of the social democratic left (Clasen, 2002, passim). As Wickham-Jones (2003, p 28) points out, as early as the 1970s, the welfare state – "the centerpiece of many social democratic reformist initiatives" – was for many no longer the solution to economic difficulties but rather their "direct and significant cause". Transnational information exchange has been an important aspect of this re-evaluation. New

Labour thinkers were clearly influenced by the American New Democrat agenda, which famously sought to end welfare as we know it (O'Connor, 2001, ch 11). Similarly, social exclusion as a concept originated in France before being adopted by the EC (Timmins, 2001, p 566; see also, for further instances, Giddens, 2000, p 30ff). At a high level of abstraction, there has thus been a trend towards convergence based on the importance of work as the route out of poverty; the role of the family; and a shift away from simply the passive receipt of welfare benefits. At an even higher (although probably meaningless) level of abstraction, we have the famous assertion by Giddens (2000, p 103) that the "need to reform welfare systems is a key part of third way political philosophy".

## New Labour and devolution

New Labour came to power promising political devolution to Scotland and Wales. The concept of devolution, however, has more than a simply territorial dimension. Bodies such as the Scottish Executive have sought to devolve powers to frontline staff in areas such as health, in this case with much being made of the rejection of the supposed command and control version of the NHS. For the moment, however, we focus on creation of a Scottish Parliament by the first New Labour government.

The Prime Minister appears to have gone down the devolution road somewhat reluctantly. He might, that said, find intellectual sustenance in his guru Giddens, who has recently supported devolution as a means of rebuilding civil society and an accompanying stable and rooted sense of self (Giddens, 2000, p 63). More immediately, Blair has little sense of the intricacies of Scottish politics and apparently little empathy with the country itself, a view that may well be reciprocated (Rawnsley, 2001, pp 236, 241ff). Nonetheless, he is a shrewd political operator. As Driver and Martell (2002, p 152) observe, Blair made a point, in a 1998 speech in Glasgow, of responding to the challenge of the pro-independence Scottish National Party (SNP) and the "centrifugal political forces unleashed by devolution". He did so by "asserting a sense of Britishness rooted in values and institutions such as social justice and the welfare state, likely to go down well with a Scottish audience". This was indeed a clever move, as well as a rather different message to that being sent to Middle England. As Paterson (2000a, p 74) points out, an important part of the Scots' "inheritance from Britain" is "a firm belief in public welfare as a means to promote equality"; hence, he suggests, "one of the reasons why Scots do remain attached to Britain – a sense that many supposedly Scottish values are in fact British". We might also note here that during its long period in the political wilderness, Labour in Scotland was able to present itself as the "natural protector of 'traditional' Scottish values and institutions – in the sense that the party sought to defend the post-1945 Welfare State" (Hutchison, 2001, p 148). The use of 'defend' is significant here. While Blair and his colleagues in England were rethinking the Keynes/Beveridge paradigm, it was being, on this account, upheld in Scotland. Again, this is discussed more fully in Chapter Six of this book.

## Enacting devolution

Whatever the Prime Minister's true feelings for the country in which he was (privately) schooled, soon after the 1997 General Election the government published a devolution White Paper. In Scotland this was followed, in September 1997 and at Blair's insistence, by a two-question referendum. This asked whether there should be a Scottish Parliament; and, if so, whether such a body should have tax-raising powers. The percentage of votes cast in favour of these propositions was, respectively, 74.3 and 63.5. Consequently, there followed the 1998 Scotland Act, which laid down the powers of the new parliament. As Lynch (2001, ch 2) remarks, these powers were in fact "implicit rather than explicit": using the precedent of the 1920 Government of Ireland Act, the Scotland Act was more concerned with what the parliament could not do than with what it could (Paterson et al, 2001, chs 1 and 2; for a practical guide to the parliament, see Hassan, 1999).

Six points stand out:

1. The UK Parliament remains sovereign and has the right to overrule the Scottish Parliament. It could do so if, for example, any proposed Scottish legislation would adversely affect a law that was covered by London's reserved powers. Scottish law – like UK law – must also conform to EC law. New Labour, at both British and Scottish levels, has repeatedly asserted its commitment to the integrity of the Union. The Parliament itself has a fixed term of office of four years[3] and is a unicameral body; that is, there is no revising chamber. Elections to it involve an element of proportional representation.

2. Certain powers are reserved to London, for our purposes the most important being macro-economic management and social security. The latter is particularly interesting: there was never any intention of it being devolved and current Scottish ministers seem uninterested in it being so. Nonetheless, there is, in the case of Northern Ireland, a precedent for exactly this sort of devolution. As Parry (1997, pp 38, 46) pointed out at the time, reserving social security was "not inevitable" – there were historic precedents as well as that of Northern Ireland – and this "largely unthinking" decision was a "major constraint" on the new Parliament's sphere of action in the field of social policy. Laws passed in London, moreover, can impact on areas at first sight the exclusive reserve of Edinburgh. Lynch (2001) points to the example of the 1999 Immigration and Asylum Act, which altered the terms of, inter alia, the 1995 Children (Scotland) Act. Overall, and again quoting Parry (2002, p 315), devolved Scottish government is "a policy system with incomplete responsibilities", these being concerned with non-cash social services such as health and education.

3. The importance of the reserved powers notwithstanding, Edinburgh clearly has competence in major areas of welfare provision. This provides

opportunities for policy divergence from some or all of the rest of the UK, as we shall see.

4. Leading on from the previous point, commentators such as Mitchell et al (2003) have pointed to the legitimacy issue. They argue that, by the end of the 20th century, the Scottish Office's ability to act as if it had a popular mandate was increasingly called into question. The creation of a Scottish Parliament resolved this issue; they remark (2003, p 127) that "there can be little doubt that [policy] divergence has been more extensive" than under the Scottish Office. What devolution also allows for is the transfer of ideas and policies from countries other than England but still within the UK. It seems likely that this will become more pronounced as devolution further unfolds. Scottish ministers have spoken of looking not only to other parts of the UK but also to other small European nations such as the Republic of Ireland.

5. There is the question of money. This is dealt with more fully in Chapter Two, but here we should note that while the Edinburgh Parliament has the right to vary the rate of income tax by 3%, in effect it has, as Lynch (2001, p 23) puts it, "in reality no independent source of funds". It is thus primarily reliant on Treasury funding and the Barnett formula.

6. Leading on to our next section, devolution (as noted earlier) was increasingly seen as a way of allowing the Scots to resolve particularly Scottish concerns and so to make a difference (see also the similar rhetoric in Wales: Davies, 2003). Finlay (2001, p 248) has pointed to the paradox whereby, from around the 1980s, Scotland's socioeconomic profile increasingly came to resemble that of England, while at the same time the two countries were diverging politically. By the 1990s, there existed a strong body of opinion which sought greater autonomy from what was seen as an overbearing – and overbearingly Conservative – London-based political system.

## The elections to the Scottish Parliament 1999

Much of the argument for devolution revolved around not only Scotland voting Labour but still being governed by the Conservatives, but also the threat this seemed to pose to particularly Scottish institutions. An important body here was the broadly based Scottish Constitutional Convention (on which see Hutchison, 2001, pp 147-51), which had in part been stimulated by Thatcherite attacks on Scotland's alleged dependency culture. The convention, as Nottingham (2000, p 175) points out, in its discussions of health policy posited "a direct relationship between constitutional reform and good health policy"; rejected post-1979 health policies as addressing English, not Scottish, concerns; and saw the "intractability" of Scotland's health problems disappearing with the introduction of "democratic accountability and decentralisation" (see also Chapter Five of this book). Similar claims were made for education (see also Chapter Four). Scotland therefore engaged in a distinctive debate about welfare, and from the 1980s this "became the basis for a new Scottish nationalism – the now familiar claim that Scotland did not share the New Right preferences of Margaret Thatcher" (Paterson, 2000b, p 48). So, Parry (1998, p 213) argues, on the eve of devolution, "Scotland's welfare state remained more old-fashioned, better-resourced and less privatised than England's and those involved in it could see the way to a field of action in the Scottish Parliament".

The first election to the re-established Scottish Parliament was held on 6 May 1999. The campaign itself was relatively low key, although Labour fears about the SNP's challenge led to Brown taking control of strategy and attempting to bolster Donald Dewar (who was to be, until his untimely death, Scotland's first First Minister). This Brown did by, most notably, attacking Nationalist proposals for increases in public expenditure funded by tax rises (Rawnsley, 2001, pp 242, 251ff). In the end, as Lynch (2001, p 32) points out, the manifesto of the eventual and highly predictable winner, the Scottish Labour Party, was "extremely limited in terms of clear policy goals and financial commitments". It was made clear, for example, that Edinburgh's tax-raising power would not be invoked, so mirroring the Chancellor's macro-economic strategy and rebutting those who had raised fears about a tartan tax. Had a first-past-the-post election system been in place, the Labour Party would have had a clear overall majority of seats – and hence Members of the Scottish Parliament (MSPs). However, because of the element of proportional representation, this was not the case. Although the SNP had the second-largest number of MSPs, Labour went into coalition with the Liberal Democrats. The new First Minister, Jim Wallace, speedily (and under pressure from Blair) appointed the leader of the Liberal Democrats as his deputy. The latter dropped his condition for coalition that student fees be abolished in favour of a review of student finance (Rawnsley, 2001, p 254). Two Liberal Democrat cabinet ministers out of a total of 11 were also appointed. Clearly, then, the structure of the electoral system had important implications for the election outcomes – not only in political terms but also, by extension, in terms of what policies were, and were not, to be pursued (Paterson et al, 2001, ch 2; Denver, 2003, pp 173-5).

The actual government of Scotland lies with the Executive. This consists of both ministers and civil servants, the latter having been taken over directly from the Scottish Office while continuing to be part of the UK civil service. Both ministers and civil servants have been, by their own admission, on a steep learning curve since 1999. It was intended that the new system would be different from what was seen as the adversarial Westminster form of politics. For instance, emphasis was to be placed on consensus and consultation in policy formation, and we have already remarked on these as historic characteristics of Scottish governance. It is worth observing in this text how often the word 'partnership' occurs, whether to describe the relationship between Scotland and the rest of the UK, between Labour and the Liberal Democrats in their coalition, or more widely. Paterson (2000b, p 52) sees consultation as both "enshrined in [the Scottish Parliament's] founding principles" and, in his review of the Parliament's early life, a notable success, especially when compared with the non-consultative habits of recently preceding Conservative Scottish

Secretaries. A further aspect of this was the Committee system, designed as a counterbalance to the Executive itself. As Lynch (2001, p 2) puts it, the "unchallenged ability of civil servants and ministers to dominate policy has gone".

To this is it is worth adding that Scotland is, at least in population terms, a small country. Historically, the political and administrative classes have been drawn from a relatively small number of individuals, so allowing for, as we shall see at various points, a policy villages effect. This has also given pressure groups greater access to government than occurs in larger polities. Mitchell and Dorling (2002, p 175) suggest that, because of the very nature of their work, Scottish politicians routinely encounter a wide range of social experience. Consequently, devolved Scotland is "at a tremendous advantage in dealing with its own diversity". It is run by a relatively small group of individuals whose aim is to provide a "voice" across a range of constituents to whom they are democratically accountable. This is over-optimistic, but it does make a useful point about Scotland's relatively compact administrative and political classes.

The main opposition party in Scotland is not as in England (or, for that matter, the UK as a whole) the Conservative Party, but the SNP. While this party's principal aim is Scottish independence, it has over the past quarter of a century or so positioned itself on the political centre-left, and on at least some issues to the left of Labour. The former SNP leader Alex Salmond even claimed in 1999 that the Scots wanted to push beyond what New Labour was doing. In Scotland, the social democratic tradition was much stronger, and should Scotland eventually achieve independence "one cause will be New Labour's abandonment of social democracy" (quoted in Mooney and Johnstone, 2000, p 157). Despite (or because of) this, the Nationalists are Scottish Labour's main opponents and between the two parties there is little love lost. Playing on fears of tax rises and the economic implications of full independence as advocated by the SNP at the 1999 elections, Labour relentlessly stressed, and has continued to stress, that divorce is an expensive business. The existence of a large centre-left opposition party does not necessarily mean that Scotland is inherently more left-wing than, especially, England. Scottish Toryism was extremely powerful in the 1950s, for example, although we should also bear in mind the point noted earlier, its own strong tendency towards corporatism and consensualism. Parry (2002, p 318) still finds among post-devolution Conservatives "a residual attachment to Scottish collectivist welfare".

Nonetheless, the Scottish Parliament does tend to the political left, not only because of Labour and the SNP, but also because of the coalition partners, the Liberal Democrats, and the presence of smaller but vocal groups such as the Scottish Socialist Party. Add to this Labour's long-standing grip on Scottish politics, an element of scepticism within Scottish Labour about the Blair project, a scepticism signalled early on regarding the Private Finance Initiative (PFI) – since renamed Public Private Partnerships – and student fees (Rawnsley, 2001, p 241), and the very nature of the devolved powers themselves, and all this makes the Edinburgh Parliament, as Paterson et al remark (2001, p 142), "the focus of the politics of the welfare state in Scotland". The point about the differences in political outcomes does need to be emphasised. In Scotland, the elections of 1999 and 2003 produced coalition governments with Labour as the dominant party and the opposition coming primarily from the left. The British General Elections of 1997 and 2001 produced large majorities for one party, Labour, with the main political opposition coming from the right. Scottish politics is not only currently more inclined to the left; it has also, with its coalitions and plethora of small parties, experienced what Davies (2003, p 1) describes as "Europeanisation". In short, there are significant differences in political position and culture as well as political structure north and south of the border.

Given, therefore, Scotland's particular political and administrative approaches, its ability to shape at least some areas of its welfare provision, and the current overwhelming dominance of centre-left parties, is it the case that it is more inclined to a social democratic rather than Anglo-American liberal welfare regime (on welfare regimes see, in the first instance, Esping-Andersen, 1990 and 1999)? Fuller consideration is given to Scottish welfare distinctiveness and the underlying reasons for this in Chapter Six of this volume. Nonetheless, we can usefully cite here Paterson's (2002, passim) recent contrast between what he calls Scottish social democratic communitarianism (a social philosophy with deep and diverse historical roots and embracing both Presbyterianism and Catholic social thought) and Blair's individualistic version of liberalism. Again, this suggests the potential for differences between Scotland and, especially, England, and a particularist counterbalance to the alleged tidal waves of globalisation and welfare state convergence.

On the other hand, Mooney and Johnstone (2000, p 177) argued, shortly after the first elections to the Edinburgh Parliament, not only that Scottish Labour had "embraced Blairite thinking on poverty", but also that many architects of New Labourism were Scottish MPs and that, more broadly, the main Scottish parties seemed to be converging in their social and welfare policies. Such convergence was, they claimed, "characterized by a strong managerialism, an emphasis on individual responsibilities and opportunities and on the role of the private sector". While having significant elements of truth, this is, as we shall see, an overstated case. However, it does alert us to the fact that, as with all social policy and historical analysis, there is ample scope for differences of interpretation, not least because of the ambiguities, tensions and contradictions in much welfare policy and rhetoric.

## New Labour's constitutional and welfare reforms

What, then, have analysts made of New Labour's constitutional and welfare reforms? On devolution, Driver and Martell (2002) comment that it has reinforced regional and national identities, so bringing into question New Labour's ability to deliver a New Britain and opening up opportunities for its political opponents. They also make the point, long a complaint of the Scots anyway, that in wooing Middle England, New Labour has "forgotten that middle England is not England, let alone Britain" (p 151). On welfare, they argue that there were indeed continuities with the Thatcher era. However, there had also been an attempt, not least through budgetary policy, to "increase spending and investment on the public services, especially on education and health, as well as increasing the incomes of the 'working poor', in particular those with children". There was, then, a "progressive and social democratic side" to welfare reform. Equally, however, it could not be argued that New Labour was somehow Old Labour in disguise – post-1997 reform crossed "ideological lines" (p 200).

Atkinson and Savage (2001, p 14) broadly agree over the possible unintended consequences of devolution; that New Labour had "altered the political landscape of Britain"; and that, while it had persisted with certain Thatcherite ideas, nonetheless it was both rhetorically more inclusive and had a "genuine desire to tackle problems of inequality and poverty through providing equal opportunities for all". They do sound a note of caution over the last point, however, suggesting that "whether [New Labour] will be prepared, or able, to provide the resources necessary to put such a strategy into practice is another matter". Coming at the issue from a different angle, Johnson (2001, p 74) comments that New Labour's welfare policy had been constructed "very much within the UK paradigm", and was thus clearly distinguishable from the "top-heavy social insurance systems of continental Europe". Equally, however, there was "little sign of a move down the truly minimalist American route". In common with other commentators, he also remarks that in welfare there is "little sign of concern about sacred cows".

Powell (2002a, pp 4-5; 2002c, passim) points to the difficulties in actually measuring success in social welfare; to the differential impact of government policy; to the fact that some government aims are long-term and can only be judged as such; and to the very range of opinion offered about social policy during New Labour's first term. Essentially, however, he argues that the contributors to his edited volume had a "broadly positive" view when analysing by way of "intrinsic evaluation". Such evaluation is "based on comparing stated aims and objectives with achievements", or, to put it another way, "measuring success on the government's own terms". Using "extrinsic evaluation" – that is "evaluation from some external reference point", whether comparative or temporal – his contributors are, however, "more critical"; for example, because some New Labour's famous welfare "pledges" were limited in the first place. If Powell is cautious, incidentally, this characteristic was shared by a number of these commentators: it was pointed out more than once that, for example, fully blown Thatcherism was not identified until Lady Thatcher's second term and that, in many respects, the jury was still out on New Labour.

The very complexity of what New Labour seeks to achieve thus makes assessment difficult, a difficulty encapsulated in another piece written around the end of the government's first term in office. Lister (2001, pp 427-8, 442 and passim) points to the "contradictions and tensions" in New Labour's welfare policy. At the heart of this lay the undermining, through pragmatism and populism, of "the many progressive policies" the government was pursuing. This was leading to such policies being at best inhibited or undermined, with a worst-case scenario of "a more reactionary stance". Populism and pragmatism also resulted in an unwillingness to grapple with redistribution. Without what she describes as a "firm compass of values" for welfare policy, Lister predicted that "a second term Labour government could simply drift in the seas of populism and pragmatism" and so fail to achieve "the transformation that, according to Tony Blair ..., is the raison d'être of a Labour government". Similarly Wickham-Jones (2003, pp 38-43), in many respects highly sceptical of New Labour, acknowledges that between 1997 and 2001 Chancellor Brown did bring forward redistributive policies, despite ambivalence (to say the least) in Blairite rhetoric about the need to address socioeconomic inequalities. This was a strategy in some respects strengthened by the first post-2001 General Election Budget where National Insurance contributions were raised specifically to fund increases in NHS spending – hence the "complexities and ambiguities" surrounding New Labour. As we shall see throughout this text, the Scottish Executive's actions and attitudes too can be characterised as beset by contradictions and tensions, by populism and pragmatism. The question is, however, whether these characteristics have the same content and outcomes in Scotland as in England.

Whatever the verdict of academic commentators, New Labour's 2001 Election Manifesto picked up familiar themes such as the importance of the family; investment in children as human capital; and a route out of poverty via work (Powell, 2002b, p 24). Furthermore, the manifesto claimed that of the welfare commitments made in 1997 significant progress had been made, although it was also acknowledged that much remained to be done (Powell, 2002c, pp 234-6). The current Scottish Executive also makes the claim that welfare reform is a long-term project. There were ongoing popular concerns, as revealed by polling, about schools and hospitals; and a belief, at least as far as Blair was concerned, that New Labour had to be about more than just economic competence. New Labour had to have a vision, and it was here that social welfare had an important part to play. As the Prime Minister put it, he had "a mission for reform of public services" (Rawnsley, 2001, p 488), central to which was the end of "the tradition of monolithic, centrally driven public services" (p 496) and an acceptance that this would involve private sector involvement in areas such as health and education. As Davies (2003, p 1) remarks, by 2002, Blair was proclaiming service delivery as the "core mission" of the "third phase of New Labour".

Service delivery is equally a Scottish Executive preoccupation, although again the question remains as to whether it is directed to the same ends as those of the UK government, and whether it is to be carried out by the same mechanisms. We shall encounter in later chapters of this book, for instance, Scottish scepticism about the role of the private sector in both health and education. Welfare thus remained central to New Labour's reforming strategy and, as Parry (2002, pp

315-6) remarks, the dominant partner in Scotland's governing coalition was, during its first two years, both cautious and clearly influenced by New Labour ideas. Equally, however, there were ambiguities. There were, Parry continues, even in the period down to the 2001 British General Election some highly visible policy issues that had been handled differently than would have previously been the case. These included, famously, free care for the elderly (see, further, Chapter Five of this book).

## The Scottish Executive and social welfare

The preceding analysis can be further illustrated by debates leading up to the second set of elections to the Scottish Parliament, elections described by Blair as "among the most important in Scotland's history"[4]. These took place on 1 May 2003 and so the run-up to them was against the backdrop of the Iraq War which, as one prominent academic commentator remarked, had the effect of highlighting "how limited the powers of the Scottish parliament are, compared to Westminster, which has managed recently to look like the cockpit of the nation"[5]. For Labour, there was a further problem in that party demoralisation seemed to have set in. Consequently, politicians such as First Minister Jack McConnell – the third holder of this post in its brief life – saw the need, in the words of one newspaper, to "make amends for a disappointing start and restore faith in devolution"[6].

McConnell himself has been characterised as a "safe pair of hands willing to work in parallel with London" – particularly when compared to his predecessor who had appeared to be "pushing the boundaries of devolution". This predecessor was Henry McLeish who, as we shall see in Chapter Five, had an important personal role to play in the 'free care for the elderly' episode. McConnell has also been seen as committed to managerialism, a sign of his New Labour credentials, and as laying particular emphasis on public service delivery (Mitchell et al 2003, pp 124-6). Having said all that, it will become apparent as this book progresses that he has also made some very non-New Labourish commitments (for example, to comprehensive schooling) and has sought to emphasise the potential for a distinctively Scottish path inherent in the devolution settlement. As the rapid turnover of First Ministers also suggests, the Parliament's brief existence has not been without trouble and controversy (for detailed accounts, see Mitchell et al, 2001, 2003). Such excitements notwithstanding, newspapers such as *The Herald* were suggesting at the start of the campaign that indifference seemed to be the mood of at least younger voters[7].

Three further contextual points should be made. First, during the campaign, National Insurance contributions were set to rise and thereby have an immediate effect on take-home pay, a further reminder of the limitations on Edinburgh's social policy powers. Second, and in a curious constitutional issue, the campaign also chronologically embraced Chancellor Brown's Budget. The latter was thus in breach of the rule that such statements were not made during election campaigns. One consequence was that the Budget itself had little to say directly about Scotland, which may explain its rather hostile reception in parts of the Scottish press and predictions of tax rises in the near and medium terms[8]. Third, as the campaign drew to a climax, there was a timely reminder of New Labour's approach to social welfare. Peter Mandelson, one of New Labour's architects, argued in a piece infused with notions of post-industrialism and globalisation that the party should have "no sacred cows" when redefining for what it stood. Specifically on social policy the left had to "rethink the role of the welfare state in providing 'cradle to grave' security in a more complex, fractured society where 'entitlements' are not a sufficient moral basis on which to provide a fair system of social protection". It perhaps goes without saying that there was no mention of direct wealth redistribution[9].

The campaign was preceded by statements from the Executive and Scottish Labour emphasising what had been achieved and, even more important, what was planned for the future. In language that was, at least in places, some way from standard New Labour rhetoric, McConnell in July 2002 told the newly formed Scottish Centre for Research on Social Justice (SCRSJ)[10] that "today we see both the start of our landmark policy on free personal care for the elderly and the opening of this important Centre". From the outset, he continued, "social justice has been central to our ambitions for Scotland", a claim emphasised throughout the speech. Crucial to this achievement was, in rather more New Labour mode, "sustaining economic growth and prosperity". Such economic success could not be gained without giving "economic opportunity to those who are excluded because their skills are outdated or unrecognised"; if schools could not provide "the basics of literacy or numeracy"; if children were not inspired to learn; or, a rather more Scottish touch given the remoteness of some parts of the country, if "we ignore the practical problems of the single family struggling to cope on low income in a physically isolated community". However, and again with a rather more Scottish (and indeed traditionally social democratic) flourish, economic growth alone would not result in "the ambitious Scotland I want .... It will not be built without fairness and equality". McConnell then went on to the issue of poverty (see Chapter Three of this book), and to outline his government's major proposals and initiatives. These included a strong emphasis on children, including child poverty, and education (and hence human capital); some standard remarks about getting people back into work; and an improvement in the delivery of public services alongside the need to cooperate with the private sector in regenerating and rebuilding communities "in the knowledge that the success of the private sector itself depends on successful regeneration". This last remark alludes to the Executive's housing strategy, briefly noted earlier in this chapter.

In McConnell's concluding remarks, however, social justice predominates and this section of the speech is worth quoting at length. The ideas and policies outlined were:

the foundation of the Scotland I want us to build. A Scotland where we use the riches we inherit and the wealth we create to pay attention to those who need our commitment and our energy most. Those whom the accident of birth or circumstance has left excluded and isolated. The young person in care, the old person in poverty, the family struggling against debt. Each of them with dreams and hopes, each with talent and ability. The Scotland I want will not exclude them. It will work with them, involve them and build with them a sustainable future. Because in that Scotland, we understand that social justice for any one of us only comes through social justice for all.

While not incompatible with much New Labour rhetoric, such a case could equally well have been argued by a traditional social democrat such as Anthony Crosland, especially as McConnell at one point defined social justice in Scotland as "founded on the values of fairness, equality and opportunity"[11]. Of course, what was crucially missing was any obvious reference to wealth redistribution and we cited Lister (2001) earlier to the effect that this was true of New Labour in general. However, wealth redistribution was not an issue shied away from by other Scottish ministers in other contexts. In the following case, as we shall see, it came about through downplaying its significance.

In September 2002, the Finance Minister, Andy Kerr, introduced his three-year spending plan. Noting that over the first six years of devolution (that is, up to 2005) resources would rise by over 25%, Kerr emphasised a number of key points. First, that devolution itself was a success under Labour, not least because of Scotland's partnership with the UK. This was a not-very-subtle attack (much utilised during the election campaign itself) on the SNP and a rerun of the 'divorce is expensive' argument of 1999. Second, the budget was a "budget for growth and opportunity". The latter was to be secured, inter alia, by prioritising investment in skills and, once again revealing New Labour's concern with human capital, by "investing in our children and Scotland's young people to give them the best start in life, more choices and the opportunity and confidence to build their future". Third, and again indicative of New Labour's agenda and its unwillingness openly to address economic inequalities, Kerr claimed his government was "concerned less with how we divide up what we have and much more about how we use all that we have to secure growth and prosperity for Scotland". Fourth, the minister set out a "new approach" in the form of performance indicators. This very New Labour emphasis on targets, portrayed as a form of accountability, was present throughout the election campaign and beyond. Summing up, Kerr suggested his proposals would result in a Scotland that would be healthier, wealthier, safer and growing – a land of "opportunity for all". Laying it on thick, his government thus advocated "better public services not constitutional wrangling; stability in devolution not risk from separation; investment in growth, schools and hospitals not tax increases to fund divorce"[12].

The Finance Minister was aggressively New Labour in his approach. It is instructive to compare his rhetoric with that of his colleague Margaret Curran, the Minister for Social Justice. The very existence and title of this post, created at devolution and without a direct counterpart in London, was of itself significant, suggesting a particularly Scottish drive for social justice. Interestingly, the post was given the more anodyne title of Minister for Communities after the 2003 elections, presumably to present a more inclusive public face. Curran and her civil servants used the occasion of the publication of the 2002 Social Justice Annual Report to outline, in a summary leaflet, her role and that of her department[13]. After a rather unpromising, if honest enough, start ("As Minister for Social Justice, I am often asked what 'social justice' means. There is no short answer to the question"), Curran articulated five key aims:

- to end child poverty in a generation;
- to help young people to contribute and develop life skills;
- to provide work opportunities for all those who are able;
- to support older people by providing a decent quality of life;
- to build strong communities.

Inequalities were to be (at the very least) reduced with the ultimate target being a "fair and decent society" for all. Since 1999, real progress had been made in "many areas", although the new government had "inherited many deep-rooted problems and it will take time to put things right". Nonetheless services were already improving and, in a curious phrase that implied a strongly positive role for government, "people's lives are getting back on track". Further emphasising this role for government, it was noted that, "under the new Scottish budget 2003-2006, unprecedented levels of resources are now available to tackle social injustice in Scotland".

The campaign for social justice was not a task for any one department – on the contrary. One of Curran's key roles was to chair the Cabinet Sub-Committee on Social Justice and to "drive the need for social justice solutions across all the Executive's work". Here, then, was an instance of the joined-up government so beloved of both New Labour and the Executive as well as an holistic approach to social policy. It would be wrong to suggest that this document paid no attention to labour market issues. On the other hand, the text also laid considerable emphasis on equality and fairness. Much was made, for example, of policies aimed at "closing the opportunity gap". The latter illustrated a mix of labour market approaches – for example, via the New Deal scheme (a series of UK-wide measures aimed at getting particular groups back into the labour force) – and more obviously social democratic aspirations, notably closing the gap "in educational achievement between the most disadvantaged children and young people and the average", and promoting "equality, inclusion and diversity". And it is also worth noting the emphasis on the level of resources to tackle social injustice, for implicit here is some form of redistribution.

## The 2003 elections

Clearly, there was to be no slowdown in the pace of reform. Indeed, one theme of the 2003 election campaign was that what had been achieved was "just the beginning" and Scottish Labour had a website[14] dedicated to showing why this was so. Moreover the future held not simply a continuation of existing policies: a change of gear could be expected. As the First Minister indicated mid-campaign, the "next four years would be very different were Labour to be returned to power". In what *The Scotsman* found his "most Blairite speech to date", McConnell "argued that extra money was no good on its own but had to be matched by reform to make public services more responsive to the needs of patients, parents and pupils". Injecting a serious sense of urgency, he suggested that there "was no time to lose". So, in an example of New Labour's desire to affect a shift from the producers to the consumers of welfare, the days when public services were "run for the system, or those who work in them" were gone. The priorities now were flexibility, choice and efficiency[15]. While it may have been a coincidence, it is instructive to compare this speech with Mandelson's almost exactly contemporaneous comments, noted earlier in this chapter.

What the Executive had purportedly already achieved was laid out in Scottish Labour Party publication, *Four years, forty real achievements* (Scottish Labour Party, 2003). These included distinctively Scottish initiatives such as free personal care for the elderly and, in education, the abolition of tuition fees and the introduction of student bursaries. This idea of a checklist – of past achievements and of commitments for the future – was again explicitly laid out during the launch, by McConnell, of Labour's manifesto on 7 April 2003. This offered a "Check against delivery". In "four short years", Labour had begun to "build a better Scotland", although of course much remained to be done. Highlighting Scottish particularity, albeit Scottish particularity within the Union, Labour proposed "Policies *made* in Scotland, *for* Scotland", policies that were "built on our values and on our principles". So, McConnell concluded, "I *guarantee* leadership that takes a long term view, that reforms as well as cuts waste and treats taxpayers' money seriously, that stands up for Scotland"[16].

Three points might be made here. First, the idea of better, but also more efficient, public services combined with economic growth and stability were recurring election themes. Attacking the SNP, McConnell stressed Labour's commitment to "more teachers, more nurses and more police", while contrasting this with what he claimed would be the effect of the Nationalists' policies: "tax rises and cuts to the public services ... to pay for the costs of separation from the rest of the UK"[17]. Second, McConnell also exhibited a New Labour tendency to think the unthinkable, in that he announced that he would be prepared to "hand over more control to individual schools and intervene to remove failing headteachers". This was characterised – quite rightly – as a "major departure in Labour's approach to education"[18]. Third, as in 1999, a commitment was made not to utilise Edinburgh's tax-raising powers.

Of course, on one level what all this points to is simply the powers the

Scottish Parliament has. Similarly, it indicates that Labour in Scotland and Labour in Great Britain have huge amounts in common in policy terms and attitudes. On the other hand, it is clear that welfare, and welfare reform, was perceived as an important way of selling both the Parliament and Scottish Labour to the Scottish electorate. As *The Herald* noted of McConnell's manifesto launch, the "tone of the Labour leader's remarks was positive, dwelling on Labour's ambitions and record in office, and was in marked contrast to the strongly negative anti-SNP rhetoric of four years ago" (this did not stop the campaign itself being, in the great traditions of Scottish politics and despite the consensual approach devolution was supposed to bring, vicious). The report also remarked that the manifesto contained nothing very new, and that Labour's proposed programme had "economic growth as (its) first priority"[19].

In a rather more critical leader on the same day, the newspaper found, despite McConnell's rhetoric, a lack of "vision and ambition for Scotland and its parliament". It conceded, nonetheless, that Labour did appear to have a long-term strategy and that its policy proposals were indeed detailed. Revealingly, it saw the latter in the following way: "some old, some new, some borrowed, but definitely more Old Labour red than blue". Investment in public services was going to require "record sums", hence the acknowledged prerequisite of a "dynamic economy"[20]. Taking a rather different slant, *The Scotsman* characterised the manifesto as part of the "battle for Middle Scotland" and constructed an imaginary family of the type that Labour sought to woo. Believers in social equality, they were thus firmly in the Scottish tradition of support for state welfare – such as free care for the elderly – and as such perhaps unwittingly contrasted with the stereotype of Middle England. However, the adult members of this family were also aspirational, one reason why they would welcome another key part of the Labour manifesto, the promise not to raise business taxes and, crucially, not to use the income tax varying power[21].

If Labour primarily focused on devolved welfare powers, then this was also true of the other parties (see the summary of manifesto commitments at www.election.scotsman.com/manifestos.cfm). The SNP promised, for example, a £2 billion increase in the health budget, an end to PFI involvement in healthcare, and smaller primary classes. In so doing, it highlighted the two key areas of concern to the Scottish electorate, health and education, while tuning in to Scottish scepticism about private-sector involvement in welfare provision (an issue we return to in Chapters Four, Five, and Six of this book). The Nationalists, however, had also taken to heart the charge that their proposals were potentially expensive and so focused on improvement in services, not just their expansion. They also promised tax cuts so as to make Scotland more economically competitive than England, a strategy that not only made them less vulnerable to the charges laid against them four years previously but also coincided with Chancellor Gordon Brown's raising of National Insurance. Nonetheless, the Nationalists' first election broadcast was based on the theme "Why are we waiting?", arguing that nothing had changed under Labour in respect of, for instance, hospital waiting lists and child poverty; and that the wealth gap between Scotland and the rest of the UK in aggregate had actually widened[22]. Indeed, the Nationalists upped the stakes with another election broadcast that depicted the death of an elderly person waiting in a lengthening queue for NHS treatment. The SNP leader responded to criticism of this broadcast by further arguing that waiting times had risen significantly at Yorkhill Hospital, Glasgow, where seriously ill children were treated[23].

The Liberal Democrats promised, inter alia, the abolition of dental and eye test charges and the raising of the school entry age to six. The Conservatives continued to emphasise market-based policies in health and education, notably through hospitals, GPs and schools being given more power to manage their budgets. The Scottish Socialist Party's proposals, much derided by both Labour and the SNP, included free school meals and an end to all public–private partnership projects.

The election thus, and as might be expected, revolved around welfare issues. An opinion poll published on 14 April was of particular relevance, for it revealed that around three quarters of respondents wanted their parliament to have more influence over events than London's. Around half thought, furthermore, that Scotland should pay for its own services out of revenues collected in Scotland, while some 61% thought that Holyrood "should set welfare benefits"[24]. Against this background, Blair's visit to Scotland the following day, and an interview he gave, take on an even greater significance. Asked how he would "persuade people to vote" – apathy continued to be a concern, quite correctly as it turned out – Blair replied that, first, he would stress the Scottish Executive's achievements, for example in "extra help for pensioners". This was richly ironic for, as we shall see in Chapter Five, his own government had declined to go down this particular path. Such achievements were, he claimed, "big, big things for Scotland that have been delivered by the partnership between Britain and the Scottish Executive". This last point alluded to his second theme, for the only serious alternative to Labour was the SNP, which, whatever it said, was "still up for divorce and separation and all the disasters that come with it"[25].

The final days of the campaign saw further claims in social and economic policy. Chancellor Brown asserted that SNP proposals for greater fiscal autonomy would result in public spending cuts, while the Nationalists continued to focus on the health service, claiming that emergency readmissions to hospitals had "rocketed" under Labour. The Tories called for an "open market" in university provision funded by, essentially, a voucher scheme, while the Liberal Democrats reiterated their proposal for free eye and dental tests, estimated to cost some £22 million per annum[26]. Indeed, the relationship between the former coalition partners proved problematic as the election approached. On the eve of McConnell's speech promising that, should Labour be returned to power, the next four years would not just be a continuation of what had gone before, Liberal Democrat leader Jim Wallace made a major policy statement. Anxious to escape the taunt of being the then least admired dog around, a poodle, Wallace "savaged" four of the Labour leader's priority policies. On health, for example, he claimed that his party had "driven the case for health promotion and prevention in the past four years. If you read the Labour manifesto, they still don't seem to have grasped the importance of that agenda"[27].

Equally worrying for Labour was the opposition parties' tactic of attacking convergence (the Nationalists) or divergence (the Conservatives) from practice elsewhere in Great Britain. This was most obviously so during a visit by the Education Secretary, Charles Clarke, to a school in Edinburgh being built under a private–public partnership. For the Tories, Clarke's visit served to highlight the "stark differences in education policy between England and Scotland", while for the SNP, "the Scottish Labour Party was increasingly being forced down an agenda that was led by London"[28].

From within the Labour Party, former cabinet minister Roy Hattersley claimed that, while in Wales and Scotland concessions had been made to "New Labour rhetoric – presumably in the hope of moderating Tony Blair's hostility" – nonetheless in both countries Labour had remained true in word and deed to social democracy. Hattersley argued that here Labour, "free from the shackles of the London party", was offering programmes that amounted to a rejection of much of Blair's domestic policy. As one instance of this, he pointed out that the "Scottish manifesto asserts that the 'comprehensive system has improved educational opportunity for all our children' – a declaration Tony Blair would reject out of hand"[29]. As we shall see in Chapter Four, on this subject at least Hattersley had a point.

Back in Scotland itself, Blair made a further visit in an attempt to bolster Labour support[30]. In one sense this simply highlighted the fact that McConnell and the British Prime Minister were not necessarily singing from the same songbook. As one commentator put it, there was a sense of dislocation in Scottish Labour politics that might be further heightened should the party win on 1 May. In areas such as education, health and social justice, Labour in Scotland had been "moving in different directions from Labour at Westminster – and the gulf in policies and principles could widen still". So, for example, Scottish Labour had "rejected the idea of foundation hospitals" and there were to be no top-fees in higher education, the deferment of tuition fees notwithstanding. This contrast was made especially marked by a speech by Blair that stressed the need for the "radical reform of key public services". While the values of the post-1945 welfare state were to endure, policies such as foundation hospitals were nonetheless to be pursued, despite the opposition of powerful figures such as Gordon Brown[31]. Blair's determination to pursue these reforms was to be repeatedly stressed over the coming months.

## Outcome and consequences

On polling day, *The Scotsman* suggested that the five-week election campaign had been too long: after all, "there are only so many times you can argue about the number of hospitals built under the PFI scheme …. Undoubtedly, however, one of the reasons the campaign felt drawn out was because the main parties were so similar", not least on social welfare issues[32]. The last point is a rather jaundiced version of Scottish collectivism and consensualism in social policy matters. In the event, Labour remained the largest party, with the SNP again second in terms of MSPs. However, such a bald summary does not do justice to a highly problematic election. For one thing, only around half the electorate bothered to vote. All the establishment parties – Labour, SNP and Liberal Democrats – performed poorly, the first two losing seats, the third standing still. The smaller parties, such as the Greens and the Scottish Socialists, by contrast performed (relatively speaking) extremely well and brought to the new Parliament radical social policy agendas.

There were also two particularly noteworthy victories by independent candidates. A representative of the Scottish Senior Citizens Unity Party gained a list seat, claiming that his increasingly vocal supporters "will no longer tolerate tired, sick and vulnerable old people being ripped off by the Jack McConnells or Jim Wallaces of the this world". Given that Scotland had already gone down a route more favourable to the elderly than in England, this was to say the least an interesting statement. Even more impressively, a previously solid Labour seat was captured by a retired GP, Dr Jean Turner, campaigning against the downgrading of a local hospital and on health service issues generally. Overall, the election result was, as one newspaper put it, a "shock to the system"[33]. McConnell attributed Labour's problems to the public concern over the pace of reform, for example in the health service[34]. The 2003 election thus showed a degree of disenchantment with the devolution process combined with an ongoing concern among the electorate about the shape and direction of the Scottish welfare state.

Labour was again required to enter into a coalition with the Liberal Democrats. Reflecting on the lessons of the election and the tasks before his administration, McConnell stressed the need to focus on the "people's priorities" – a phrase that had also featured in the Social Justice Annual Report and embraced health, education, crime, transport and jobs (Scottish Executive, 2002a, p 8)[35].

The coalition deal was underpinned by the joint document, *A partnership for a better Scotland*. A long and detailed text, this was divided into sections dealing with:

- the economy;
- delivering public services;
- supporting stronger and safer communities;
- developing a confident, democratic Scotland;
- working together.

There were two overarching themes. First, emphasis was again placed on work still to be carried out, for instance to "tackle poverty and disadvantage". Second, the coalition partners expressed their determination to improve public services and that this process be accountable and measurable. The Scottish people deserved and expected public services "of the highest possible quality" and offering "the greatest possible choice". The "record level of investment" would thus be used to "secure new and better facilities, particularly for our schools and hospitals". Investment would be matched with "continued reform" so that services would be "designed and delivered around the needs of individuals and the communities within which they live". To ensure such service delivery, "national standards" would, where appropriate, be set. Expanding on this last point, it was stated that progress would be monitored by "both regular and targeted independent inspection of performance and action against common standards"[36].

Not everyone was entirely impressed. *The Scotsman* found at least some of the (many) policy pledges "statements of the obvious, the self-explanatory and the confusing" and urged its readers to be "afraid, very afraid" of what they could expect from Holyrood in the coming four years. *The Herald* too had its doubts, noting that McConnell had "set out his priorities for the next four years: to make the economy grow, tackle crime, and reform the public services". Whether this could be achieved or not was, however, another matter[37].

## Conclusion

The Scottish press may have been sceptical, although it was quite right in drawing attention to some of the rather obvious statements in the coalition document. Nonetheless, the path was now clear for the administration to press on with its plans for public service reform. And, in what may have been a straw in the wind, the new Parliament opened with calls for further powers to be devolved to Holyrood[38]. McConnell continued, over the summer of 2003, to emphasise the necessity of reform and that "more of the same" was not an option. This took place in a difficult political and economic climate. Chancellor Gordon Brown expressed concern over the relatively poor performance of the Scottish economy, a point echoed by the First Minister at the opening of Holyrood's new session in September. Fears were raised about the economic implications of a declining population (a situation unique in Europe), with two academics prophesying that Scottish society was "in danger of developing into a culture where fewer young people are charged with providing for an increasingly old population". The First Minister, meanwhile, publicly agreed that there was a problem for his party in the significant gap between the support given by Scots to Labour in Scottish elections and that given in British elections. The Scottish Office was effectively abolished in suitably rancorous fashion, while some commentators revived the issue of Scotland being over-funded. There was a clear illustration of one of the central paradoxes of devolution when some Scottish Labour MPs twice voted in the London Parliament in support of Blair's policy on foundation hospitals, a policy that, as we shall see in Chapter Five of this book, has been rejected in Scotland itself[39].

Like its predecessor, the new Scottish government thus continued to have a bumpy political ride. As a consequence of the very nature of its powers, this clearly had implications for major areas of social welfare. However, as we have seen, the Executive continued to emphasise its commitment to pursuing a modernised Scottish welfare state. Introducing his Draft Budget in the autumn of 2003, the Finance Minister claimed that, over the lifetime of the new Parliament, "we are determined to continue to improve public services and tackle the real issues that matter to people in Scotland". His spending plans would help deliver "better public services, greater economic prosperity, and an improved standard of living for the people of Scotland"[40]. This leads on to our next chapter, where we discuss welfare funding and expenditure priorities.

## Notes

[1] The absence of overarching descriptions and analyses of welfare in Wales and in Ireland can be explained in similar ways.

[2] The expression 'Great Britain' is chosen deliberately here, since so few works attempt or claim to deal with Northern Ireland, and hence the UK as a whole.

[3] However, under the terms of the 1998 Scotland Act, there are provisions for dissolution. (I am grateful to an anonymous referee for reminding me of this point.)

[4] *The Guardian*, 17 April 2003, 'SNP win spells end of Britain, says Blair'.

[5] *The Guardian*, 1 April 2003, 'Scots campaign overshadowed by war'.

[6] *Scotland on Sunday*, 30 March 2003, 'McConnell's campaign of divide and conquer'.

[7] *The Herald*, 1 April 2003, 'Indifference the enemy as poll booths beckon'.

[8] *The Scotsman*, 2 April 2003, 'Budget date "breaks tradition"'; 10 April 2003, 'Conjuror Brown's rabbit'; 10 April 2003, 'Iron Chancellor's prudent façade rusting'.

[9] *The Guardian*, 25 April 2003, 'We need to rethink the welfare state'.

[10] For the aims of this body, see SCRSJ (2002, 2003).

[11] www.scotland.gov.uk, 1 July 2002, 'Social justice in Scotland'.

[12] www.scotland.gov.uk, 12 September 2002, 'Spending Plans 2003-2006'. For the financial dimensions of this statement, see Chapter Two of this book.

[13] www.scotland.gov.uk/library5/social/emsjs-00.asp

[14] www.justthebeginning.org.uk

[15] *The Scotsman*, 25 April 2003, 'McConnell disdains "more of the same"'.

[16] www.scottishlabour.org.uk – emphasis in the original.

[17] *The Scotsman*, 15 April 2003, 'McConnell: SNP deceiving voters'.

[18] *The Scotsman*, 8 April 2003, 'Labour's education right turn'. For further discussion, see Chapter Four of this book.

[19] *The Herald*, 7 April 2003, 'Labour pins hope on the economy'.

[20] *The Herald*, 8 April 2003, 'Scotland needs vision'.

[21] *The Scotsman*, 15 April 2003, 'The battle for Middle Scotland'.

[22] *The Scotsman*, 1 April 2003, 'SNP on tune to get their message across'.

[23] *The Herald*, 15 April 2003, 'Swinney defends "negative" campaign'. On the significance of waiting lists, see also Chapters Five and Six of this book.

[24] *The Scotsman*, 14 April 2003, 'Call to beef up Holyrood'.

[25] *The Herald*, 17 April 2003, 'Scotland can be proud of us'.

[26] *The Herald*, 23 April 2003, 'Brown rounds on SNP fiscal plans'; 'Conservatives call for open market on university costs'; 'A case to be won, says Swinney'.

[27] *The Herald*, 24 April 2003, 'Wallace and McConnell go to war'; for McConnell's response, see *The Scotsman*, 25 April 2003, 'McConnell sets out powershare conditions'.

[28] *The Scotsman*, 24 April 2003, 'Opposition highlights Labour's "great divide"'.

[29] *The Guardian*, 28 April, 'Why I wish my vote was in Llangollen'.

[30] *The Scotsman*, 28 April 2003, 'Blair flies in as Labour nerves fray'.

[31] *The Guardian*, 29 April 2003, 'Scots take the high road' and 'Blair sticks by reform of public services'.

[32] *The Scotsman*, 1 May 2003, 'With so little to argue about, five weeks is a very long time in politics'.

[33] *Scotland on Sunday*, 4 May 2003, 'The people didn't want him to be First Minister' and 'Will Independent's Day bring fringe benefits or chaos to Holyrood?'; *The Herald*,

2 May 2003, 'Hospital champion pulls off stunning victory' and 'A shock to the system'; *The Guardian*, 3 May 2003, 'Hostile voters shake up Holyrood'.

[34] *The Scotsman*, 3 May 2003, 'Leader of a weakened Labour Party says voices of protest will be heard'.

[35] *The Guardian*, 15 May 2003, 'Holyrood deal agreed'; *The Scotsman*, 21 May 2003, '"Fixer" McConnell reshuffles the pack' and 'Little change as McConnell names Cabinet'; *The Herald*, 21 May 2003, 'The new executive' and '"Cut down" ministers join cabinet'.

[36] www.scotland.gov.uk/library5/pfbs

[37] *The Scotsman*, 16 May 2003, 'Future is clear as a policy muddle'; *The Herald*, 21 May 2003, 'McConnell's new team: public yet to be convinced it can deliver for Scotland'.

[38] *The Herald*, 23 May 2003, 'MSPs want more powers: call to take control from Westminster'.

[39] *The Scotsman*, 13 June 2003, 'Signs of chaos contradict Liddell's claim that resignation was planned'; 1 August 2003, 'Population plunge threatens Scotland's future prosperity, warns CBI'; 26 August 2003, 'First Minister admits Scottish voters prefer London Labour'; *The Herald*, 27 August 2003, 'Brown calls Scots council of war to tackle ailing economy'; 20 November 2003, 'Scots save Blair from humiliation'; www.bbc.co.uk, 6 September 2003, 'Economy and crime on the menu'; *The Guardian*, 23 June 2003, 'Hammered by the Scots'.

[40] www.scotland.gov.uk/library5/finance/db05s

# TWO

# Income and expenditure

## Introduction

In January 2003, Lord Barnett asked a government spokesperson in the House of Lords whether the administration had "any plans to scrap the Barnett formula with respect to the allocation of public expenditure". Since it was Lord Barnett who, as chief secretary to the Treasury, had allegedly created this formula, here was a question with an agenda. The subsequent exchanges brought out the controversies, methodological problems and misapprehensions surrounding the mechanism that determines the level of incremental expenditure changes to Scotland, Wales and Northern Ireland. Lord McIntosh, for the government, made four points. First, the formula was not the basis on which Scotland and Northern Ireland in particular received proportionately higher levels of funding. Second, the formula worked and provided "a degree of security and certainty", being based on "known facts about the population and the known baseline". Such advantages should not be "taken too lightly". Third, in any event there was no practical or attractive alternative. Finally, in principle, if not so far in practice, the Barnett formula would ultimately lead to convergence in public expenditure levels across the UK.

Lord Barnett himself, however, felt the formula to be "grossly unfair". It was not, moreover, a formula when he introduced it – it had only become so under the Conservative governments of the 1980s and 1990s and the current Labour administration. Lord Stoddart was even blunter: was the minister aware, he demanded, that:

> people in the south of England, who are being told that their rates might increase by 20 per cent, and people in the north of England, who see Scotland being treated in a preferential way, feel great resentment, especially when they see that in Scotland students are treated better than they are in England, Wales and Northern Ireland? Moreover, old people get better treatment in Scotland than they do in the rest of the United Kingdom. Does he understand that the resentment will boil over one day and cause the Government much trouble? (Hansard, House of Lords, 27 January 2003, cols 913-16).

As will become apparent, Lord Stoddart was either confused or misinformed about certain aspects of Scottish public expenditure. Nonetheless, he raised important questions about how funding is allocated to Scotland, and about the matter of equity (as we shall see in Chapters Four and Five, respectively, student funding and care of the elderly are indeed areas of policy divergence between Scotland and England).

Nor is it just members of the House of Lords who are unclear about the operations of the Barnett formula. Just before the announcement of the 2002 Spending Review, a BBC report, headlined 'Fears for Scottish spending', claimed (somewhat misleadingly) that, for Scottish politicians, the "burning issue" was whether the Barnett formula was to be reviewed. The formula, the piece continued, "was created in the 1970s to allocate public spending for all the regions within the UK" and had "resulted in Scotland, Wales and Northern Ireland receiving much higher spending levels per head than England". The article then quoted former SNP leader Alex Salmond who suggested that the only guarantee of the Comprehensive Spending Review was that "the Scottish share of UK spending will continue to fall as a result of the Barnett Squeeze". Salmond further claimed that there was "no doubt that New Labour want to cut Scottish spending even further and faster"; that Scotland was in a "funding straightjacket"; and that the priority must therefore be "financial independence for the Scottish Parliament", this being the only way in which adequate investment in Scotland's public services could be guaranteed. Unsurprisingly, Scotland's coalition government rejected these claims. Spokespersons for both Labour and the Liberal Democrats agreed that there might, at some point in the future, be a need for a revision or review of the Barnett formula – but not yet. In the meantime, public expenditure should be targeted on Scotland's social problems[1].

On the volume of Scottish public expenditure, during the 2003 election campaign, research carried out by *The Scotsman* claimed that:

> Scotland's government spending is set to become the highest in the developed world, relative to the country's economic size, as a result of Gordon Brown's tax-and-spend bonanza.

Scotland was about to overtake Sweden in this respect as well as being significantly ahead of the rest of the UK. For *The Scotsman* at least, this was going to "torpedo the argument that more funding will solve Scotland's problems", an important issue given that all the main political parties had, in their election manifestos, at least one commitment for increased public expenditure. However, this was not a new phenomenon. Gordon Brown's "spending bonanza" was aimed at "lifting England to public spending levels enjoyed both by Scotland and the rest of Europe". However, as the Barnett formula left the Chancellor "unable to decouple Scotland from the equation", then more money was added to "Scotland's already high base". Pointing to one of the central paradoxes in this situation, it was remarked that, while Scotland spent a higher proportion of its national income on health than any other comparable country, health outcomes were, nonetheless, poor[2].

The way in which Scotland is funded clearly generates considerable heat if not necessarily always much light. The volume and results of Scottish public expenditure are, equally clearly, also contentious issues. The aim of this chapter is to provide a context for understanding the opportunities and constraints on social welfare expenditure afforded by the devolution settlement and the way in which the Scottish Executive has handled these. My discussion is in three parts. First, I examine the Barnett formula. Second, I look – for reasons that will become apparent – extremely briefly at the so-called Tartan Tax; that is, the Edinburgh Parliament's ability marginally to vary the rate of income tax. And, finally, I discuss the Executive's spending opportunities and priorities since devolution. There is, as we have already observed, a strong argument that Scotland is particularly advantaged in public expenditure terms. Equally, we shall see that there are those who defend this advantage on historical, political and social grounds. Once again, this provides an important context for the volume as a whole.

## The Barnett formula

In the first part of this section, an attempt is made to explain simply what is meant by the Barnett formula, and in so doing we draw heavily upon a number of useful official publications (House of Commons Library, 1998; Scottish Parliament Information Centre, 2000; House of Commons Library, 2001; HM Treasury, 2002). The Barnett formula (a non-statutory mechanism, then and now) was devised by the then Labour government in the late 1970s (its precise origins remain somewhat obscure) and applied to Scotland in 1978 and thereafter to Wales and Northern Ireland.

At this stage, three fundamental characteristics need to be understood. First, the formula "does not determine the overall size of the [Scottish, Welsh and Northern Irish] budgets but provides that, where comparable, changes to programmes in England ... result in equivalent changes in the budgets of the territorial departments calculated on the basis of population shares". In other words, the formula does not decide the total allocation but, rather, incremental change. It does so automatically, however, and on the basis of population ratios. Since its inception, therefore, there has been no need for direct negotiation by the Scottish Office or, latterly, the Executive – hence the "security and stability" identified by Lord McIntosh. Rather, the negotiating is done by the spending ministers of the UK government.

Second, beyond population, this is not a needs-based formula (House of Commons Library, 1998, pp 5, 6, 8; see also later in this chapter). Higher per capita public expenditure, such as there is in Scotland, cannot be attributed to Barnett but, rather, is a situation that developed historically and was present at the point at which the formula came to be applied – Lord McIntosh's baseline. Indeed, because of the way it was set up a strict operation of the formula "could lead to slower increases in public sector provision for Scotland, Wales and Northern Ireland than for England". This is the so-called Barnett Squeeze, alluded to by Alex Salmond and the reason why the formula can be seen, in principle, as leading to convergence of public expenditure levels (House of Commons Library, 2001, 'Summary of main points').

Third, although incremental change is based on changes in English programmes, it has been the case, from the outset, that once monies have been allocated to Scotland, there is an element of discretion as to how these are employed. That is, if we take the situation pre-devolution, the formula was used to determine "the aggregate size of the block which the relevant secretaries of state are then free to allocate between services as they see fit" (House of Commons Library, 1998, p 9).

Although often described – including by Barnett himself (Barnett, 2000, p 69) – as a "temporary expedient", the formula remained in place under the Conservatives. More than this, however, it became integral to the devolution settlement. As a recent Treasury statement put it, the funding arrangements for Scotland, Wales and Northern Ireland were for the most part a "continuation of long-standing conventions ... prior to devolution and are consistent with the Devolution White Papers and the Devolution Acts". In 1997, the chief secretary to the Treasury articulated 'A statement of principles' which, in effect, summarised a number of our central points so far:

> The key to these arrangements is block budgets which the devolved Administrations, like the Secretaries of State now, will be free to deploy between the functions under their control in response to local priorities. Changes in these block budgets will be linked to changes in equivalent English spending plans by the Barnett Formula which gives Scotland and Wales a population-based share of planned changes in comparable spending in England.

The chief secretary added that, while this system had by then operated for 20 years, this was the "first time that these principles have been spelt out in public" (HM Treasury, 2002, p 1 and annex A).

How has this all worked in practice? First, as the opening section of this chapter illustrated, convergence has not as yet taken place. Scotland is, so it continues to be claimed, especially advantaged at the expense of England in particular and, especially, those parts of England with their own share of social problems. So, for example, in 1999-2000, identifiable expenditure on education was some 30% higher in Scotland than in Yorkshire and Humberside and overall Scotland had a clear advantage in identifiable public expenditure per capita over England and Wales (although not Northern Ireland) (House of Commons Library, 2001, pp 17-18; for 2000-01 data at national level, see Glennerster, 2003, p 192). (The definition of identifiable expenditure is dealt with later in this chapter.) There is thus an issue of equity which, as Bell and Christie (2001, p 139) remark, is most acutely felt in the North East of England. They point, for example, to the MP for Gateshead asking the chief secretary to the Treasury in summer 2001 if there were any plans to review the operations of the Barnett formula, a question that should be put in the broader context of the Executive's policies in respect of university students and the elderly. A couple of years earlier, a Newcastle newspaper had gone so far as to claim that, in British society, there was a "less talked about divide – a divide not between the North and South, but between the English regions and the Celtic nations" (quoted in Morgan, 2001, p 346).

Second, there is a complex range of reasons as to why such inequities – if that is what they are – remain. Given that the Barnett formula deals only with incremental change, this means that levels of public expenditure in Scotland were relatively higher than those in England prior to its implementation. As one official commentary puts it, the "higher per capita spending in Scotland is a reflection of historical developments" (Scottish Parliament Information Centre, 2000, p 7). Nonetheless, the Barnett formula was supposed to bring about, eventually, convergence. Here we might note four points. First, the Barnett formula applies only to the block grant from the Treasury, not to all identifiable public expenditure (most notably, it does not apply to social security, which is, of course, reserved to London). Second, the formula has occasionally been bypassed – especially, so it would appear, in the 1980s and early 1990s, although this is less important now (Heald and McLeod, 2002a, p 150). Third, in an era of low inflation and tight public expenditure the formula, which applies to change, has as McCrone puts it "little to bite on". Finally, and most famously, the formula relied on population data that were, in effect, overly favourable to Scotland. This situation has been rectified since devolution (McCrone, 1999, pp 146-7; Scottish Parliament Information Centre, 2000, pp 3-4).

Third, we have to recognise nonetheless that the allocation of Scottish funding is about more than technical matters to do with population estimates. It is frequently suggested, for instance, that allocation should be determined by need. As McLean (2000, p 78) argues, "public policy should aim not for equal public spending per head for each territory, but for public spending at the correct level in relation to each territory's need". According to this argument, Barnett fails on at least two counts: it was not based on need – except in the limited sense of population – in the first place, while it in theory aims for convergence, again not a needs-based concept. Attractive as such an argument might be, there are problems. As one commentary points out, determining need is not unproblematic "nor would the findings be beyond the reach of political debate and argument". Nonetheless, such an exercise was carried out in the 1970s, around the first attempt at political devolution. Leaving aside all sorts of methodological and technical questions, the same commentary remarks that if "the relative need of the regions were similar to that in an exercise carried out in 1979 the result would be an immediate and substantial fall in provision for [Scotland, Wales and Northern Ireland]" (House of Commons Library, 2001, pp 15-17, 'Summary of main points'). However, we also need to take account of asymmetry. As McLean (2000, p 78) puts it, in a polity (that is, the UK) with "asymmetric devolution, the parts with a credible threat of causing trouble [Scotland and, for different reasons, Northern Ireland] have a bargaining advantage over those without". Put another way, whether or not Scotland is receiving more than its share for Westminster politicians challenging this might cause more political grief than it is worth.

We are thus dealing with a highly politicised issue, and this leads us on to our final point in this section. Analysts such as Midwinter argue that Barnett has the "virtue of simplicity and objectivity". Furthermore, proponents of needs assessment purport to be offering technical solutions to matters that are, in fact, based on political judgement – it thus "requires political judgement as to what constitutes need". Indeed the "block and formula" approach is the one that is "politically rational", not least in the ongoing context of imprecise information. But even when the Barnett formula was introduced, Midwinter argues, the "historic baseline expenditure" in fact reflected "political judgements made about relative need". Given the particular problems Scotland continues to experience – for example in health – these political judgements not only had historical validity but continue to have contemporary validity. Midwinter further notes, incidentally, that if convergence does take place – and he thinks this unlikely – it will be as a result of the operations of the formula and not because it has ever been a policy objective. In short, different patterns of expenditure developed historically, and with justification, and continue, with justification in the light of evidence to the contrary (Midwinter, 1999, pp 53-4; 2000, pp 73-4; 2002a, pp 564-5).

Although it is unlikely that this argument will go away – Glennerster (2003, p 191) has recently remarked that "devolution has brought the funding mechanisms into the public domain and exposed their results" – there can be equally little doubt that in the short to medium term neither will the Barnett formula and block grant funding. Morgan points out that certain areas of the UK – Northern Ireland, Wales, North East England, Scotland – are both highly dependent on public expenditure as a constituent of their Gross Domestic Product (GDP) and, at least in some cases, strongly pro-Labour (Morgan, 2001, p 345 and passim). The suggestion here, once again, is that the current London government would be taking a big political risk in changing the Barnett formula in ways that would be seen, in Scotland, to disadvantage Scottish public expenditure. Barnett (2000, p 70) himself argues that the Conservative administrations of the 1980s and 1990s declined to tamper with the funding mechanisms because they feared yet more vote losses in Scotland and Wales and that New Labour operates under a similar, self-imposed constraint.

It is certainly the case that Scottish, and many British, Labour politicians are unwilling to countenance change. On the same day as an earlier Lords debate on the abolition of the formula, again led by Barnett himself, the Scottish Secretary told a Parliamentary Committee that it delivered a "good and fair deal for Scotland"[3]. More pointedly, the Scottish Finance Minister claimed during his September 2002 budget statement[4] that devolution – "our partnership with the United Kingdom" – guaranteed Scotland a:

> fair share of resources. The agreed formula (ie. Barnett) delivers for each
> person in Scotland pound for pound, person for person, the same increase as

in England. That comes as a right. Every extra pound for the people of Gateshead, matched by an extra pound for the people of Glasgow.

## Some implications of the current funding mechanism

In viewing the funding of the Scottish Parliament (and hence of its policies) through the operations and underlying principles of Barnett, a number of important points emerge. First, we have noted that the Executive has the discretion to use the monies given it as it chooses. So, for example, any increase in health spending in England automatically leads to a proportionate rise for Scotland, but Scotland need not spend the resulting funds on health. Nonetheless, this does not affect the total volume of funding itself. As Bell and Christie (2001, p 139) succinctly put it, devolved authorities "have a cake they can divide however they choose, but they cannot take a policy decision to change the size of the cake". Giving a specific example, Lynch (2001, p 25) notes that, from 1997 to 2000, the Executive moved money into health and education at the expense of local government. There was no new money, simply funds taken from one sector to be given to others. This tactic thus had the "essential facet of robbing Peter to pay Paul, as most Scottish local authorities will testify".

Even so, the power to determine where money is spent once allocated is not all it at first seems. As one analysis points out, "as much public spending is on-going or demand-led, the scope for the exercise of this discretion is limited in practice" (House of Commons Library, 2001, p 10). In addition, we need to take account of the Treasury's determination to maintain as much influence as possible over the economy. Again to quote Bell and Christie, the very survival of the Barnett formula attests to the Treasury's strength "and its determination to control the key macroeconomic variables in the UK economy". The formula is thus "part of a political process that allows the centre to retain tight control over the resources available to the devolved administrations and thus the extent to which they can differentiate policies" (Bell and Christie, 2001, pp 137, 139). In short, as Heald and McLeod put it, the devolved administrations are "embedded into the UK public expenditure system" with "highly centralised and unified control over public expenditure and taxation, exercised directly by, or on behalf of, the Treasury" (Heald and McLeod, 2002a, pp 147, 154; see also *Scottish Affairs*, 2002). Given Chancellor Brown's engagement with domestic affairs and his own political background, in reality none of this is especially surprising.

Second, as a result of the Barnett mechanism, Scottish ministers may well be spared bruising annual battles with the Treasury; but on one level, this simply highlights their dependence on their London counterparts. Bell and Christie (2001, p 139) report that, certainly in economic terms, the UK devolved authorities are "in a very weak position in comparison to their counterparts in Germany or Spain". Furthermore, in the developed world, only the UK "allocates resources at a sub-national level using a formula based on changes, rather than levels of spending in relation to assessed need". In a more detailed comparative study, Darby et al (2002, p 48) argue that, in sticking with Barnett, the UK is "one of the few countries that have resisted the trend towards needs-based formulae and stuck with history and political expediency". While the current UK and Scottish administrations remain committed to Barnett, while the former can in some way defuse the unhappiness of, most notably, north-eastern Labour MPs, and while both Westminster and Holyrood remain in Labour hands, then as a political issue it seems likely that the current method of funding will remain in place. But these circumstances may not prevail forever. As Lynch (2001) has put it, given Holyrood's "fiscal dependency", it is possible to imagine circumstances where the UK government could be blamed for "limited policy choices or expenditure cuts" in Scotland. The focus on perceived Scottish advantage by some English politicians means, he continues, that "the politicisation of Barnett and the block grant process is inevitable". Although, he argues with equal conviction, this politicisation has "been contained by Labour holding office in Scotland and Westminster, such containment will not survive a change of government in either institution". Having said that, Lynch also suggests that the "fiscal weakness of the devolved Parliament and its financial dependency on central government look set to continue" (2001, pp 24-5).

Third, the nature of the funding regime has led Heald and McLeod (2002a, p 147) to state that the UK remains "essentially a unitary state, not a federal one". This is somewhat overstated, but it does correctly point to a phenomenon noted in subsequent chapters whereby there is a tension in New Labour ideology and practice between devolving powers on the one hand, and centralising control on the other. It is the realisation of this form of dependency, however, that has resulted in demands for financial independence for Edinburgh. This has led to a debate about fiscal autonomy, usefully encapsulated in a special edition of the journal *Scottish Affairs* based on a 2002 symposium. As Heald and McLeod point out, the debate was "brought to life" during the 2001 General Election campaign by a letter to *The Scotsman* from a group of economists who had argued, without defining the term, for a greater degree of fiscal autonomy (Heald and McLeod, 2002b, p 6). This has clearly struck some sort of chord. So, for example, we noted in the last chapter opinion poll findings published during the 2003 elections that showed that around half the population thought that Scotland should pay for its own services out of revenues collected in Scotland.

This is not the place to go into the detail of the debate. However, the following points can be taken from the symposium contributors while recognising, as Heald and McLeod (2002b, p 23) point out, that no attempt was made to "forge a consensus". First, Heald and McLeod (2002b, pp 5-6) themselves remark that, while Scotland is ultimately dependent on grants from the UK government, nonetheless its Parliament derives around 15% of its spending from taxes under its control.

Second, Midwinter (2002b) again defends the current arrangements as providing "relative stability" and "flexibility" in funding. Once more emphasising the political and historical nature of the devolution settlement and the associated financial arrangements, he argues that it would not be in Scotland's interest to change the current system and that anyway such a change would not be politically acceptable. However, he also recognises "structural weaknesses" in devolved finance that may only be resolved by a "constitutional conflict" that persuades the Treasury – once again the key player here – of the need for some form of change. Midwinter reiterates the point that, although clearly sceptical of needs-based assessments himself, nonetheless Scotland continues to score highly on indicators of deprivation such as morbidity and poverty (2002b, pp 116-18). Finally, Bell and Christie (2002) start by making the obvious, but important, point that while devolution radically changed Scotland's political system "its fiscal settlement was substantially unaffected". Unlike Midwinter, however, they are sceptical of the long-term sustainability of the Barnett formula and suggest the likelihood for the consideration of a "new fiscal settlement" in the medium term. At either end of the spectrum lie, on the one hand, a needs-derived form of assessment; and, on the other, the "radical alternative" of fiscal autonomy (2002, pp 122, 136-7).

## The Tartan Tax

Of course, as Heald and McLeod have reminded us, the funding of devolved Scotland does not derive entirely from the Treasury. Furthermore, the Scottish Parliament does have a revenue-raising power of its own. For reasons that will soon become obvious, we now move into one of the shortest sections of this book, a discussion of the so-called Tartan Tax.

As we saw in Chapter One, the 1997 Scottish referendum asked, at the insistence of the New Labour leadership, two questions: should Scotland have a parliament; and should such a body have tax-raising powers? We also saw that both of these propositions received significant majorities, albeit larger for the first than for the second. Accordingly, under the 1998 Scotland Act, the new Parliament – and here it differs from the Welsh Assembly – was given the right to vary the basic rate of income tax by three pence in the pound. During the 1999 General Election, only one major political party, the SNP, made a definite pledge to utilise this power in order to finance its manifesto pledges. The immediate context here was Gordon Brown's recent announcement of a cut in the basic rate of income tax by one pence in the pound (the SNP's proposals, had they been implemented, would simply have returned the situation to what it had recently been) (Paterson et al, 2001, pp 17-18).

The broader context, however, was New Labour's commitment to stick with Conservative spending plans during its first term of office. Labour in Scotland followed this general line of financial responsibility, pledging not to use the Parliament's fiscal powers if elected. So, for instance, in early 2002 a BBC poll revealed that the Scots were significantly more willing to accept tax rises to improve the NHS than their counterparts elsewhere in Britain. Nonetheless, the health minister went out of his way to say that there were no plans to utilise the Tartan Tax to this end[5]. By the time of the 2003 elections, the SNP was beginning to argue a fiscal independence case, and thus its manifesto, like that of Labour, declared for no deployment of the tax-raising power[6]. In the event, of course, the Scottish people acquired a second Labour/Liberal Democrat coalition. Although the Liberals had hinted, during the election, at the possibility of using Holyrood's fiscal powers under certain circumstances, the document produced by the coalition on the successful conclusion of their negotiations appears unequivocal: "We will not use the income tax varying power of the Scottish Parliament"[7].

It would be wrong to argue that the very limited tax-raising powers vested in the Scottish Parliament could go a long way in addressing some of the issues discussed in subsequent chapters. Utilisation would cost a lot to set up; possibly, although not necessarily, be unpopular; and would produce relatively little revenue. Hence Lynch's (2001, p 25) caustic remark that the tax power "exists more as symbol than an effective financing scheme". Nonetheless, the powers are there; are among the few powers the Parliament has in this field; were strongly argued for up to the devolution settlement; and, although they might not raise much, would raise something. As a journalist for *The Herald* (a newspaper that has recently argued for more fiscal autonomy) put it: "So the mystery endures. The Tartan Tax. Why?"[8]. Part of the answer to this might be that the use of this power has not been ruled out quite so unequivocally as at first appears.

Even in the present circumstances, however, we might also note an important point made by Simeon (2003, p 230) in her discussion of free personal care for the elderly. The separation of expenditure and income-generating responsibilities, she suggests, "changes the shape of political debate in Scotland". It allows for relatively generous policies for which the Parliament is not under any obligation to directly raise money. To put it another way, Edinburgh has only limited powers to raise income that in any event it has not employed, while its main responsibilities are to spend large sums of money on social welfare programmes, some of which are not followed or even approved of by the London government. Of course, this has to be put in the context of the aforementioned points that such schemes have to operate within an overall budget allocation; and that the Treasury appears determined to exert its authority over spending as often as possible. It is in this context that we return to the issue of Scotland's apparent funding advantage when compared with the rest of the UK, and then to the Executive's welfare spending priorities.

## Comparative funding

Much important work has been done to understand Scottish public expenditure, notably through *Government expenditure and revenue in Scotland* (GERS). The most recent edition of GERS was, at the time of writing, from January 2003 and dealt with the period 2000-01 (Scottish Executive, 2003a). From this wide-ranging and complex document, we can extract the following points. First, total government expenditure on Scotland in the period was estimated at £36.3 billion, this being 9.9% of the UK total. To put this in context, Scottish GDP was 8.2% of the UK total, while its population share was 8.6%. Second, GERS breaks down public expenditure into identifiable and non-identifiable: that is, respectively, "expenditure undertaken in providing services for the benefit of the population in a particular part of the UK, in this case Scotland"; and "expenditure which is incurred on behalf of the UK or GB". It is identifiable expenditure with which we are concerned here (non-identifiable consists largely of defence) for the simple reason that this includes the welfare services dealt with in this volume. Third, within identifiable expenditure the largest single category is social security, as we know reserved to London. However, as a point of reference, it is worth noting that this constituted, in the period 2000-01, around one third of overall identifiable expenditure; and that if a value of 100 is ascribed to the UK in this category, then relatively Scotland scores 110.

Fourth, if we compare expenditure per head, we find that, again taking the UK as 100, in 2000-01 the Scottish index figure was 118, that for England 96, that for Wales 113, and that for Northern Ireland 136. The Scottish and English indices have remained relatively steady over a five-year period, while those of Wales and Northern Ireland have fluctuated. Hence, in Scotland's case, identifiable expenditure was around 18% above the UK average or, to put it another way, was "around £4.3 billion higher than if UK expenditure had been apportioned strictly by Scotland's population share" (Scottish Executive, 2003a, p 17). Fifth, differences between Scotland and the UK are also evident in individual programmes, including those dealt with in later chapters. Health and personal social services (the second largest category of identifiable expenditure after social security – together they constitute nearly two thirds of the total) has an index figure of 116 compared with the UK's 100, while another large spender, education, has a figure of 124. The overall pattern of expenditure in Scotland is broadly similar to that for the UK. Commenting on these comparatively higher levels of Scottish spending, the document remarks that the there are "many complex reasons for the differences in expenditure priorities". Among these are population distribution – here, as is often the case, the cost of providing education in remote areas is alluded to; see also Chapter Four – while in "health expenditure, Scotland's needs are greater for a number of reasons, including high death rates from circulatory disease and cancer" (Scottish Executive, 2003a, p 18).

A longer-term perspective has been provided by the author of the GERS report and chief economic adviser to the Executive in the symposium on fiscal autonomy encountered earlier in this chapter. Allowing for concerns about the nature of the data, for our purposes what stands out is that "Scottish aggregate government expenditure has consistently exceeded that of the UK as a proportion of GDP" (Goudie, 2002, p 62) for the past two decades; that over the same period government expenditure per capita in Scotland has been between 10% and nearly 20% higher than that of the UK; and that identifiable expenditure has, from the beginning of the 1990s to 2000, averaged 17.5% higher than that of the UK. Goudie (2002) has also used this data to argue that overall Scotland has a structural deficit; that this too is long-standing; and that this therefore implies that "a continued net fiscal transfer to Scotland remains necessary to maintain the current service provision" (p 84). The GERS report thus appears to confirm the points noted earlier:

- that Scottish public expenditure in general is higher than that of England especially;
- that, within this, Scottish expenditure is higher on social welfare than in the UK;
- that Scotland is thus advantaged over England and indeed Wales, although not to the same extent as Northern Ireland;
- that this is a long-standing situation;
- and that, furthermore, the Scottish economy is presently not paying its way.

We have already encountered some of the arguments as to why this might not be as unreasonable as it at first appears and these will be elaborated upon in Chapter Three. Nonetheless it is important to acknowledge that critics from, in particular, North East England undoubtedly have a point when they complain about Scotland's apparently privileged position.

## Spending priorities

What, however, have been the spending priorities? In its 2000 Spending Review, the Treasury remarked that the extra monies allocated would provide a "major boost to the public services in Scotland, Wales and Northern Ireland". Such increases would "allow the devolved administrations to improve public services and determine their own particular public expenditure outcomes" according to their own particular needs[9]. Two years later, the Treasury announced a further rise in monies available to Scotland, again remarking that these would enable the Executive to improve Scottish public services in ways appropriate to Scotland. The Scottish Secretary, again defending the Barnett formula, also highlighted the continuing benefit to the people of Scotland of the country's membership of the UK and claimed that the Blair government's "successful management of the economy and sound public finances" had led to the "substantial additional resources for Scotland". It was now for the Executive to "translate this into the best possible public services for the Scottish people"[10]. As Parry (2003, p 31) points out, the Treasury announcement was the third "to confirm real-term increases in non-cash social policy going way beyond those thought sustainable in the previous 25 years". This longer-term perspective is particularly illuminating, confirming that at least in some respects New Labour has shown its commitment to investment in public services.

In the light of the 2002 Spending Review, how did the Executive respond? We sketched in broad terms the thrust of Finance Minister's 2002 Budget

Statement in Chapter One and earlier in this chapter his defence of Barnett. We now look at this statement in more detail with a view to assessing spending priorities. The minister noted, first, that by 2005-06 the total resources available would be some £25 billion and that the "significant increases to our budget" that he was announcing were a result in turn of "the increase in public expenditure across the UK" – that is, of Barnett. In other words, the annual average rise up to 2005-06 would be of the order of 4.6%, and over the coming three years "we will be investing over £70 billion pounds in Scotland". The big-spending portfolios – over one billion pounds per annum, and together constituting well over three quarters of total expenditure – were in descending order:

- finance and public services;
- health and community care;
- enterprise, lifelong learning, transport;
- environment and rural development.

More discursively, the minister emphasised that his was a budget for "every man, woman and child in Scotland". For the young, the Executive planned to build on its "delivery of a free nursery place for every three and four year old" by, for example, refurbishing schools and improving the nutritional quality of school meals. As the last point suggests, the Executive thus believed investing "in Scotland's health is investing in Scotland's future and is one of our key priorities". Health improvement was to have the resources available to it doubled and the Executive's objective was, as we see further in Chapter Five of this book, "nothing less than a major change in life expectancy for people across Scotland" (and see Chapter Four for pre-school placements). All this would constitute unprecedented levels of investment in health. Further reworking these official figures, health and community care constitutes around 31.5% of total expenditure in 2002-03, rising to around 33.2% in 2005-06.

Of course, there was also, in true New Labour style, emphasis on the need for economic growth and the achievement of centrally imposed targets accompanied by a dismissal of the significance of wealth redistribution. And, as we have noted on more than one occasion, the Executive spends money in the various fields of social welfare because that is mainly where its devolved powers lie. Nonetheless, the commitment to improve the quality of Scottish life through programmes of government spending is also clearly present. The Finance Minister notably rounded on the "scare mongers" who had said that:

> we wouldn't be able to afford our ambitious agenda. We can. We were told there wouldn't be enough money to deliver on student support, to modernise the teaching profession or to provide free personal care. There is.[11]

Once again, we can see in this document one of the many tensions inherent in New Labourism: on the one hand the stress on economic growth and indifference to how its benefits are distributed, on the other ambitious plans to improve, through state action, social conditions.

This strategy was essentially unaltered during and after the May 2003 election when, as we have seen, much was made of improving and investing in the public services. The Draft Budget of September 2003 slightly revised the 2002 plans in the light of the commitments given in the coalition document *Partnership for a better Scotland*. In real terms (at 2003 prices), total expenditure was to increase between 2003-04 and 2005-06 from £22.8 billion to £24.4 billion, up by some 7%. The levels of expenditure now determined for portfolios of particular interest to this volume were as follows. Health and community care spending was to go from £7.3 billion in 2003-04 to £8.1 billion in 2005-06, a rise of around 11%. In the same period, the education and young people portfolio was to increase from £281 million to £386 million, a rise of 37%; enterprise and lifelong learning from just under £2.4 billion to just over £2.4 billion, a rise of approximately 3%; and communities (formerly social justice) from £833 million to £860 million, a rise of just over 3%[12].

Overall, then, in spending terms the Executive does appear committed to improving the lives of the Scottish people, not least in areas such as health. We begin to address why this should be deemed necessary in the first place in the next chapter.

## Notes

[1] www.bbc.co.uk, 17 July 2002, 'Fears for Scottish spending'.

[2] *The Scotsman*, 22 April 2003, 'Scottish public spending highest in the world'. (Health expenditure and outcomes are discussed in Chapters Five and Six.)

[3] www.bbc.co.uk, 7 November 2001, 'Liddell defends Barnett formula'.

[4] www.scotland.gov.uk, 12 September 2002, 'Spending Plans 2003-2006'.

[5] www.bbc.co.uk, 21 February 2002, 'Scots back tax for health service'.

[6] *The Herald*, 1 May 2003, 'What the parties promise'.

[7] www.scotland.gov.uk/library5/pfbs

[8] *The Herald*, 14 April 2003, 'Mystery of the Tartan Tax: why do the parties simply dismiss it?', 1 May 2003, 'The vision to build a dynamic Scotland'.

[9] www.hm-treasury.gov.uk, 'Spending Review 2000'.

[10] www.hm-treasury.gov.uk, Press Release 15 July 2002, 'New spending plans for Scotland'.

[11] www.scotland.gov.uk, 12 September 2002, 'Spending Plans 2003-2006'.

[12] www.scotland.gov.uk/library5/finance/db05s-01.asp

# THREE

# Poverty, inequality and social disadvantage

## Introduction

> Tackling poverty and social exclusion [have been] seen as a major priority for the re-established Scottish Parliament.... Since 1999 the Scottish Executive has sought to present that attack on poverty as a central organising principle of the new Parliament. In some important respects this has involved a degree of divergence between Holyrood and Westminster. While it should not be overstated, nonetheless it is also clear that a different language is often mobilised in Scotland. Thus there is a greater stress on social inclusion (as opposed to exclusion), on partnership, equality, and, importantly, on social justice. There is now a Minister for Social Justice with responsibility for these issues. (Brown et al, 2002, pp 6-7)

> Child poverty is at the heart of the UK and Scottish governments' agendas .... The political context of a devolved Scotland (in which responsibility for some poverty-related matters is devolved), the subtlety of variation in political priorities that results (such as the greater emphasis on social *in*clusion in Scotland ...) and a quantitatively and qualitatively different experience of poverty in Scotland ... necessitate a Scottish-level analysis of poverty. Nonetheless, it should be acknowledged that responsibility for most of the economic factors which would tackle child poverty are reserved at Westminster.[1]

The first of these quotes, from a joint publication of the Child Poverty Action Group (CPAG) and the Scottish Poverty Information Unit, neatly encapsulates a number of themes of this chapter and of this book as a whole: the possibility of policy divergence, the Executive's addressing of the issue of poverty, and the emphasis on classic social democratic preoccupations such as equality and social justice. The second, from an Executive publication of autumn 2003, illustrates that body's commitment to the issue of child poverty in particular, while also drawing attention to the policy constraints embedded in the devolution settlement.

This chapter:

- describes the historical and contemporary context of poverty in Scotland;
- examines New Labour attitudes to the issue, and its expansion into the more all-embracing concept of social exclusion;
- outlines analyses of Scottish poverty by both independent and official commentators;
- and discusses how the Executive has gone about addressing the problem.

As particular instances of socioeconomic disadvantage, it then focuses briefly on health inequalities and child poverty. It does so for five reasons.

First, child poverty has been identified by the administrations in London and in Edinburgh as a major policy concern both for its own sake and as a means of improving human capital. Second, health inequalities are often seen as organically linked to other forms of inequality. This in turn highlights the more general point that there are significant inequalities within Scotland itself. Third, tackling child poverty and health inequalities – and, more generally, every aspect of social exclusion – is seen as the task not simply of one government department, but as part of a total strategy. This is particularly noteworthy in Scotland where the role of the Minister for Communities (previously Social Justice) is to provide precisely this sort of cross-government collaboration and where the stress has consciously been on social inclusion. From the outset, the emphasis on inclusion embraced three particular priorities: young people, communities, and the impact of anti-poverty action (Munn, 2000, p 116). Fourth, there is clearly a resources issue in tackling such complex problems as child poverty and, as we have seen in Chapters One and Two of this book, the Executive does not have powers over important policy areas such as social security. Even within the Executive's remit, the difficulties of utilising resources effectively and implementing joined-up government were forcefully brought home in autumn 2003 by reports that individual departments "do not know how much efforts to pursue an inclusion agenda are costing"[2]. Fifth, an understanding of the nature and scale of these problems forms an important background for our discussions in Chapters Four and Five.

## Historical background: from Industrial Revolution to deindustrialisation

While Scotland, like the rest of the UK, is a rich country when compared with much of the rest of the world, nonetheless poverty and inequality have long, and quite correctly, been seen as blighting Scottish society. As Gordon Brown is probably fed up being reminded, in the mid-1970s he argued that any examination of contemporary Scotland "must start from where people are, the realities of day-to-day living, extremes of wealth and poverty, unequal opportunities at work, in housing, health education and community living generally" (quoted in Mooney and Johnstone, 2000, p 167). The totality of this analysis is worth remarking upon. While it comes from a more left-wing phase in Brown's career, it also sees an organic interrelationship between poverty and other social phenomena.

Historically, the existence of poverty in what was at one point a highly advanced industrial society can be attributed to the nature and consequences of its modern economic development. The manner in which Scotland industrialised from the late 18th through to the 20th centuries resulted in a concentration of population in the central belt. This in turn gave rise to the notorious overcrowding in urban slums, many later replaced by equally notorious and vast municipal authority housing estates. The situation was at its most acute in Glasgow, which has long had the dubious honour of the worst housing conditions in Britain and continues to be the focal point of Scottish poverty, but could also be found in other towns and cities. Accompanying these problems were high rates of morbidity and mortality. Over-reliance on a limited range of industries meant that when world economic conditions changed, as they did in the course of the 20th century, the economy was increasingly vulnerable. So even in the relatively affluent 1950s and 1960s, unemployment was persistently higher than in England, a phenomenon with roots going back at least to the inter-war period. Furthermore, wage rates tended to be lower than their English counterparts. Scottish industrial capitalism, of the sort traditionally based on heavy and extractive industries, received its final deathblows in the 1980s (Harvie, 1998, ch 7).

Surveying a long period of Scottish history, Houston and Knox (2001) remark that recent changes in labour market structures and social structures have afforded new opportunities to particular groups within Scottish society. This is not unproblematic, however, given the rising volume of poorly paid, unstable jobs. Moreover, they also note that there are significant differences between mainly affluent cities such as Edinburgh and Aberdeen (the latter largely as a result of the oil industry) and more deprived urban centres such as Dundee and Glasgow. They thus conclude (2001, p xxxvii) that, as a result of these historic trends, west-central Scotland in particular is one of the poorest parts of Great Britain; and that "large numbers of poorer Scots remain excluded from the discourses of civil society" (see also Levitt, 1983; Lee, 1995; Harvie 1998; Mooney and Johnstone, 2000; Mitchell and Dorling, 2002). To give this a sense of particularity, Harvie (2001, p 514, 2002, p 229) points out that, in 1991, the (in)famous Easterhouse council estate in Glasgow was home to some 40,000 residents, had an unemployment rate of 48%, and a car ownership rate of around 20%; and, more broadly, that between 1979 and 1993, "families on or below half the national average income rose from 9 per cent to 24 per cent" (for an account of life in Easterhouse, see Holman, 1998). Here again we are reminded of the significant disparities within Scotland itself, given that not that far from Easterhouse, at least in a geographical sense, are Bearsden and Eastwood, among the least deprived areas not only in Scotland but in Britain as a whole (Mooney and Johnstone, 2000, p 171). This urban emphasis should not, incidentally, be allowed to obscure long-standing problems of rural poverty and, by extension, social exclusion.

On the eve of devolution, Lee (1995) drew up a "balance sheet" of the Union. One of his major conclusions was that, while economic restructuring had indeed taken place, by "most economic and social indicators ... Scotland remains, with the exception of a few favoured locations, troubled by unemployment, poor housing and most other characteristic features of relative deprivation". Lee pointed to the origins of Scottish poverty in its historically (and continuing) low-wage economy; and, once more, to its regional dimensions. Again using the example of Easterhouse, he pointed out that, here, "the principal ingredients of multiple deprivation were large households, several children, male unemployment and single parent families. Many pensioners lived in poor circumstances" (Lee, 1995, p 214). A couple of years later, Peat and Boyle (1999a, pp 8-12; 1999b, p 56), in an economic survey of Scotland, further confirmed, first, the significance of regional disparities. In a telling statistic, they pointed out that, in 1977, "the gap between the richest and poorest region was 18 per cent. By 1995 it had leapt to 62 per cent". At this latter date, the two most affluent regions, by some way, were Grampian and Lothian, while at the bottom came the Borders, followed by the Highlands and Islands and Strathclyde. Second, Peat and Boyle showed that Scottish per capita Gross Domestic Product (GDP) had grown steadily since the early 1970s but was still somewhat lower than that for the UK as a whole (although higher than that of Wales, Northern Ireland, and some of the English regions). Furthermore, when compared with other European countries, Scotland scored poorly with, at this stage, only Portugal and Spain worse off. By contrast, some of the Scandinavian countries had around double GDP per capita.

## Acknowledging, measuring and thinking about poverty

Clearly, then, New Labour and, subsequently, the Scottish Executive inherited huge problems. Commentators such as Mooney and Johnstone and Toynbee and Walker point out that, since 1979, poverty had become a serious problem in the UK as a whole with, most notably, large numbers of children living in poverty, a doubling of the number of households where nobody had a job, and a widening gap between rich and poor. This was not only unprecedented since 1945; it also made the UK one of the most unequal societies in the western world (Mooney and Johnstone, 2000, p 156; Toynbee and Walker, 2001, p 12). So, in crucial respects, there were changes with the defeat of the Conservatives for, as commentators such as the CPAG have noted of the outcome of the 1997 General Election, "Labour's willingness to resurrect the concept of poverty, and to locate anti-poverty policies high on the political agenda for the first time in decades" was a major attitudinal shift. While problems arose with how poverty was actually to be tackled, neglect of the concept of poverty was "not an accusation that can be levelled at the current government" (Brown et al, 2002, pp 3, 157). Indeed among the government's major commitments were Blair's pledge to end child poverty within a generation and Brown's adherence to full employment, important given the emphasis on work as the best way out of poverty (Toynbee and Walker, 2001, pp 11-12, 14).

In a Scottish context, we have observed that poverty was a long-standing problem and, with both the election of New Labour and the prospect of devolved powers to Edinburgh, a considerable body of literature – official and independent – engaged with the issue, suggesting potential areas to be addressed by the impending Scottish administration. Before examining some of this, however, it is important to note a couple of important points. Poverty is clearly a far from unproblematic concept. Should it be seen in relative or absolute terms? How can a poverty line be agreed? Over what time period do we measure success in combating poverty and its effects? (For a useful discussion of definitional issues, see Scottish Poverty Information Unit, 1998, section 1; Bailey et al, 2003, ch 2.) For the purposes of this volume, what is important is less the issue of detailed measurement and more the sense that poverty is generally agreed to be an issue to be addressed with a degree of urgency.

Nonetheless, it is worth observing that it was long the case that inadequate statistical data existed for its proper analysis at the Scottish level. Addressing this was one of the Executive's early tasks – as that body itself acknowledged – although some problems clearly remain (Scottish Executive Central Research Unit, 1999, pp 87-8; Scottish Executive, 2000a, p 29)[3]. Serious steps forward, however, have been taken by the Executive's Annual Reports on Social Justice (Scottish Executive 2000a, 2002a); its analyses of households below average income; and its commissioning of the 2003 Indices of Deprivation[4]. We should likewise note the Scottish Centre for Social Justice's work (commissioned by the Executive's Central Statistics Unit) on developing the means to measure deprivation in a more nuanced way (Bailey et al, 2003).

This in turn resulted in a recommendation in autumn 2003 that the Executive should accept the definition of poverty embracing the idea that deprivation was a "multi-dimensional concept, concerned not merely with material goods but also with the ability to participate in social life". Deprivation was also a "relative" concept, intimately associated with poverty, and both "financial resources and outcomes should be captured in measures of multiple deprivation". It was further suggested that separate standards should be used to measure adult and child deprivation, with research on the latter building on the "views and experiences of children" (see Chapter Four for a discussion of children's rights). As to the adult measure, this should be able to "disaggregate results for different social groups based on: age, gender, ethnicity, disability, sexual orientation, household type and other factors such as health or employment status"[5]. For the Executive in particular, the ability to measure problems is an important part of policy formulation, just as successfully hitting targets is a key part of policy outcomes.

At a broader, conceptual level, much Third Way thinking has stressed the idea of social exclusion. For Giddens (2000, p 105), social exclusion extends beyond material deprivation to, for example, "not sharing in the opportunities that the majority have" (p 105). It is thus, for those affected, an experience that touches the totality of their lives. The Third Way approach to welfare is thus that it does not just "react to" inequality and poverty; rather, it enters into "the life circumstances of individuals and groups involved" (Giddens, 2000, p 121). What is important here is that, first, we have a concept that seeks to move away from a simply income-based definition of poverty to one that embraces a whole range of factors – educational, familial, geographic, age-related, and so on – shaping and even determining individual lives. Second, such a strategy involves solutions that rely not on direct wealth redistribution, as in much previous social democratic thought and action, but rather on labour market participation. The latter is seen as a means not only of bringing people out of poverty but also of ensuring their active engagement with the wider society – attacking, in other words, social exclusion. This approach is central to the New Labour project. Indeed as Lister remarks, a principle characteristic of New Labour is its "reluctance to acknowledge the power of deep structural inequalities". It welfare philosophy is thus "a paradigm shift from a concern with equality to a focus on social inclusion and opportunity, with which comes responsibility" (Lister, 2001, p 431). Third, this kind of approach also involves both the active engagement by all branches of government and the targeting of particular groups in the population.

## Scottish analyses of poverty and social exclusion

By the late 1990s, Scottish public discourse on social exclusion revolved around, to put it very crudely, three particular points:

1. that New Labour had, in 1997, inherited a severe poverty problem and that this was an area in which Scotland had long suffered and was particularly badly affected;
2. that devolution might of itself be important in tackling this issue;
3. that the concept of social exclusion/inclusion provided a new way forward for tackling the problem in an holistic way.

As our first illustration of these points, we take the document published in 1998 by the independent Scottish Council Foundation and evocatively entitled *Three nations: Social exclusion in Scotland* (McCormick and Leicester, 1998). A rich and complex text, for present purposes four themes emerge. First, the document placed the whole issue of tackling social exclusion in the context of recent history; hence, for instance, the significance of the Commission on Social Justice set up in the early 1990s by the then Labour leader, and advocate of devolution, John Smith. The commission's brief had been to examine, inter alia, welfare policy and its recommendations included some measure of Scottish and Welsh political devolution. The creation of the Social Exclusion Unit in the Cabinet Office by the incoming New Labour administration had been shortly followed by the setting up, in the Scottish Office, of the Social Exclusion

Network. Furthermore, the authors saw welfare reform and devolution not as separate parts of New Labour's political agenda but, on the contrary, as intimately linked. Hence the "common thread" linking social exclusion, welfare reform, and devolution was "the acknowledgement that social justice cannot be realised without better coordination between government departments and between tiers of government". The creation of a Scottish Parliament was thus "potentially a useful step towards the goal of a more inclusive and just society" (p 6).

Second, in 'Explaining exclusion', the authors of the report commended an approach to social welfare that "placed an emphasis on prevention rather than cure". A multiplicity of factors was involved in exclusion from society – poverty, and its duration and concentration, were especially noted – but in the end, the "strongest cause of exclusion is lack of work". This was not unproblematic, however, for while "a job remains the best route out of poverty, it offers no guarantees". In a further reminder of the country's long history as a low-wage economy, it was claimed that more "people are earning their poverty than in the past. The lowest-paid tenth of Scottish workers now take home around 55 per cent of the average wage – the lowest share yet recorded" (McCormick and Leicester, 1998, pp 8-12).

This leads on to the document's third point: 'Is Scotland different?' While careful to note the complexity of comparisons of poverty and deprivation, made more complex by the then relative paucity of data, it was suggested that there was "some evidence that the depth, duration and nature of poverty in Scotland differs from the UK average". The key word here is 'differs'. There were undoubtedly some causes for optimism: some of Scotland's "distinctive" welfare features already worked to its advantage, for example in education and child welfare. Nonetheless, there was also highly negative features of the Scottish experience, most (in)famously in health. Scotland was, more generally, divided in three ways: "Excluded Scotland, Insecure Scotland, and Settled Scotland".

Finally, then, what was to be done about this? The document pointedly remarked that the healthy state of the economy notwithstanding, the persistence of a group of long-term unemployed and their families was a "sharp reminder – if one were needed – that economic growth is not enough by itself to tackle exclusion". In summary, the authors suggested that stress should be placed on Scotland as "A Working Nation"; "A Learning Nation" (education being a "powerful weapon against exclusion"); "A Healthier Nation", with concern being expressed about health inequalities within the UK and Scotland itself; and a series of other measures including "a new approach to retirement". Overall, a more inclusive Scotland would not be "one without risk, uncertainty, unemployment, low pay or inequality. But that is not to say that all of these cannot be reduced. Our central argument is that it is essential to reduce them" (McCormick and Leicester, 1998, pp 5-6, 8-12, 14-17, 18ff). As we shall see, the Executive's approach to social welfare clearly mirrored these analyses in crucial respects.

If the Scottish Council Foundation's prognosis was relatively optimistic, at least at this stage, there was also a recognition elsewhere that problems might not be immediately solved by a devolved government. Paterson (2000a, passim), commenting on papers given at a 1999 symposium on social inclusion and exclusion, made the following important observations. First, he quite correctly pointed out that social welfare was a political project and, particularly at a time when a new democratic institution was being set up, "claims that there could ever be any type of apolitical solution to the problem of social exclusion" (p 68) were untenable. Second, if a pessimistic view of the new parliament was taken, then it might have no impact on social exclusion or inclusion because the tools that could fundamentally address these issues remained with Whitehall. A public debate on the acquisition of further powers might therefore be necessary. Third, and on the other hand, the parliament could be argued to have at least some powers to promote social inclusion because of its "legislative competence … its capacity to promote social cohesion, and … its role in articulating a sense of common identity" (p 70). To focus on legislative competence (the latter two issues are discussed in Chapter Six of this volume), Paterson emphasised the virtual independence of Scottish education and the effect educational provision could have on labour market supply.

So, as the Scottish Parliament came into being, poverty and social exclusion, and how to deal with them within the constraints of the devolution settlement, were high on the political agenda. In 1999, research on the experience of social exclusion in Scotland concluded that, in policy-making terms, the problem involved "addressing multi-layered, overlapping and deep-rooted problems". Consequently, there were "no easy messages or lessons for policy development. Tackling social exclusion poses an immense challenge" (Scottish Executive: Central Research Unit, 1999, p 82). This challenge had "implications for every area of policy-making" and so a need for "integration and coordination in policy design" (p 84). The concept of social exclusion could itself be seen as recognition of "the multiplicity of individual needs, and emphasises the need for a holistic approach to meet them". There was, however, a concern that the concept "might pathologise and stigmatise individuals in a way that would be disempowering and unhelpful" as well as a fear that "a term which lacks precision or poignancy" might be used as a euphemism masking "the reality of disadvantage and inequality faced by individuals in Scotland". In short, the "key challenge" posed by the concept of social exclusion was to ensure its efficacy as a model for analysing society and one that would aid those "involved in formulating and delivering policies to tackle discrimination, disadvantage and inequality" (Scottish Executive: Central Research Unit, 1999, p 87).

We might note here three points:

- the perceived complexity of the issue;
- the consequent, repeated, need for policy coordination (soon to be embodied in the form of a Minister for Social Justice);
- and an unease with the expression 'social exclusion'.

In the same year, the Scottish Social Inclusion Network (note here the shift to 'inclusion') commissioned a report to examine ways of tackling poverty at a local level. In line with other analyses, this pointed to the worsening situation since the late 1970s and put forward a plan for immediate and medium-term Executive action. It also suggested that a society "without poverty and exclusion would offer all its citizens a range of affordable choices and give everyone an adequate income through employment or, for those who cannot work, through benefit", an interesting acknowledgement that the labour market was not the only mechanism for achieving income security. The freeing up of markets had left certain groups vulnerable to poor quality services – public and private – and in any case, and echoing the Scottish Council Foundation's remark, "the market has its limits when it comes to social justice, and very significant numbers of people in Scotland remain in poverty" (Strategy Action Team, 1999, p 1). These various rejections of the market's efficacy sit uneasily with New Labour ideology, at least in its purest form and as much more explicitly utilised in England.

Unsurprisingly, then, the commitment to attack poverty was affirmed by the new Parliament and its leading figures, and especially those representing Scottish Labour. First Minister Dewar, for example, claimed that "Scotland today is an unequal society" in which "(t)oo many families live in poverty". Such "misery", he continued, "demands action" (quoted in Mooney and Johnstone, 2000, p 167). Indeed, the attack on poverty was, according to a Scottish Labour Party document produced before the 2003 elections, the very reason for the party's existence:

> The battle against poverty and injustice gave birth to the Labour Party. For over a century, we have continued to fight to create a society in which everyone is valued and to which everyone can contribute.[6]

So far, this might be seen for the most part as highly positive. We should acknowledge, however, that an overly optimistic view of the Executive and its strategy has not been universally shared. Paterson's (2002a) remarks on devolution's limitations and the need for at least a discussion of an extension of powers, for example, have already been cited. Mitchell and Dorling (2002, pp 173-5), although far from pessimistic in their overall analysis, nonetheless make the obvious but crucial point that "Scotland has become an increasingly segregated society over recent years". For Mooney and Johnstone (2000, pp 176, 168, 158ff, 177), while "there are some references to 'poverty' in Scottish policy documents, overwhelmingly the terms social exclusion and inclusion tend to be used". Hence, they continue, there is "little indication that the approach to poverty being adopted by the new Scottish parliament is different from that of the Westminster government" (pp 176-7). They claim that the Scottish Council Foundation's depiction of the "three nations" of Scotland is both definitionally imprecise and, like other such studies, of limited value when they fail to "explore the relationship between the poor and the wealthy" (p 168). Mooney and Johnstone further caution against mythologising Scottish difference on the grounds that this obscures as much as it reveals, not least in underplaying socioeconomic divisions within Scotland itself. They too also comment on the limits to the Executive's powers, notably in the field of social security.

Once again, we have here a variety of interpretations, a further salutary reminder of the contested and politicised nature of social policy. Mooney and Johnstone's comments are particularly useful in reminding us that New Labour, and its approach to poverty and wealth distribution, is not an unknown phenomenon in Scotland.

## Poverty and the Executive

How, then, has the Executive viewed its role in combating poverty and social exclusion? We briefly examine some key documents and speeches to gain a sense of its overall strategy and a useful starting point is the report on social justice published in 2000. Six issues stand out:

1. The commitments to end child poverty, to bring about full employment by way of opportunities for all those who can work, to secure "dignity in old age" (p 5), and to build strong, inclusive communities are stressed.
2. The Executive emphasised its determination to break "the cycle of deprivation and disadvantage". A number of complex, long-term and deep-rooted factors had led to poverty and social exclusion, with outcomes detrimental to individuals, families, the community and the nation. No "civilised nation" could afford to tolerate this "shocking waste of human potential" – a further reminder of the aim of enhancing human capital. Real and lasting change, it was nonetheless cautioned, "needs a long-term strategy" (pp 5-6). As we saw in Chapter One, the depth and scale of Scotland's problems, and the consequent time needed to address these, has been a recurrent theme.
3. The complexity and interrelatedness of these problems required a strategy embracing "economic, education, health, justice and communities issues" (p 5) – holistic welfare, once again.
4. There were particularly Scottish characteristics to be addressed, most notably high rates of child poverty and the existence of some of "the most deprived communities in Europe" (p 6).
5. It was reiterated that social progress "must be founded on a strong economy", although it was also immediately acknowledged that, equally, "a successful economy depends on people achieving their full potential" (p 6).
6. Finally, and again exhibiting the New Labour fondness for targets, success (and, implicitly, failure) in the battle against social exclusion was to be measured, for in so doing "we have the best opportunity for delivering social justice in Scotland" (Scottish Executive, 2000a, p 29).

Individual ministers and the Executive continually reiterated the need to fight poverty on a number of fronts and to encourage social inclusion. The issue of inequalities within Scotland, for example, was addressed by a Working Group on rural poverty. This brought forward two key points. First, measuring "the extent of deprivation, and progress towards tackling poverty and social exclusion" was difficult in rural Scotland not only because of population dispersal and heterogeneity, but also because until now "there has been very little hard evidence to measure the effectiveness in rural areas of policies designed to promote social justice". Second, the evidence that the Working Group itself had collected suggested that:

> the effects of poverty and social exclusion in rural areas are similar to those in urban areas, but the causes of and solutions to poverty and social exclusion in Scotland's rural areas can be very different. (p 3)

There was a need, therefore, to "tailor the delivery of policies in rural areas" to get the best out of such policies (Scottish Executive, 2001a, p 3), an interesting instance of a policy approach both focused and flexible.

First Minister McConnell, in his July 2002 speech to the Scottish Centre for Research on Social Justice, spelled out why poverty was such a vital issue[7]. On coming to power, New Labour "faced the challenge of poverty on a massive scale". Two years later, on the opening of the Scottish Parliament, "the first steps of progress had been taken at a UK level, but there was still much to do. The problems were, and are, complex". McConnell offered several reasons why this situation had arisen in both Scotland and the UK as a whole. First, changes in the labour market resulting from the decline in traditional industries had left "people and communities jobless and excluded", a situation exacerbated by globalisation and new technology. The decline in traditional industries is an incontestable fact. Globalisation, however, is a rather more contentious proposition and one that has been, for New Labour, both an explanatory tool (or excuse) and an aspiration.

Second, social change had led to children facing "more disruption in their family lives", with, in the particular case of Scotland, a majority of children not living with both their natural parents and the highest teenage pregnancy rate in Europe. Children who experienced "severe poverty and disadvantage early in life" were more likely to "suffer long-term damage to their prospects in adulthood". In turn, and in the absence of "practical steps and support", this disadvantage could be passed on to the next generation "and the cycle will repeat itself". This last is an analysis of poverty that has been highly contested but has, all the same, a long historical pedigree. Third, the public services had, historically, experienced under-investment. Consequently, services such as health had been "undermined" and so unable to respond to changing socioeconomic circumstances.

Overall, the emphasis on children is noteworthy, as is McConnell's historical explanation of the origins of the present crisis. He also stressed that poverty was about more than just income, being "critically linked to health, to education and to housing", and was a communal as well as individual concern. The First Minister then claimed that:

> we know that the best route out of income poverty is through work. This is where our children's policies and economic objectives make common purpose.

What was needed, therefore, was the creation of the "right conditions for parents"; a strong economy; and a situation whereby work paid. As was observed in Chapter One of this book, this important speech clearly contains elements of both New Labour – work as the route out of poverty – and more traditional social democratic rhetoric.

Before focusing on responses to the battle against social exclusion in Scotland, we look at one final statement, the 2002 Annual Report, *Social justice: A Scotland where everyone matters* (Scottish Executive, 2002a). We have already commented in Chapter One on some of its broader points, but it is worth returning to both for its statistical data and because of the nature and purpose of its analyses, and it is the latter on which we concentrate. The Report reiterated the aims set out in the 2000 Annual Report and sought to assess the progress that had been made in tackling social exclusion and poverty. It stressed, first, that previous interventions had, in now familiar terms, "failed to recognise sufficiently that the reasons that people face social exclusion are complex and inter-related". What was required, therefore, was a "joined-up, cross cutting approach", an approach that had been successfully initiated and was "delivering results" (p 6). Second, resources backed up this strategy. The recently announced Scottish Budget 2003-06 had "given us the means – an unprecedented level of resources – to sharpen the attack on poverty and lack of opportunity that too many people still face". To give one particular, but of course particularly significant, example, from 2004 £20 million had been allocated to "help parents in (the) deprived areas into work by ensuring that availability of childcare is not a barrier to getting into education, training or employment" (p 3).

Third, while there remained difficulties with the lack of data, nonetheless, there was now sufficient information to evaluate the Executive's strategy. Of the 29 "milestones" identified in the report:

- 16 had "data moving in right direction" (pp 14-15);
- seven had "data broadly constant, no clear trend";
- four had "insufficient data";
- a mere two (relating to truancy and to the proportion of working age people on low income) had "data moving in wrong direction".

Using what in fact is a clear case of intrinsic evaluation, the Executive claimed that it was "beginning to break the cycle of deprivation". In so doing, it was "making real differences to people's lives" – a deliberate echo of devolution making a difference – and it was "by that standard that we have to measure everything that we do" (p 2).

This leads on to the fourth point, that while success had undoubtedly (as far as the Executive was concerned) been achieved, there were no "grounds for complacency" (p 7), yet a further instance of the rhetoric of there being 'much to do'. Finally, there was an underlying purpose behind the Executive's approach. Indeed, the "whole of our social justice strategy" was "only a means to an end". Success could only be claimed if it "gives people new opportunities to improve their lives – closing the opportunity gaps which they face". All policies and actions were to be, and embracing the evaluative point made above, "measured against success in closing the opportunity gap, to ensure we live in a society founded on fairness, equality and opportunity" (p 8). Interestingly, given the language of fairness, equality and (criticisms noted earlier notwithstanding) poverty, one rather throwaway remark also stands out in the report. Briefly discussing the Executive's *Cities review* (p 11), it is claimed that this recognised that the "wealth creation and wealth redistribution agendas are intimately related". Wealth redistribution is not a phrase that readily slips off the New Labour tongue (Scottish Executive, 2002a, pp 2-3, 6-8, 11, 14-15).

## External evaluations

If, then, these were the Executive's aspirations, and if their self-created scorecard was fairly positive, how do others see their overall performance? The press release accompanying the CPAG's publication *Poverty in Scotland 2002* also marked the government's scorecard – but in this case as "trying hard but must do better". As it explained:

> Leading experts on poverty today launch a report that shows the reduction in poverty in Scotland has stalled and still remains at disturbingly high levels. It questions whether Westminster and Holyrood are doing enough to end poverty even within a generation. (CPAG Scotland, 2002)

This, clearly, was of a somewhat different tenor to the contemporaneous Social Justice Annual Report. Where did the emphasis in the CPAG report (Brown et al, 2002) lie? It again agreed that poverty had come back on the political agenda since 1997, that the Scottish Parliament had explicitly seen the tackling of poverty as one of its defining aims, and that in some areas progress had been made. So, for instance, in child poverty (although see the completion of this quotation below), Scotland had seen a decrease from "34 per cent in 1996/97 to 30 per cent in 2000/01. Progress, albeit slow, is in the right direction". It also agreed that poverty was hard to define (as was social justice) and that data for poverty's measurement in Scotland had, to say the least, a chequered past.

Nonetheless, problems remained, and among the most important of these were as follows.

1. As with many other external commentators (for example, Kenway et al, 2002, p 14), the CPAG was clearly wary of the way in which officially determined, and abundant, indicators became the UK government's or the Executive's measures of success in combating poverty.

2. The document was extremely careful to note that there were, in some areas at least, differences between UK and Scottish experiences and that these did not necessarily show that Scotland was uniquely disadvantaged. Nonetheless, average Scottish incomes were lower than those for the UK, a higher proportion of the Scottish population received income support, a higher proportion of Scottish households claimed income-related benefits, and unemployment had declined more sharply in the UK than in Scotland.

3. Whatever government intentions, inequalities in wealth remained high throughout Britain, and certainly higher than in most industrialised countries. In (as we shall see) a prescient remark, it was noted that after a period of stabilisation, such inequalities might again be on the increase (and see also Shephard, 2003, p 1: "there has been little impact upon the slight upward trend in inequality that has been experienced over Labour's term in government"). The point here is that the existence of such inequalities raises particular problems in attempts to combat poverty when it is defined, as it is by most analysts, as relative.

4. Leading on from the previous two points and something we have seen to be an historic characteristic, there remained profound inequalities within Scotland itself. Although always a complicated issue (see later in this chapter), above the most micro levels of disaggregation – to give a crude example, Edinburgh as a whole is relatively affluent (in Scottish and UK terms) while containing areas of severe poverty – there is "a spatial concentration of poverty" (Brown et al, 2002, p 98). Although in general Scotland fared reasonably well, it has areas, "particularly within Glasgow, which are ranked among the poorest in the UK" (p 83). By the standard of the 1998 Scottish Deprivation Index, Glasgow contained 22 out of the most 25 most deprived postcodes in Scotland – as is often remarked, there is a Glasgow effect when discussing Scottish poverty, inequality and deprivation. This was a further part of the rationale for targeting and area-based approaches typical of the New Labour project.

5. Again leading on from the previous points, while there was a clear sense that New Labour and the Executive deserved credit for a shift in emphasis from previous administrations, it had also to be recognised that things were not necessarily going all that well, or at least not as well as the "29 Milestones" appeared to suggest. Most notably, if the overall child poverty situation was improving, nonetheless, and to complete the quotation earlier, "but there is serious danger of not attaining the next PSA targets" (p 98), these being the Public Service Agreement targets set up by the Treasury in 1999 that had promised an end to child poverty by 2019 (within a generation) with further defined milestones in 2010 and 2004. There was, in other words, a strong sense that in this and other areas reform had stalled.

---

6. Finally, and citing the work of Mooney and Johnstone already noted, the CPAG suggested that at the outset there had been "hopes in Scotland that devolution would bring locally-appropriate policy initiatives". In some areas, for example student financing and care of the elderly, this had materialised, but overall "the differences are so far fairly limited, and tend to reflect pre-existing institutional and organisational differences". Generally, therefore, in both Scotland and Britain "policies on poverty, inequality and social inclusion/exclusion ... continue to show strong similarities" (Brown et al, 2002, p 162). This again reminds us of devolution's constraints. There were thus inherent tensions and contradictions in policy aimed at combating poverty and social exclusion – for instance, between reserved powers and devolved powers; and between nation (however defined), region (an equally problematic term), and locality (which might be urban or rural).

Other contemporary reports also pointed to the complexities of tackling Scottish poverty. The Joseph Rowntree Foundation/New Policy Institute analysis, also published in 2002 but after that of the CPAG, came to two broad conclusions. First was the "stubborn refusal of so many of the key measures of poverty and exclusion in Scotland to show any signs of movement", again a rather different point from that being made in the Social Justice Annual Report and its 29 Milestones. Using its own 'Summary of Indicators', performance, over five years, had in the 34 categories identified:

- improved in seven (for example, school leavers' qualifications);
- remained steady in 15 (for example, households without work for two years or more);
- worsened in six (for example, and damningly, inequality);
- and, for the final six, information was not available (for example, community participation).

In other words, this was a situation where around two thirds of the indicators were, at best, much the same as they had been at the beginning of the period.

Second, Kenway et al pointed out that "a strategy to reduce poverty that is built on getting people into work" – the heart of New Labour's welfare strategy – was problematic given that "40 per cent of the working age poor are actually already in work". This again points to the historic problem of Scottish low wages and is a further example of scepticism about the market's role in solving social problems. If to some extent this strategy depended on tax credits and the minimum wage then, and largely echoing the CPAG analysis, "it is a UK matter at least in the first instance". This was so, furthermore, "especially as the problem is no worse in Scotland than elsewhere". There were, on the other hand, areas of quite clear Scottish particularity, namely "in the very high proportion of its economically inactive who are sick or disabled". "Since", Kenway et al continued, "people in this position are not expected to work, the question of how they are to escape from low income and poverty is one that at the moment is without an answer". Here again was a sense of momentum stalled. These general conclusions were backed up by more detailed analysis – it was important, the authors rather pointedly asserted, "to go beyond the *Social Justice Annual Report*" (Kenway et al, 2002, pp 10, 14).

## The dimensions of poverty and inequality in Scotland

We now use the platform of both the CPAG and the Joseph Rowntree Foundation/New Policy Institute work and, latterly, that of other commentators to make the following broad points on the dimensions and nature of Scottish poverty and inequality.

First, in European terms, neither Scotland nor the UK fare well in terms of income poverty, with both, on admittedly now relatively old data, coming joint second to Greece in the European poverty league.

Second, both organisations are clearly concerned with the issue of income inequality. Although the gap in Scotland was not as wide as that for England and Wales, nonetheless both bodies found that it was widening – over a seven-year period, according to the Joseph Rowntree Foundation/New Policy Institute, this held true for both the highest and the lowest earners. For the CPAG, this raised the fundamental point that it is "not possible to offer real equality of opportunity" – a key Executive aspiration – "in deeply unequal societies" (Kenway et al, 2002, pp 23, 25 tables 4a, 4b; Brown et al, 2002, pp 52-4). This sense of a serious issue regarding inequality was reinforced by analyses of income inequality in the early summer of 2003, which appeared to show that it had returned to the levels of the early 1990s. As one commentator put it, inequality in disposable income had "gone up both in absolute terms and in terms of average inequality as compared to the situation under the Conservatives". This, he continued, was something that might be found surprising "given Labour's commitment to redistributing income via the tax and benefits system" and that would be bad news for Chancellor Brown[8].

Third, we have noted the CPAG's point – a point made in both historical and contemporary terms by other commentators – that there is a geographical dimension to Scottish poverty. The Joseph Rowntree Foundation/New Policy Institute did not necessarily disagree, while observing that around two thirds of local authority areas had at least one ward that could be characterised as having a high rate of low income and that some of these occurred in otherwise relatively affluent areas. This is indicative of poverty's pervasiveness throughout Scottish society while continuing to justify the targeted approach noted earlier. More generally, however, the paucity of useful data was once again commented upon (Kenway et al, 2002, pp 26-9). This last point reinforces the significance of the Executive's initiatives in this respect. While it is perfectly correct to note the widespread geographical distribution of poverty, it is also salutary to observe that Executive data show the City of Glasgow scoring first on all deprivation indicators. At the other end of the spectrum, Aberdeenshire, East Renfrewshire and East Dunbartonshire experienced the lowest average scores[9]. As Bailey et al (2003, p 20) comment, Glasgow's recent economic successes notwithstanding, "the city continues to dominate patterns of deprivation in Scotland". This point was further reinforced by analyses in autumn 2003 that showed the city to have high levels of one-parent families – with more than half of these parents being economically inactive – and overcrowding. In the case of the former, only three local authorities (Manchester, and two London boroughs) scored higher in the UK, while overcrowding was double the Scottish average[10].

## Health inequalities

We now focus briefly on health inequalities, a serious social issue in modern Scotland and one that has been the object of considerable attention on the part of the Executive and of policy analysts. Health policy is dealt with in Chapter Five of this book, but here we examine some analyses put forward in this area focusing on the interaction with poverty. The CPAG volume, using the starting point of Wilkinson's (1996) famous and important interpretation, argues that the "association between poverty and poor health is now largely incontrovertible". Low income was not an "absolute arbiter" of poor health (although it clearly does not help); inequality also had a key part to play. So the "experience of powerlessness, exclusion and discrimination" had a profound effect "through various psychological and physiological mechanisms" (Brown et al, 2002, p 151). At a more obviously empirical level, in 2002 Scots were still "the sick women and men of Europe", a situation unlikely to change for the better "without addressing the causes of poverty and structural inequality" (pp 153-4). As we shall see in Chapter Five, Scotland's health record remains poor in UK and European terms.

The Joseph Rowntree Foundation/New Policy Institute brought forward some depressing data, based on close statistical analysis. So, for example, children from poor households were much more likely to be injured in road accidents than their wealthier counterparts, and consultations for mental health problems were "considerably higher" in the most deprived areas (Kenway et al, 2002, p 74). The commentary on this part of the volume argued, unequivocally, that one of the "main reasons" for Scotland's poor health record was "the perpetuation of health inequalities between rich and poor people and communities within Scotland". With "few exceptions", the notable differences in "behaviour, disease, disability and premature death are associated with area deprivation, household poverty and occupational social class". While other factors might also contribute to such a poor state of health, "inequalities in social circumstances" were "significantly reducing Scotland's health potential". There was no escaping the "unacceptable fact that social injustice causes preventable illness and avoidable mortality" (Kenway et al, 2002, p 86).

To varying degrees, other analyses have confirmed these positions. In the late 1990s, Shaw and her colleagues examined and explained "a simple fact: that at the end of the 20th century inequalities in health are extremely wide and are still widening in Britain" (Shaw et al, 1999, p 1). They then demonstrated that "52% of the worst-off million people in terms of health live in Scotland" (p 16); tabulated the 15 parliamentary constituencies where people were most at risk of premature death, of which nine were in the West of Scotland (with Glasgow constituencies in the top six places); and concluded that health inequalities could "only be effectively tackled by policies that reduce poverty and income inequality" (Shaw et al, 1999, p 209). A further report in 2002 (Blamey et al, 2002) noted the "complexity" of the challenge of health inequalities; the clearly evident relationship between health and other forms of inequality; the Executive's positive attitude towards the issue; and the ongoing difficulties of measuring. The document had "many messages but two simple points" for emphasis. First, "inequalities in all their manifestations" were a key issue for Scottish society; and, second, that unless these were confronted "Scotland's health will continue to lag behind the rest of the United Kingdom and many of our European counterparts" (Blamey et al, 2002, p 47).

However, in a brief, but useful and suggestive, discussion of social capital and its relationship to health, Crawford (2001) points out that recent research has indeed shown Scotland's health in a poor light compared to the rest of Europe. In addition, however, "the gradient of health inequalities within Scotland appears to be sharper than elsewhere in Great Britain and this now cannot be completely accounted for by deprivation. This unexplained part of the health gap has been called the 'Scottish effect'". One possible explanation for this phenomenon was "psychological, social or behavioural factors". There was, therefore, a need to "make greater efforts to understand what factors within Scottish society determine health status and engage with less tangible and disputed ones such as social capital". Crawford thus raises important questions about precisely why the Scots are as unhealthy as they are: for the preceding analyses, the prime factor was poverty. Here it is being suggested that there may be more to it than this – cultural factors, broadly defined, are also significant. So while income inequality is certainly a serious issue and has a clear impact on health, Crawford pinpoints an important social phenomenon in her notion of a Scottish effect. This is further pursued in Chapters Five and Six.

## Child poverty

Finally, we need to say something about a key priority for New Labour and the Executive – child poverty. Just prior to the 2001 General Election, Bradshaw reviewed progress thus far. He noted, first, the situation inherited by New Labour whereby, inter alia, Britain as a whole had experienced rising rates of child poverty resulting in one of the highest in the industrialised world: only the US and Russia were worse off. While there were a number of causal factors involved, Bradshaw (2001) stated unreservedly that children were "more likely to be poor in the UK than in other countries because of the failure of policy makers to protect them – to protect children as well as other countries do" (p 11). Herein lay the background to Blair's "welcome and brave ... historic commitment" (p 10) to end child poverty within a generation. Second, after a further deterioration in the first two years of office the plight of at least some poor children had improved. This was "a great achievement" that had come about partly because of propitious economic circumstances but also because of "redistributive social and fiscal policies" (p 9). Nonetheless, and third, the timescale and measures adopted did not go far enough, not least when international comparisons were made and the resources technically available were taken into account. For Bradshaw, therefore, the "objective of abolishing child poverty will eventually entail policies which are much tougher politically and much more redistributive" (Bradshaw, 2001, p 25).

Brewer and his colleagues found, in 2003, that throughout Britain there remained some 3.8 million children (around 30%) still in poverty using one of the standard definitions, namely living in households with income below 60% of the median income after housing costs. This level was the lowest since 1991 and following the coming to power of New Labour some half million children had been lifted out of poverty. Despite these obvious successes, however, it seemed unlikely that the government would hit its target, and indeed was further behind schedule than previously. While this lag was in part attributable to generally rising incomes (a problem in tackling poverty if this is defined relatively), nonetheless, more direct action might be needed if Labour's own targets were to be met (Brewer et al, 2003, pp 1, 6). What both analyses suggest is a sense of opportunities not taken. Or, as Hendrick (2003, p 216) puts it, the current New Labour administration "is not yet a government that has earned our trust in honouring its commitment to end child poverty".

Are such perceptions shared by specifically Scottish analyses? A reworking of the Households Below Average Income data for the Executive showed, if the same definition of poverty was applied as by Brewer et al, that in 2001-02 over 300,000 Scottish children remained in poverty. In percentage terms, this was around the same as for Great Britain as a whole. This was down from the recent historic high point of 34% in 1996-97 but up from the 28% of 1999-2000[11]. For CPAG Scotland, it remained the case that, in 2000-01, around one third of children lived in households that could be defined as poor; and that there had been, over the preceding year, a marginal increase in child poverty. As noted, the CPAG was quick to praise both the UK and the Scottish governments' commitments to end child poverty while remarking that data showed that it remained "at a disturbingly high level" with a "relatively slow" rate of change. Those who had benefited most, it further observed, were children in households with incomes "just below the poverty threshold" (Brown et al, 2002, p 21): as it was put elsewhere in the report, the government had "completed the easiest job first" (p 101). Scottish children were, moreover, the social group "most likely to be poor and most likely to remain poor for a long period of time" (p 97). Younger children were particularly vulnerable. For Scottish child poverty to be eliminated, it was thus crucial that there be built a "social consensus that children are a collective investment and the responsibility of us all, rather than a private cost and the sole responsibility of their parents" (consciously or not, an argument with a very long historical pedigree; see Stewart, 1995). It was "simply unacceptable in a rich nation such as Scotland that children should go without bare necessities or be socially excluded [from mainstream society]". Only with the ending of child poverty could Scotland "call itself a modern country" (Brown et al, 2002, p 101).

Analysis by the Joseph Rowntree Foundation/New Policy Institute confirmed this depressing Scottish picture. The proportion of children "with relative low income showed little change over the four years to 2000/01" – hovering just over the 30% mark – and the proportion of children "with relative low income is about 7 percentage points higher than for the population as a whole" (Kenway et al, 2002, p 19). From another angle, 40% of households with children on low income were "more than £50 a week short of the low income threshold" (p 38), while more than half of all lone-parent families fell into the low-income category.

The consequences of child poverty, furthermore, involve more than access to material resources. We have already cited this report's observations on road accidents as they affect poor children; to this we might add, for example, its data on low birth weights. In 2001, this revealed that "babies born of parents who were the most deprived were twice as likely to be of low birth-weight compared with babies born of parents who were least deprived". So, while the percentage of babies in the low birth-weight category overall was around 2.5, for those in the most deprived category it was a full percentage point higher. Lest it be thought that this is simply a medical matter with no further consequences, the report's authors comment that:

> Low birth-weight babies face a future range of health problems both immediate and longer term, including poor health in the first four weeks of life, a higher risk of death before the age of two and delayed physical and intellectual development in early childhood and adolescence. There is, again, a clear socio-economic pattern to the risk of low birth-weight babies. In addition, their levels of occurrence indicate the way in which the historical disadvantage of children's parents can be transmitted from the very outset. (Kenway et al, 2002, p 73)

We see here the recurring nature of poverty and child poverty; how these lead to inbuilt disadvantages that may then reproduce themselves in future generations; and how simple poverty is part of a broader problem of inequality, disadvantage and exclusion (see also Bailey et al, 2003, p 64).

## Summary

This chapter has raised five specific points.

1. There has been a persistent, historically rooted, problem of poverty in Scotland, notwithstanding that in global terms it was and is a rich country.

2. This has contributed to other social problems, most notably ill health, an area where Scotland traditionally does extremely poorly.

3. The governments in both London and Edinburgh have especially targeted child poverty. Child poverty is seen as not just a problem in itself, but also as something that disadvantages children for the rest of their lives in numerous ways and is replicated in subsequent generations. Human capital concerns clearly come in here.

4. New Labour has sought to address the issue of poverty not by way of direct wealth redistribution, the traditional social democratic approach. Rather, the focus has been on moving individuals into paid employment. Moreover, emphasis is placed not on poverty per se, but rather on the broader concepts of social exclusion/inclusion that, by definition, require coordinated action across all branches of government.

5. Finally, and most importantly and problematically, New Labour's emphasis on paid employment as the best cure for poverty is, unsurprisingly, frequently echoed in Executive statements and policies. The Executive, however, has consciously set out to pursue what it calls (although is rather coy about defining) 'social justice'. Indeed, this can be seen as embodied in a particular minister with a stated responsibility for, among other policy areas, poverty[12].

Furthermore, the very creation of a Scottish Parliament has been seen by many commentators, as well as by the Executive itself, as a fresh start in poverty policy and an opportunity to address fundamental problems in Scottish society. Political discourse in Scotland has thus hinted at a more radical agenda than its southern counterpart, notably through its emphasis on social inclusion and on the pursuit of social justice, and through a more public acknowledgement of issues of poverty and deprivation and the need for these to be addressed by government. One important instance of this, which brings together a number of these summary points so far, can be found in the new 2003 government's first major statement, *A partnership for a better Scotland*. Discussing 'Social Justice', it argues that:

> Too many lives are damaged by poor housing, a blighted environment and poverty…We will tackle the social, educational and economic barriers that create inequality and work to end child poverty by tackling deprivation and social need.[13]

The problem is, of course, that whatever the Executive's own agenda may be, it once again runs up against constraints built into the devolution settlement. In particular, its lack of powers over macro-economic policy and the benefits system must be viewed as a major drawback in its no doubt well-intentioned assault on Scottish poverty. As in other fields, devolution thus offers opportunities, but opportunities of a limited kind. It is in this multi-faceted context that we now move to specific policy areas.

## Notes

[1] www.scotland.gov.uk/library5/social/lili

[2] www.bbc.co.uk, 19 September 2003, 'Social justice spending "unknown"'.

[3] See also McCormick and Leicester (1998, p 27); Mooney and Johnstone (2000, p 168); Brown et al (2002, ch 2); Kenway et al (2002, pp 15-16); Bailey et al (2003).

[4] Respectively, www.scotland.gov.uk/library4/FCSD/OCEA; www.scotland.gov.uk/library5/social/siods

[5] www.scotland.gov.uk/library5/social.mdis

[6] www.scottishlabour.org.uk, 'Policy documents: social inclusion'.

[7] www.scotland.gov.uk, 1 July 2002, 'Social justice in Scotland'.

[8] *The Independent*, 12 May 2003, 'Poverty levels have grown under Labour', quoting Maurice Fitzpatrick, head of economics at the business services group, *Numerica*.

[9] www.scotland.gov.uk/library5/social/siods, appendix C.

[10] *The Herald*, 22 September 2003, 'Glasgow has the most one-parent families in UK'.

[11] www.scotland.gov.uk/library4/FCSD/OCEA

[12] See the descriptions of ministerial posts at www.scotland.gov.uk, 20 May 2003, 'New Cabinet named at Bute House'.

[13] www.scotland.gov.uk/library5/pfbs

# FOUR

# Children, education and lifelong learning

## Introduction

The Executive's Education Department has among its aims promoting social justice for children and young people; raising educational standards; modernising schools and enhancing professional responsibilities and rewards; guaranteeing early learning and quality care for all children; and, overall, ensuring that "every child or young person is able to develop to their fullest potential". It seeks to achieve these through its Children and Young People's Group, whose remit includes children's rights and pre-school education; its Social Work Services Inspectorate, among whose responsibilities are "social work issues affecting children and young people" and liaison on such matters with other departments; and the Schools Group, responsible for a range of issues, including the National Priorities in education and, once again, social justice[1].

This wide-ranging brief says much about Executive attitudes, not least the overarching concerns for social justice and joined-up government. Education, moreover, deals with more than simply the young. Equally, policy aimed at children is more than simply to do with education. In this chapter, we discuss in this broad sense educational policy and aspects of child welfare. We begin with a variety of commentaries and analyses that set the scene and alert us to important themes. Next we move on to a short historical account of Scottish education, following this with discussions of New Labour and education and of the Executive's policies. Finally, we examine child welfare both as an important policy area in its own right and as a means of reinforcing points about human capital and the attempt to pursue an holistic welfare policy.

For Giddens (2000, p 165), investment in human capital, and the necessary reaction of governments to the "knowledge economy", require "placing a premium on education". This need might be seen as especially important in Scotland, with its low birth rate and declining population. Famously, New Labour campaigned in 1997 on a platform of 'Education, education, education'; as Muschamp et al (1999) point out, a very different set of priorities from the 1979 Labour manifesto. In the intervening period there had been the plethora of changes brought in by the Conservatives. Writing in 1999, Muschamp et al (pp 101-2) claimed that there were strong elements of continuity between New Labour and Conservative education policy, for example in Labour's abandonment of "the principle of comprehensive education".

Reviewing the election campaigns to the first Scottish Parliament, *The Guardian* noted the commitment of the SNP, the Liberal Democrats, and the Conservatives to the abolition of student fees (the only supporter thus being Labour), and predicted that, consequently, education could be an early political battleground. Equally importantly, however, the question was posed: what further divergence might take place between Scotland and England, given their existing differences? Ten areas were listed where Scottish education was already distinctive, including four-year undergraduate degrees at most of Scotland's older universities; and the Higher exam system, whereby students could gain qualifications at the end of their fifth year of secondary education and so apply for university a year earlier than A-level students in England. The Higher system was at this stage being remoulded under the Higher Still programme (discussed later in this chapter) aimed, inter alia, at introducing more vocational elements. The strategy here was to reduce the number of pupils leaving school with no qualifications, a clear attempt to address changing labour market demands. Also noted were: higher levels of teacher flexibility than in England – Scotland has no compulsory national curriculum, apart from religious education; the 5-14 programme, which gave curriculum guidance across the primary/secondary divide (and so made this transition easier); a high level of support for comprehensive education and an associated low level of support for the independent sector; and the power of the Schools Inspectorate and the organised teaching profession[2].

The following year, an official consultative document (Scottish Executive, 2000b, p 3) stressed that raising school standards was the Executive's "number one objective". This would benefit all children and young people, a reference to education's perceived key role in promoting social inclusion. Picking up on this last point, Labour's pre-2003 election education policy document stressed a continuing commitment to education's role "in delivering social justice". The 2000 Standards in Scotland's Schools Act, for example, was evidence of the party's "commitment to fostering equality of opportunity in education and a recognition of the potential for education to empower and lift people out of poverty"[3]. Furthermore, and this was equally important, education was not simply what happened during compulsory schooling. "Lifelong Learning" was necessary because of changes in population structure and in the world economy, and to close the "opportunity gap". It sought to foster "personal fulfilment and enterprise, employability and adaptability, active citizenship and social inclusion" and so embraced "formal and informal learning and workplace learning" and the "skills, knowledge, attitudes and behaviours that people acquire in their day-to-day experiences" (Scottish Executive, 2003e, p 2).

One way in which these goals were to be achieved was through reducing the number of 16- to 19-year-olds not in employment, education, or training and increasing support to those in this age group from low-income families to stay at school or go on to some form of tertiary education. The outcomes of such a strategy embraced making "social justice a reality", as well as both increasing individual income and helping people achieve other goals, for example civic participation. Society would further benefit through, for instance, a reduction in crime (Scottish Executive, 2003e, p 2). Such was importance of lifelong learning that, as another Executive publication put it, it lay "at the heart of our vision of a *Smart, Successful Scotland*" – a direct reference to the Executive's economic strategy (Scottish Executive, 2003c, p 1). Here was a classic New Labour vision of education – Whitehall ministers too shared the desire for lifelong learning (Timmins, 2001, p 585) – with its emphasis on the labour market and its role in attacking social exclusion.

Finally in these opening remarks, comparative analysis by Reynolds (2002) raises important issues for this chapter. He notes, for example, that the non-English parts of the UK customarily exhibited higher levels of achievement at the higher end of the ability range (especially in Wales and Scotland). Underpinning this is an educational philosophy as much concerned with equality of outcomes as of opportunity and an historical commitment to state education as a means of personal and collective advancement. In consequence, there has been resistance to market-based solutions to poor educational performance, an approach more pragmatically justified on the grounds of physical and human geography. On this last point, Scotland, like Wales and Northern Ireland, has a much higher proportion of its population in rural or small-town settings than England. We saw in Chapter Two that differences in funding levels (Scotland historically has spent more per capita on its school pupils) could be justified on this basis. Indeed, Midwinter (1999, p 53) has argued that:

> the provision for educating children in rural Scotland is a mere 2.4% greater than in England, despite the high proportion of the rural population in Scotland. This is less than the provision of sparsity costs made in the Scottish Revenue Support Grant.

Moreover, and here Midwinter is again arguing that the Barnett formula is flexible and historically based, he points out that Scotland's rural schools have lower pupil-teacher ratios than are found in urban settings, "reflecting a professional and political judgement that ought to be recognized" (2002a, p 565); and that Treasury estimates suggest that rural pupils cost 8% more per capita to teach. Reynolds (2002, p 97) adds that the idea of competition between schools in rural or small-town Scotland is implausible, given the distance between institutions. The issues raised by these extracts – for instance, Scottish particularity, human capital, education and the labour market, and Scottish attitudes to public sector education – will all be picked up throughout this chapter.

## Scottish education: history and identity

It is a fundamental premise of this volume that, to understand the present, we require knowledge of the past. Nowhere is this more so than in Scottish education, which, as one of its foremost historians has commented, "has been characterised by a peculiar awareness of its own history" (Anderson, 1999, p 215). Even before the Union, Scottish society saw itself as placing a particular premium on education, and after 1707 it remained under Scottish administrative control and was the subject of separate legislation. The Scottish Education Department (SED) soon became, as Anderson (1999, pp 218-19) comments, a "powerful bureaucracy, giving Scotland a more centralised and uniform state system than England". Paterson (2000c, p 16), a leading educationalist as well as a contributor to historical and sociological analyses of Scotland, adds that the SED was, when compared to its English counterpart, both a firmer advocate of state provision and held in higher esteem as a department.

Three factors contributed to an ongoing sense of distinctiveness from the Union through to the 20th century. First, Scotland had a vigorous form of elite education in the shape of its universities of which there were, post-Reformation, five. Paterson (2000c, p 14) contends that these were widely seen as "the property of the nation, much more like the public system of Germany or France than the private colleges of England". Second, as secondary education developed, it was open to both boys and girls. A significant proportion of schools charged no fees and were socially mixed, with the middle classes largely content to send their children to local schools rather than to fee-paying institutions, local or otherwise. Third, the education delivered at all levels was, it was widely held, of particularly high quality. Taken together, these points led to one of the enduring perceptions of Scottish education, that it was notably democratic. So, it was believed, the 'lad o' pairts' – a boy from a modest background – could, through application, scale the educational ladder. Again to quote Anderson (1999, p 215) this, like other national myths, certainly idealised reality while also containing "a core of truth".

These points continue to have resonance. Scottish parents, for instance, adapted much more easily than their English counterparts to comprehensive education – Paterson (2000c, p 23) comments that comprehensive schools in Scotland appeared to benefit working-class pupils without harming those of the middle class – and remain significantly less inclined to look outside of the state system. As we shall see, considerable emphasis continues to be placed on the comprehensive principle – the contrast here being with the death of comprehensive education in England noted earlier in this chapter – and on Scottish education's place in the world. As the Scottish Labour Party put it prior to the 2003 elections, the country had a "strong educational heritage" and Labour was committed to "restoring Scotland's educational system to the position of a world leader"[4]. The idea of restoration is important, indicative of Labour's frequent assertion that public services had been seriously damaged under Conservative rule. As we see in Chapter Five, this notion also occurs in post-1997 health policy.

Scottish education, furthermore, is commonly viewed as of itself a key constituent of Scottish national identity. McCrone (1999, p 243), for example, asserts unambiguously that "Scottish education is central to Scottish identity".

This was significant in that as long as the British state declined to interfere with Scottish education, then this was one reason why no form of political nationalism was deemed necessary. Like Anderson, McCrone sees the myth of Scottish education as containing a strong element of truth and its ongoing significance as due to it being "a key ideology to the Scottish education system and its cadres". This also, he continues, helps explain why "a perceived attack on the Scottish education system is perceived as an attack on Scottish culture and identity itself" (McCrone, 1999, p 240). Paterson (2000c, p 11) likewise sees education as one of the "pillars" of national identity. Throughout the Union, the education system was perceived as "self-governing". It could and did borrow ideas and practices from elsewhere but "the important point was that the borrowing was freely chosen and was chosen on Scottish terms".

Problems therefore began to arise after 1979. So, for example, while many English schools opted out of local authority control under Conservative legislation, only two did so in Scotland (Pickard, 1999, p 230). When the relevant Bill was going through Parliament it was denounced by Scottish Labour and Liberal MPs, as well as by the SNP, as alien and anglicising, claims that highlighted the Conservative's failure to win a majority of Scottish parliamentary seats. The Bill was thus an attack on Scottish traditions, traditions ill understood by English MPs (Paterson, 1994, p 1). Other issues too further alienated both the Scottish professional class and the wider electorate. A bitter strike by teachers – led by their union, the Educational Institute of Scotland (EIS), the very name of which tells us much about the profession's view of itself – gained widespread public support and went undefeated, something of an achievement for organised labour in the mid-1980s.

School boards were created by legislation, in itself relatively uncontroversial since some form of administrative reform had been put forward by all major political parties at the 1987 General Election. However, as Pickard (1999, p 228) observes, the way this was handled constituted an "affront to the educational establishment", with much consumerist rhetoric that appeared to suggest a highly interventionist role for parents in individual schools. More generally, many leading Conservative politicians did little to hide their scorn for the teaching profession and their desire to make it more accountable through market and other mechanisms. Scottish parents, however, remained unimpressed and candidates for the school boards mostly "stood on a minimalist platform, tacitly or explicitly rejecting the government's philosophy" (1999, p 230). Indeed for Paterson (2000c, p 25), the "most notable" political impact of this exercise was the boards' resistance to "compulsory standardised tests in primary schools" with parental opposition so widespread "that it forced the tests to be severely modified, and placed under the control of teachers".

In short, the Conservatives' educational policies were unpopular with the powerful Scottish educational establishment that sought, in its own eyes, to operate in a consensual way and was committed to the comprehensive principle. Just as important, they were unpopular with the Scottish electorate, which retained a high degree of respect for the teaching profession and which, because of its own educational experiences, was likewise committed to the comprehensive principle. This unpopularity undoubtedly contributed to Scotland's wholesale rejection of the Conservatives in 1997 and is thus an instance of the centrality of welfare to the Scottish electorate and further evidence of education's particular role in Scottish identity.

Before moving on to New Labour's education policy, it is important to make one crucial further observation. It would be wrong to suggest that all aspects of Scottish education were in good shape and that, with the return of Labour (much welcomed by Scottish educationalists), life would carry on as before. In 1999, a report for the Scottish Council Foundation, for instance, noted the significance of a coalition government statement that had used the phrase "earning the reputation for a world class education system" for Scotland. This, it continued, challenged "the complacent view that there is nothing wrong with Scottish education that more money could not solve" (Innes, 1999, p 14). Other commentators also drew attention to, in Pittock's (2001, p 135) words, the "cosy corporatist consensus" that certainly avoided producing the sort of badly performing schools found elsewhere, but also failed to deliver really high-quality schooling. This, rather than the "legend" of Scottish education, was contemporary reality. Complacency was indeed going to be challenged, sometimes in unforeseen ways.

## New Labour and education

There can be no doubt about the centrality of education to New Labour. As Kendall and Holloway (2001, p 154) put it, underpinning its policies:

> are the beliefs that education enables individuals to obtain employment and stable income sources in a competitive global economy, that education is crucial to overcoming the low-skill equilibrium of the British economy.

Education is also central to combating social exclusion and thus the "cycle of dependency". Drawing up a provisional balance sheet around the end of its first administration, they note that New Labour's strategy involved ongoing control of classroom activities; continuing public access to outcomes through, for example, league tables; and the maintenance of regulatory regimes. In varying degrees these approaches had been inherited from the Conservatives and in some cases expanded upon or tightened up. Added to this, however, was increased public expenditure aimed at both overall improvement in standards and a decrease in educational disparities within the UK. As Kendall and Holloway (2001, p 173) suggest, none of these approaches were "by themselves especially new or distinctive" but nonetheless there was "a particular combination of approaches which no previous post-war government has attempted". As Hendrick (2003, p 218) remarks of this eclectic policy mix, there is now a consensus "that most of what New Labour is doing in education is not new in itself, but that the combination of approaches is innovatory".

Naidoo and Muschamp (2002) argue that the historic link between Labour and the comprehensive system has been effectively broken with "diversity and a competitive environment ... central to the drive to raise standards" (p 145). Summing up to around 2001, they conclude that, by both extrinsic and intrinsic evaluation, "New Labour has kept its pledge to make education its number one priority through its efforts to ensure a decent education for all". On the other hand, educational reform means that the system will be "characterised not only by less equality of opportunity, but also by greater highs and lows of quality". This will result, they continue, in a "less inclusive higher education system and lower overall standards", (p 162) outcomes inconsistent with New Labour's stress on the need for a highly skilled workforce.

Glennerster (2001) acknowledges that, in the first two years, the term 'priority' could not be applied to state education spending; and, indeed, that during New Labour's first four years, education spending fell to its lowest point in 40 years. Using 1995-96 as a base, spending declined in both England and Scotland, but in 1999-2000 exceeded the baseline in England for both primary and secondary education; in the same year exceeded the baseline for primary education in Scotland; with, in the following year, Scottish secondary education moving above the 1995-96 base. Glennerster also makes the point that, while many of the quasi-market reforms in health were diluted by New Labour, "the Thatcher education reform package was retained and, if anything, strengthened" (2001, p 12). Problems notwithstanding, he finds much to praise in New Labour's approach. So, for example, in identifying education as a key area, the government has unquestionably got "the diagnosis right", because in addressing child poverty and social exclusion, "the key is to raise the basic skills of those at the bottom and ensure an adequate supply of more highly educated people so that they do not get paid scarcity wages" (p 3). Glennerster is particularly positive about achievements in primary education, which has seen a significant improvement in standards due to "a series of measures begun by the previous government and pushed further by this one". Secondary and higher education, however, still had problems (Glennerster, 2001, pp 25).

From this brief survey of commentaries on New Labour's education strategy, the following points stand out:

1. Investing in education is investment in human capital, essential for individual, social and economic progress.
2. Education, therefore, is not simply (or, some would argue of New Labour, not even) a cultural good in itself. It is also a key mechanism for pulling individuals and their families out of poverty. Education should thus be available to all – in other words, equality of educational opportunity.
3. Education is thus deeply integrated with other areas of welfare policy, not least because of its role in combating social exclusion.
4. Performance indicators are to continue, and to be made available to parents in their capacity as proxy consumers of education.

However, this approach also raises critical questions. First, can equality of opportunity be achieved if the comprehensive principle is rejected and schools encouraged to diversify and to compete against each other? Second, Hendrick (2003, p 218) suggests that during the era of the post-war consensus education was used, "in part at least", to promote "not only wealth creation, but also social justice". The emphasis on human capital formation and social discipline, and the social depredations of the Conservative 1980s and 1990s, however, have resulted in a New Labour project of "redefining the meaning and practice of education" (2003, p 223). This is a somewhat romanticised view of the post-war era, but it does make a point. Third, and leading on from the two previous points, New Labour's is a purportedly pragmatic approach: what works, works. Pragmatism is another New Labour characteristic, but we need to be aware that its supposedly practical approach is not what it seems. Pragmatism is as ideological as any other mode of thought, and as several of our commentators have implied, there is clearly something else going on in this (and other) aspects of New Labour's welfare policy. At the very least, there appears to be a fundamental reassessment taking place of the aims, nature and desired outcomes of educational provision. Given this general context, how has education policy developed in Scotland in recent years?

## The Scottish Executive and education

Reynolds (2002, p 98) remarks that, while "harsh rhetoric" has characterised discussions of educational standards and the role of teachers in England, this has not been the case elsewhere in the UK. At anecdotal level, this is borne out by the former Labour Cabinet Minister, Roy Hattersley, who in the summer of 1999 recalled a conversation with Donald Dewar. Hattersley asked the soon-to-be First Minister "if the worst excesses of Woodheadism had infected Scottish education policy – naming and shaming and that sort of absurdity. [Dewar] was too loyal to his cabinet colleagues to discuss the subject. He simply replied: 'We don't do that sort of thing up here'"[5]. If harsh rhetoric and the philosophy of the then chief inspector of schools in England were being rejected, what did the Executive seek to put in its place?

We saw in Chapter One that the first Holyrood elections were relatively low key. They were important, nonetheless, for Scottish education and we start with the analysis made by Paterson et al (2001) of the 1999 election. Here they point out that education is an area where Edinburgh has "almost unfettered power"; is central to national identity; and had been an election issue, particularly regarding student fees. So, Paterson and his colleagues predicted, the "sheer prominence of education is one reason to expect that there will be policy divergence between Scotland and England" (p 144). In addition, they point out that opinion polls show a high level of support for prioritising educational spending (although it remains second to health in this regard); and that more than half the electorate in 1999 believed that the new Parliament would improve educational standards (although this was significantly down from the proportion two years earlier) (Paterson et al, 2001, p 144). It must be worrying for the Executive, therefore, that subsequent findings, based on material gathered in 2001, show the electorate having a diminishing belief in their Parliament's ability to improve educational standards. Indeed, the proportion of Scots who see Holyrood as responsible for educational outcomes appears to have dropped significantly since 1997 (Bromley and Curtice, 2003, pp 14-16, tables 1.3-5). This may reflect disenchantment with the devolution process – we noted in Chapter One the low level of electoral participation in 2003 – or it may simply be that not enough time has yet elapsed for real, positive change to become apparent.

Nonetheless the Executive has, as the comments of Paterson et al (2001) would suggest, consistently placed considerable emphasis on education. One early example of its commitment to maintaining a consensual approach came with the implementation of the key findings of the McCrone Inquiry. This had come about as a result of a threatened teachers' strike. For Scottish Labour, the ensuing agreement allowed the profession to be "fit for the challenges of the modern classroom, delivering a package which increases professionalism and offers an improved career route". In a clear attack on the disruptions caused by previous Conservative administrations, the document continued that Labour was "proud to have reached an historic agreement to redress the damage of the past and restore stability to the classroom"[6]. Of course, there was more to it than this: as we shall see, the Executive was going to seek more from teachers in the way of performance indicators, for example. Nonetheless, the power and standing of the profession was being recognised by the Executive, acting in a sphere where it had considerable powers. And, as Reynolds (2002, p 98) puts it, the proposal to cut hours and improve pay and conditions as suggested by McCrone "could only have come in a relatively supportive educational climate", the contrast here, as immediately above, being with England. The actual cost of the McCrone settlement was estimated as reaching some £2 billion by 2006[7].

In fact, educational reform in Scotland actually predated the arrival of the Parliament, with the introduction of New Community Schools under a three-year pilot scheme launched in late 1998. These were to be "concentrated in disadvantaged areas where children face significant risk of social exclusion and formidable barriers to learning in their everyday environment". Crucially, however, the underlying principles were "applicable to all schools" (Scottish Office, 1998, quoted in Sammons et al, 2002, p 1). As Paterson (2000c, p 54) points out, the scheme was based on the idea of full-service schools in the US. Various health and social services are located on the same site as the school "in order to deal directly and efficiently with the various social barriers to learning". Teachers are thus freed to be "educators, rather than surrogate social workers".

The New Community Schools, in the first phase from 1999 to 2002, consisted of 37 initiatives by way of 170 schools in 30 local authorities. These were funded by a specific grant from the Scottish Office Excellence Fund and generally involved clusters of nursery, primary and secondary schools. Five key goals were identified:

- modernising schools and promoting social inclusion;
- increasing the educational attainment of students confronted with the "cycle of underachievement";
- early intervention aimed at confronting barriers to learning and thereby to maximise potential;
- meeting the needs of all children;
- raising the expectations, and participation, of parents and families in children's education.

The central idea of providing a focal point for all student needs is clearly important. Sammons et al (2002, p 2) point out that all the first-phase projects were involved in "diverse other educational initiatives and most in health and social initiatives". This approach has been likened to the cocktail approach employed in English Education Action Zones. So, for instance, the Scottish Office required of schools under the scheme that from the outset they "work towards the formal status of a health promoting school". Sammons et al found that, in this particular case, nursery and primary schools were placing most emphasis on healthy eating. Secondary schools stressed healthy living, the impact of drugs and smoking, and sex education, including HIV awareness. Secondary schools also emphasised "psychological aspects such as creating a positive school ethos and raising self-esteem" (Sammons et al, 2002, pp 3-4, 6). School ethos has been important for the Executive as a means of promoting social inclusion.

New Community Schools are seen by the Executive as a major success story, although, as we note at the end of this chapter, independent research was, by the summer of 2003, calling this into question. Labour's education policy document in the run-up to the 2003 elections described the scheme as "one of the most innovative and modern initiatives ever carried out in education". Nor was this "just a passing phase". On the contrary, New Community Schools were a "stable foundation through which much can be achieved" and as such were key to the integrated strategy of raising educational attainment and promoting social inclusion[8]. In its 2003 response to the National Debate on Education (discussed later in this chapter), the Executive re-emphasised the idea of universalising the New Community Schools approach (Scottish Executive, 2003b, p 10). In the same year, another Executive publication reiterated the role of such schools in promoting social inclusion and raising educational standards and the intention to have their approach adopted by all schools by 2007. There were now some 62 projects under the scheme, each having been awarded £200,000 per annum for three years. Up to 2004, the total funding for the pilot programme, now extended to five years, would be £37.2 million. Nearly £80 million had been committed to this programme down to 2006 (Scottish Executive, 2003c, p 4).

Here we should stress two intertwined issues: the integration of education with other areas of welfare; and schools as key players in addressing social exclusion. The first of these is self-evident. New Community Schools illustrate the Executive's commitment to an integrated approach through, in particular, the associated health initiatives; and, by extension, through the wholesale adoption of this model. They feature in, for example, Labour health policy material[9] and the scheme is a good example of the joined-up government so close to the hearts of both New Labour and the Executive. Another party document stressed Labour's "holistic approach to children's services". An "integrated, focused approach" better met the needs of children than a "departmental approach" that struggled to "recognise the links between educational performance and health". New Community Schools brought such an approach into practice[10].

As to social inclusion, we saw in Chapter Three that the Social Inclusion Network had young people as one of its three initial targets. As Munn (2000, pp 116-17) put it, as early as 1999, the role of schools had "already featured heavily in policy initiatives" in this sphere. Such initiatives included, in addition to New Community Schools, funds to help tackle school exclusion on the grounds of behaviour and the Early Intervention Initiative, designed to raise literacy and numeracy levels in the first two years of primary school. The latter, a government-funded programme influenced by the success of such measures in the US, had started as a pilot scheme in the Pilton area of Edinburgh in 1997 (Croxford, 2002, p 145 and passim). A further Executive-commissioned report noted that both in Scotland and elsewhere arguments for "inclusive schooling" were in part driven by educational and social concerns about social exclusion and social justice. Despite an overall rise in educational standards, attention still had to be paid to the relative achievement of "individual pupils and groups of pupils, particularly linked to socio-economic status, gender, and 'race'". And, although socioeconomic disadvantage impacted significantly on educational outcomes, research had shown too that, and this point was emphasised, "schools can and do make a difference" (Campbell et al, 2001, pp 1-2). Echoing this is Labour's claim that education was "central" to its objective of a more equal society and that while educational attainment alone could not "right all the wrongs associated with poverty and deprivation, it can make a major difference"[11].

The acknowledgement that education cannot solve all social problems, and indeed that such problems exist in the first place, is significant here and will be met again. Equally important, however, is the emphasis on the "major difference" it purportedly can make. Commenting on policy divergence and the "contemporary enthusiasm" for education as a "driver" of economic and social change, Reynolds (2002, p 93) remarks that while this enthusiasm may on occasions be excessive, it is not unreasonably so. He finds it "particularly understandable" that "Scotland, Wales and increasingly Northern Ireland have been drawn to distinctive educational and training related policies as a possible solution to their long term social and economic problems".

## The 2000 Standards in Scotland's Schools Act

In June 2000, the Standards in Scotland's Schools Act was passed, one of the first pieces of legislation from the new Parliament. The Act was recognised at the time as incomplete, with ministers looking forward to, for example, measures to make the dismissal of incompetent teachers easier. Nonetheless it was generally welcomed, with interested parties such as the EIS commenting on the consultative nature of the legislative process – more consensualism – and the clear priority given to education by Holyrood. An official of the Scottish Parent Teacher Council remarked on the contrast between the formation of the 2000 Act and "Michael Forsyth's opting-out Bill in the late 1980s which rejected the views of everyone in Scotland"[12].

The underlying basis of Scottish education remained the Education (Scotland) Acts of 1980 and 1981 which, inter alia, gave parents the right to choose their child's school; laid down the ages between which education was compulsory; and laid a duty on parents to see that their child was educated and on education authorities to make educational provision. The Standards in Scotland's Schools Act, most of whose provisions were to be phased in over two years, nonetheless had important components of which we here note four.

1. Emphasis was laid on the child's right to education which, as Munn (2000, pp 127-8) points out, was more in tune with the 1995 Children (Scotland) Act than with previous educational legislation. The Act worked on the assumption that all children were to be educated in mainstream schools and required that schools and education authorities listen to students. Rights for vulnerable groups, such as childcarers and children excluded from school, were strengthened[13]. Here was an attempt at inclusive schooling alongside an assertion of child-centred education and welfare policy.
2. The right of schools to opt out of local authority control, as we have seen not popular and little exercised in Scotland, was abolished.
3. The Act guaranteed pre-school provision for all three- and four-year-olds, an issue worth briefly dwelling upon. Arguments for such provision had been building for some time and were not confined to Scotland (on England, see Naidoo and Muschamp, 2002, pp 150-1; Millar and Ridge, 2002, p 91; for Scotland up to the late 20th century, see Littlewood, 1998, pp 143-4; Watt, 1999, passim). As Watt (1999, p 312) points out, a significant development during the 1990s was the growing recognition of such provision as education, and of its role in long-term educational improvement. For the Executive, the aims of access for all three- and four-year-olds to "free, quality pre-school education" are clear. It helps children learn as they play; builds on home learning; develops "essential skills" for use in later life; and prepares children for primary school (Scottish Executive, 2003c, p 4). The proportion of children involved has risen from around 8% of four-year-olds in the early 1970s through 40% in the mid-1980s to 55% in the mid-1990s (Paterson, 2000c, p 47). By April 2002, some 96% of four-year-olds and 85% of

three-year-olds were receiving pre-school education, a total of over 98,000 children – as an Executive document reasonably remarks, given "the voluntary nature of take-up these figures represent full participation". The service was provided at around 1,500 local authority centres and around 1,000 voluntary and other centres, at a total cost of £137 million in 2000-01. Emphasis was again placed on "integrated service delivery" as "key to supporting well nourished, well balanced and healthy children who are well prepared to benefit from education". There was also the explicit assertion that services previously seen as care providers were now recognised as having a role in educating younger children and "nurturing their development" (Scottish Executive, 2003d, pp 13-14). Commenting on this trend more generally, Toynbee and Walker (2001, p 50) identify a defeat for the social services approach that brings Britain closer to the European norm. The demand for nursery education has been partly fuelled by changing patterns of female employment and the availability of tax credits. However, we should also note the observation, in autumn 2003, by a group researching low-income families on behalf of the Executive. Significant steps, it remarks, have been taken to improve both the quantity and the quality of childcare "for those wanting to move from welfare to work"[14].

4. The Act set up a framework for continuous improvement in schools. Ministers were required to give "strategic direction to the education system"; local authorities to produce plans "showing improvement objectives"; schools to publish their own development plans; and both local authorities and schools to produce annual reports describing their progress (Scottish Executive, 2003c, p 1). Deriving from this, and taking account of consultations that had taken place both before and after the Act's passage, the National Priorities in Education were articulated as:

- achievement and attainment;
- framework and learning;
- inclusion and equality;
- values and citizenship;
- learning for life.

The underlying rationale here was that, in the course of consultation, many had argued that young people would benefit were a shared vision of educational priorities developed. Significantly, there had also been a "clear call to look beyond attainment to other aspects of education and to focus on outputs, rather than inputs" (Scottish Executive, 2002b, p 1). Here we find a mixture of central control alongside an acknowledgement of the partnership role of local authorities and schools; and a New Labour-ish concern with performance indicators alongside, on the other hand, a sense of moving away from over-prescriptive central direction. Indeed, the tension between devolving powers and centrally imposed targets is a more general characteristic of New Labour – and Scottish Executive – social policy.

We might also note Paterson's (2002, p 125) comments on one dimension of this structure, citizenship education, a big issue in educational and political circles because of its potential impact on social exclusion. Paterson finds, however, an emerging difference here between Scotland and England – while the latter is concerned with "community duties", in the former there is also emphasis on "the right to dissent". He sees this difference as deriving from the dichotomy, noted in Chapter One and returned to in Chapter Six, between Scottish social democratic communitarianism and Blairite liberalism. We therefore have here an example of how rhetorical similarities can mask philosophical difference.

## National Priorities and the national debate

National Priorities were under consideration even as the Standards Bill was making its way through Parliament. In March 2000, for instance, a consultation document discussed where education policy was coming from and where it sought to go. The wider context was "rapid globalisation" and "the development of the knowledge economy" (Scottish Executive, 2000b, p 3). The framework for improvement was designed to be "transparent and robust" while devolving responsibility for "the best solutions" to local level, so empowering schools to work towards agreed outcomes. Elaborating on this last point, the National Priorities were to "identify the key outcomes that school education should seek to achieve" while not determining "the process for delivering these outcomes" (p 4). Local authorities – working in partnership with parents, teachers and pupils – were to do this for themselves while taking account of Executive guidance. We can again see here the potential for conflict between the centre and those to whom powers have been devolved.

In general terms, the desired outcomes were to be achieved, for example, through a flexible and modern curriculum; an ethos of fairness and achievement; highly skilled and motivated staff; a safe, attractive and well-equipped learning environment; and an efficient and accountable delivery system. These would result in confident, well-motivated and fully rounded young people who were literate and numerate to "a level at or above that of their peers in the rest of the world". They should be able to comprehend and play an active part in a modern democratic society. Their education should allow them to take available opportunities "regardless of their background" and give them "the skills and aptitudes to work flexibly and to embrace change throughout their future lives" (p 6). Various targets and performance indicators were to be set, for example reducing the number of 16- to 19-year-olds not in education, training, or employment by half. Finally, it was again acknowledged that socioeconomic factors "can and do affect performance levels in schools" and the Executive was taking steps to address these. This did not, however, absolve schools, local authorities, or parents from "the commitment to excellence or from having the highest expectations of themselves and the children they serve" (Scottish Executive, 2000b, p 9). So, and as has been frequently asserted by the Executive:

> Every child should expect an excellent education directed at raising their
> full potential – no matter where in Scotland they are educated or what
> challenges they face. (Scottish Executive, 2000b, p 9)

Overall, here we have an approach that addresses education itself as well as the
role of education in the broader context of, most notably, social inclusion and
the labour market.

The National Priorities were, after further consultation, agreed by Parliament
in late 2000. A timetable, stretching from 2002 to 2005, was established with
key points along the way, including the making available of School Development
Plans to local audiences in summer 2002; the publication of the first education
authority "progress report" in spring 2003; and the publication of independent
research findings in 2005. There was to be no doubt that performance was to
be measured. However, the "mix of performance measures and quality
indicators" had been chosen in an attempt to gain a "fuller picture of a school's
performance than is possible from statistics alone" and a support package was
being developed "to help schools and local authorities set realistic and stretching
targets" (Scottish Executive, 2002b, pp 2-3).

The National Debate on Education took place in summer 2002 and the
Executive's response again highlights important themes. The opening sentence
of the Ministerial Foreword proclaimed the vision of "excellent comprehensive
schools, at the heart of local communities". The minister asserted that the
"Scottish Budget provides historic levels of investment in education for the
next three years" (Scottish Executive, 2003b, p 2). Elsewhere the document
stressed, inter alia, the need to "substantially reduce the current overload in the
5-14 curriculum"; and to strengthen the role of inspection. Significantly, it
observed that the "vast majority of people who responded to the Debate believe
in the strength of the Scottish comprehensive system and want to build on
that" (pp 3-4). This was rather more problematic than might appear from such
bald statements, however, for another part of the document – 'Our vision for
the future' – suggested that "Comprehensive education means meeting all pupils'
learning needs, not putting all pupils through the same system, delivering
according to local needs and priorities" (p 6). Children and young people
should, however, "have a broad education and develop the skills to be active
citizens of a modern Scotland" (p 5), so preparing them for employment, training,
college or university. The reaffirmation of a traditional characteristic of Scottish
education – its breadth – is notable here. Various schedules were given for the
achievement of the National Priorities and its associated targets (Scottish
Executive, 2003b, pp 2, 3, 4, 6, 10, 5).

Finally in this section, parallel to the National Debate the Scottish Council
for Research in Education, at the Executive's behest, conducted a focus group
study on the purpose of education. Respondents were consciously selected
from socially marginal groups, for instance young unemployed men. As two of
the researchers put it, one the most "striking findings was the profound
dissonance between the perspectives, expectations and value systems of those

who framed the inquiry and those who shared their views with us". These views included, inter alia, the belief that social and citizenship skills should balance what was perceived as the current over-emphasis on academic achievement. So, the researchers concluded, until a challenge was made to "the value systems of a society that puts educational prestige in the centre of the frame, there will continue to be those who are marginalised from the mainstream concerns of schools as institutions" (Pirrie and Lowden, 2002, pp 4-5). Here, then, was a (mediated) voice from those educational policy had as one of its principal targets – the socially excluded.

## Problems?

The Executive has generally been upbeat about its educational strategy as well as continuing to pursue a broadly consensual approach. However, as we have already seen, this does not mean that everything has gone its way, that there are no dissenting voices, or that there are not more general concerns. The Executive itself, responding to the National Debate, acknowledged that what had emerged in the consultative process was that "we have much further to go. People are not complacent; they want improvement" – a further instance of the Executive's claim for a longer view of public service reform. Areas of concern included curriculum relevance and the volume of assessment (Scottish Executive, 2003b, p 4). What, then, have been among the education system's actual or perceived problems in recent years?

The most obvious example of system failure came in summer 2000 when the Scottish Qualifications Agency (SQA) – the body responsible for "the development, accreditation, assessment and certification of qualifications other than degrees"[15] – failed to deliver accurate and/or complete examination results to thousands of pupils. This caused a major scandal, with an investigation uncovering a "damning catalogue of failure and incompetence across the organisation". A number of SQA staff eventually resigned, although not in the first instance the Education Minister[16]. If this incident had simply been an example of administrative incompetence and computer malfunction, it might have rested as a distressing period in the lives of the affected students, but not necessarily anything more.

However as the episode's chronicler suggests, it also drew attention to some "fundamental questions about the character and quality of Scottish education". The new Higher Still programme had been intended as the "latest phase in the development of Scotland's comprehensive secondary schools" and sought to both maintain high academic standards and provide equal opportunities for all those in their late teenage years. Furthermore, Paterson (2000d, p 7) continues, the events of summer 2000 also provided "an early test of the new Scottish parliament. Its enquiries began to probe the role of the country's civic institutions". It was thus important to ask whether these were in need of "drastic innovation" and whether the crisis had come about because of "complacency – because people in charge of Scotland's civic life are not truly accountable".

Before taking these issues further, it is necessary to say something briefly about Higher Still. Traditionally Scottish school pupils could, after the end of their fifth year of secondary schooling, take Higher examinations in their chosen subjects. Highers were the key to university entrance as well as important qualifications in their own right. This system celebrated its centenary in 1988, but even at this point it was clear, as Pickard (1999, p 232) puts it, that "all was not well with the benchmark of dependability in the Scottish assessment system, preferable though its breadth was to the much criticised narrowness of English A levels". Among the perceived problems were an over-academic emphasis combined with a relative neglect of vocational training; the related issue of too many pupils leaving school at 16 unqualified; and the weak status of the Certificate of Sixth Year Studies, not officially recognised for university entrance. After various investigations and proposals, the Higher Still programme emerged in 1994. While the Higher itself was not to be abolished, the new programme sought to merge the academic and the vocational – similar developments were taking place in England with regard to A levels and GCSEs (Timmins, 2001, p 585; Toynbee and Walker, 2001, p 59).

Secondary pupils could still take an academic Higher from the end of their fifth year, but were also to have the opportunity to take less demanding courses with more overtly vocational content. For the academically gifted, a new Advanced Higher was to be introduced. After various postponements, the new system came into being in 2000. Despite these delays, much optimism was invested in Higher Still. One report described it as a "revolution that breaks with a 111-year old tradition". The "long-separated spheres of the academic and the vocational" were to be brought together in a "single national qualification system". Albeit with a number of hitches, consensus had again been the order of the day, with the teachers in particular being won round to the scheme. Ron Tuck, head of the SQA, argued (rather contentiously) in the same piece that Scotland differed from England in merging the academic and the vocational, and that in this respect the latter was going "against the flow of an international tide". "I can only assume", Tuck continued, "that England has different values and a different culture. If we had difficulties with reform, it would be ten times harder in England".[17] Ironically, Tuck had to resign as the scale of the problems of summer 2000 emerged but the suggestion of further divergence is notable here. Teething problems notwithstanding, it is clear why Higher Still would appeal to Executive and New Labour thinking. Such a programme could help tackle the intimately related issues of unqualified school leavers, labour-market demands for a wide range of skills, and thereby social exclusion. It is unsurprising, then, that the events of summer 2000 took on extra dimensions and were traumatic for both the Scottish educational establishment and the Executive.

In many respects, however, the crisis of 2000 was the occasion rather than the cause of serious heart searching about the nature, purpose and delivery of Scottish education. We now look at some further critical analyses of Scotland's educational system, immediately pre- and post-devolution. This approach is selective, with the deliberate intention of highlighting areas of the educational myth that, on closer scrutiny, were not quite as close to reality as its more optimistic supporters might suggest.

Even before the new Parliament assembled, concerns were expressed about the potential direction of its education remit. In 1998, Paterson (1998, p 7) suggested that reforming education would not be easy, as decades of "defensiveness bred by Scotland's unsatisfactory constitutional status have made the system resistant to change, and have developed in it all sorts of subtle ways of subverting unwelcome reforms even while appearing to go along with them". In their measured essay on the future of Scottish education, Humes and Bryce (1999, pp 1008-9) presciently pointed to, inter alia, the tensions between "control and liberation" inherent in certain policy areas. Such tension was present in the political desire to, on the one hand, "tighten up" the system and, on the other, to promote "access, opportunity, and lifelong learning". As they remarked, these "two forms of discourse may not be in direct contradiction but the relationship between them is at times uneasy". Similarly, teachers were being promised "professional entitlement" alongside plans to monitor performance more closely. In a revealing review of the volume in which this appeared, Scott (2000, pp 128-9) claimed that its tone was that of "the old Unionist Scotland, of the high-minded but collusive elites whose duty it had been to regulate Scottish civil society relatively untroubled by the unruly world of politics and ideology". This, he suggested, might well be "fundamentally challenged" by the new political order.

Around the same time, the Scottish Council Foundation produced a report that, as one press article put it, saw the education system as "stuck in a Victorian time warp". This was manifested, for example, by a "mass-production" model, which required every pupil to follow the same path, while simultaneously stifling classroom and curriculum creativity[18]. The following year, the foundation published a further report (Bloomer, 2001), written by a former local authority director of education. Bloomer had no doubt about the need for critical thinking about Scottish education at the beginning of the new century. By his account, up to the 1980s smugness and complacency ruled. During the 1990s, however, Scottish education "stopped congratulating itself and started thinking; or, at any rate, contemplating the possibility of having to think" (p 5). As evidence of the problems faced, the Third International Mathematics and Science Survey was cited. This had shown Scotland in a poor light, even when compared with badly funded East European nations; and that variations in school performance across Scotland "strongly correlated with social circumstances". From this last point, Bloomer concluded that education was "clearly having only a very limited impact on the cycle of deprivation" (p 6).

What, then, was the solution to this set of problems? The traditional emphasis on "breadth and balance" was no longer acceptable. It involved an essentially "knowledge-based" curriculum at the neglect of, for instance, the "cultivation of adaptability or enterprise" (p 17), an approach that could not meet the demands and expectations now being placed on education. The debate around the National Priorities was therefore "striking and important" because of the emergence of a consensus that "embraces a broad range of objectives focused as much on the development of the individual as on traditional concepts of curriculum design" (p 9). Bloomer also supported the idea of lifelong learning, characterising the dichotomy between it and "school education" as "absurd" (pp 23-4). Unfortunately, good general intentions did not always work out in practice. The essential problem was that "the education system has continued to act as if the best way of promoting progress is to determine centrally the one true path and seek to secure universal adherence to it" (Bloomer, 2001, p 30).

Such a brief summary does disservice to a complex text. However, from this and the preceding criticisms a number of important points emerge, points that contextualise the Executive's actions and initiatives.

1. There is the alleged complacency and rigidity of the educational establishment. We saw in Chapter One that corporatism and centralism have long been characteristic of Scottish governance, and that this had, in certain respects, served Scotland well. But such characteristics were now seen by some as obstacles in an increasingly competitive world dominated by the knowledge economy.
2. What was therefore needed was a system that was flexible and responsive to individual, and to labour-market, needs and recognised that education did not stop at 16 years of age.
3. What this further implied was that the traditional Scottish view of comprehensive education, with its emphasis on breadth and balance, and on uniformity of delivery, was no longer tenable. Indeed, such a view significantly contributed to the allegedly failing corporatist and centralist approach.
4. Education as currently practised had not succeeded in breaking the cycle of deprivation. We saw in Chapter Three that poverty in Scotland is a multi-faceted and complex phenomenon; have frequently noted the Executive and New Labour belief that it can be significantly addressed by way of educational reform; and hence that, notwithstanding the recognition that socioeconomic circumstances are important, education can make a difference.

## Comprehensives and league tables

The last point is part of a wider issue about how to combat poverty. As Croxford (2002, p 148) points out, the perpetuation of poverty by educational disadvantage "appears a very long-standing and intractable problem". While it was traditionally believed that education could of itself reduce social inequality, in fact pupils starting school with socioeconomic and educational disadvantages made poorer progress, so further widening the gap between the advantaged and the disadvantaged. What this suggests is that Scottish education, reformed or otherwise, is being burdened with too high a level of expectation in the fight against social exclusion, although here we should bear in mind initiatives such as pre-school provision and its shift from care to education.

As to how the Executive has actually responded to some of these criticisms, we start with three fundamental observations. First, we have seen repeated assertions of the Executive's commitment to comprehensive education and noted its popularity with the Scottish public. Nonetheless, the waters have, at least to some extent, become muddied. First Minister McConnell told a conference in late 2002 that he "had faith in the comprehensive system" but equally that this "should not mean a uniform system". He thus urged the need for "flexibility and choice".[19] A few months earlier, on the occasion of the Education Minister's announcement that the era of "one size fits all" was over, concerns were expressed that there had, in Scottish schools, been a "perceptible shift towards fragmentation". "Comprehensives were", the report continued, "beginning to revert to setting and streaming" and schools were, of course, by this stage also being told that they could employ a more flexible curriculum[20]. On this account, just how comprehensive Scottish education will remain is an open question. However, we shall have cause return to this issue below and, in Chapter Six, to an important speech made by the First Minister in autumn 2003.

Second, the devolving of flexibility to individual schools and education authorities also raises the questions of central versus local control, as now noted on a number of occasions a potential source of tension in education and elsewhere in New Labour social policy, and of how monitoring might take place. So, for example, in summer 2003, the Education Minister emphasised that he would be seeking a Bill to force education authorities to deal with problem schools. This was to take place in a system wherein there was a "huge degree of expertise about delivering very high performing schools" but also a need to ensure that this expertise was "more consistently and universally applied". New systems of monitoring would deal with organisations as well as pupils "to measure more effectively the education system as a whole"[21]. This point is also discussed later in this chapter.

Third, again in summer 2003 the Education Minister stressed that while in future national tests would be "less bureaucratic and time-consuming", nonetheless, they would remain, and he repeated his aim that they "measure more effectively the education system as a whole". The system put in place would be "robust" enough that schools could not "massage" results to their own advantage[22]. Then, in September 2003, the same minister denounced school league tables as "meaningless". They were characteristic of a time when "the political currency was about competition between schools", but this was no longer the case. The minister believed in "universal excellence" and he duly gave notice of the abolition of the tables. This had, in fact, been prefigured during the National Debate in 2002 when analysis showed that one of the "key comments" made was a need to "celebrate success and recognise the negative effect of league tables" (Scottish Executive, 2003b, p 6). As the newspaper in which this story broke put it, abolition would bring Scotland in line with Wales and Northern Ireland (but not, of course, England), so enlarging the gap between "the Blairite vision of school education" and that of the Executive. At the same time, it was also announced that national tests for 5- to 14-year-olds were to be abolished, partly to prevent the creation of league tables for primary schools[23]. In fact, all this proved much more problematic than originally anticipated – thanks in part to the 2002 Freedom of Information (Scotland) Act – but the Executive remain convinced that league tables were, as one spokesperson put it, "largely meaningless" and reform of the nature and scope of the information was under way in late 2003[24].

## Confidence and commitment

Problems, tensions and ambiguities notwithstanding, education remains central to the Executive's strategy. Considerable resources and energy have been devoted to it, and the Executive clearly sees itself as pursuing policies tailored to Scottish needs and attitudes. And while think tanks such as the Scottish Council Foundation may be critical of aspects of educational provision, nonetheless they are also, as Reynolds (2002, p 100) puts it, a "fertile breeding ground for ideas". This of itself clearly adds to the quality of discussion around Scottish education.

Some commentators even found positive signs in the aftermath of summer 2000. As one newspaper remarked, the exams "fiasco masked the changes that devolution was bringing to Scottish classrooms". Problems notwithstanding, there was a "high degree of confidence in the state sector", which educated 96% of children. An important deal had been struck with the teaching profession that, at least as far as the profession itself was concerned, had properly recognised its status. Officials from other countries were reported as visiting Scotland to examine the implications of this arrangement. For Paterson, quoted in the article, devolution had "changed a lot of things fundamentally", not least in the adoption of a less aggressive attitude towards teachers than was found in England. Commenting further on the myth of Scottish education, he praised the Executive for not being obsessed by it. Instead, it had adopted an approach emphasising that "education is important, Scots value education. The parliament is trying to modernise Scottish education for the present"[25]. The idea of a more supportive educational climate bears out the previously noted comments of Reynolds (2002). The latter, like Bloomer, remarks (2002, p 98) on the international maths tests but also notes that the admittedly "very disappointing performance" did not result in the sort of criticism experienced contemporaneously in England. The mood was, he suggests, one of sadness rather than of "apportioning blame".

Crucially, however, Bromley and Curtice (2003, pp 10-11) show that New Labour attacks on what was charmlessly described as the bog-standard comprehensive in England do not, on polling evidence, mirror Scottish popular aspirations. A much higher proportion of Scots responded positively to the prompt that: "All children should go to the same kind of secondary school, no matter how well or badly they do at primary school" than was the case in

England. Bromley and Curtice further suggest, quite correctly, that in general terms, and in contrast to England, the Executive has "indicated its continuing faith in the principle of comprehensive secondary schools that have a remit to teach equally well across the full range of the curriculum" – the traditional Scottish approach. They thus conclude that on secondary education "a distinctively Scottish policy does appear to reflect a distinctive strand of public opinion" and that this is of greater significance than the much more widely publicised differences over university fees.

This is a valid, well-made and correct point. Whatever the (undoubted) ambiguities, the comprehensive principle is seen as the bedrock of Scottish education by both the public and the current Executive (for a similar approach in Wales, see Davies, 2003, p 4). It is what the vast majority of Scots both experienced themselves and desire for their children. Scottish parents send their children to state schools because they want to – not because they have no choice in the matter. By the same token, there is undoubtedly private-sector involvement in Scottish education in terms of participation in construction projects. So, for instance, a scheme was announced in late 2003 for the building of 11 schools in the Highlands under a public–private partnership[26]. However, in terms of actual educational provision and regulation, the private sector is widely seen as having little part to play. This hugely significant difference between Scotland and England is returned to below, and again in Chapter Six.

Further evidence of the Executive's aim of enhancing the quality of educational provision can be found in its commitment in June 2002 to put aside £2 million for research on schools improvement, particularly in the context of the National Priorities[27]. A few months later, access to lifelong learning became a "fundamental right" of the Scottish people. A report from the Executive's Enterprise and Lifelong Learning Committee focused, inter alia, on entitlement and how to widen access to post-18 learning, whether at work, university or local college. The committee thus sought to "create a culture of lifelong learning, so that once you're out of school or university that's not it forever"[28]. And finally in this selective trawl of its initiatives, in June 2003, the Executive announced the allocation of £2 million to recruit teachers, with a view to fulfilling its commitment to radically reduce class sizes. The intention is to increase the number of teachers by 2007 from the initially projected 50,000 to 53,000 and it was anticipated that the number of primary school teachers being trained in Scottish universities in 2003-04 would increase by just under 50%[29]. Soon after, the Executive was able to report that – partly due to the decline in the pupil population, partly because of the recruitment of more teachers – class sizes had fallen further. The Education Minister claimed that the average primary class now had 24 pupils and reaffirmed the commitment to further reductions by the target date of 2007[30].

## International standards

What of the international standards already alluded to in this chapter? Around the time of the 2003 elections various alarms were sounded about levels of literacy. In fact, a document published in 2002 – *Programme for international student assessment: Scottish report* – showed Scottish 15-year-olds performing well in mathematical, scientific and reading literacy, coming out in each subject area in the top third of predominantly OECD countries. This was, it was conceded, significantly better than the performance of Scotland's 9- to 13-year-olds in mathematics and science tests carried out in 1995. Not only did Scots 15-year-olds systematically perform well above the OECD average, they also did so on a significant number of occasions when compared to the English/UK average. In an area where this advantage did not apply – scientific literacy, where the OECD average was 502, the English 533, and the Scots 522 – it was suggested that the "science strategy and the revised 5-14 curriculum guidelines" would help redress this relative shortfall. Discussing factors associated with student performance, it was remarked that while variation between countries could in part be explained by expenditure, this alone was "not sufficient to achieve high attainment". On the other hand, school ethos seemed to be important, something that had "received considerable emphasis in Scotland in recent years through school self evaluation and the Ethos Network". We noted above the Executive's interest in school ethos. Similarly, attainment seemed to correlate positively where head teachers reported high degrees of autonomy and this appeared to "support the case for devolved school management, which is well advanced in Scotland"[31]. So, there is evidence that Scottish education is in important areas in a healthy state. How and to whom, however, is it delivered?

## Organisation and delivery

As noted, the legislative framework is the various Education (Scotland) Acts and, since 1999, legislation passed by Holyrood. The responsible departments are Education, and Enterprise and Lifelong Learning. The former is responsible for pre-school and compulsory and post-compulsory school education. Quality is monitored by the requirement that schoolteachers be qualified and registered; the national accreditation of examinations and qualifications; and the work of Her Majesty's Inspectors[32].

We have already encountered the successful push for more places for pre-school education. At primary and secondary levels power is devolved to the 32 unitary councils set up in 1996. These have education committees consisting of elected councillors and representatives of the teaching profession and the main churches. Funding derives from the Executive's annual grant to local authorities. In principle the latter are free to decide how much of the allocation is devoted to education, although given the emphasis from the centre on, for example, the National Priorities, in reality there is little room for manoeuvre. The other main source of income is local taxation. Education accounts for around half of local authorities' budgets and as such is by some way the single largest item of expenditure. Under the 1998 School Boards (Scotland) Act local authorities are required to seek for each school the setting up of a board comprising members elected from the staff and parents co-opted from the local community.

Primary education runs from five to 12 years of age. There is no statutory curriculum, although the Education Department's 5-14 programme is explicitly intended as a fundamental framework to provide "breadth, balance, coherence and progression" (Scottish Executive, 2003d, p 15). In 2001, there were some 2,200 primary schools serving 420,000 pupils, with a pupil:teacher ratio of around 19:1. The number of teachers had fallen since the recent peak of 1999-2000, but the number of pupils has fallen much faster so there has been a steady improvement in the pupil:teacher ratio (and see also earlier in this chapter on primary teacher recruitment). The average annual expenditure per primary school pupil has risen from £1,642 in 1993/94 to £2,369 in 2002/03. These average figures mask considerable variations in school size, for example. Put crudely, the larger the school, the cheaper is the cost per pupil. Scotland, as a result of its geography and population distribution, however, has a considerable number of small, predominantly rural, schools. In 2002/03, of the 2,262 primary schools some 6% had school rolls of 20 or less, with an average cost per pupil of £6,587. Around one third of primary schools have rolls of 100 or less. At the other end of the spectrum, the average cost per pupil for a primary school with a roll of over 600 (of which there were 11) was £1,855, although a more realistic comparison is with the 165 schools with a roll of between 401 and 600 and an average pupil cost of £1,962[33].

Secondary education is available up to the age of 18 and compulsory between 12 and 16 years. Around 70% of Scottish secondary pupils are educated in schools with rolls of between 400 and 1,200. The numbers of both pupils and teachers have been relatively steady over the period 1997-2002, with the pupil:teacher ratio also fairly constant at around 13:1. Average cost per pupil has risen, as with primary students, from £2,686 in 1993/94 to £3,513 in 2002/03 and this too varies according to the size of school, but rather less dramatically[34]. During the compulsory phase of secondary education, the curriculum for 12- to 14-year-olds continues to be based on the 5-14 programme. The next two years are more specialised, with both vocational and academic elements, and at their conclusion pupils can begin to take the Scottish Qualifications Certificate. This is available at three levels: Foundation, General and Credit. Achievements in these examinations vary considerably, at 16 years and subsequently, by location. Most noticeably, Glasgow City scores less well at all levels and at all ages and appears to show no signs of improvement (another example of 'the Glasgow effect'). By contrast, affluent areas such as East Renfrewshire – geographically close to Glasgow – score consistently well, and some way above the average (Scottish Executive, 2002c, pp 3-4).

Post-compulsory school education is designed:

> to build on achievements in the earlier years, to prepare pupils for future
> years, whether in work, society and/or further study, and to offer a broad
> and rewarding educational experience. (Scottish Executive, 2003d, p 23)

As with all other levels of school education, we see again here the ongoing
emphasis on that very Scottish characteristic of breadth. Examinations taken
in these fifth and sixth years of secondary education are based on the Higher
Still programme discussed earlier in this chapter and can be taken at five levels:
Access, Intermediate 1, Intermediate 2, Higher, and Advanced Higher. It seems
likely that the way in which information about results is communicated will
be the subject of further investigation and simplification, in the wake of
widespread concerns about what the qualifications actually involved[35].

The tertiary sector has two principal components: further education (FE)
and higher education (HE). Both have been given a key role in lifelong learning
and social inclusion. The providers of the former are 46 colleges. Access
restrictions have been eased and the traditional audience (16- to 18-year-olds)
has been increasingly supplemented by older students. The mode of study
remains predominantly part-time, with students able to take a wide range of
primarily vocational courses, some of which can lead to formal qualifications
such as the Scottish Qualifications Certificate or Higher National Diploma/
Certificate. As from 2000, tuition fees were abolished for Scottish and EU
domiciled students taking full-time courses. Other financial support is available,
for example fee-waivers for certain part-time students on state benefits (see
further Scottish Executive, 2003d, p 27).

Funding comes from the Scottish Further Education Funding Council, a
non-departmental body set up in 1999 and charged with ensuring that colleges
"implement the priorities of Scottish Ministers". By the end of the first
Parliament, financial resources to this sector had risen by 50% in cash terms
when compared with 1998, the total current expenditure being £428 million.
A commitment to increase the number of places over the first three years of the
Parliament was easily surpassed, with an extra 60,000 enrolments filled "mainly
by students from under-represented groups"[36]. By 2000-01, enrolments in
non-advanced courses had reached some 600,000, with data for a slightly
earlier period showing that just over 50% of enrolments were female and the
same proportion from the over-25 age group. The actual number of FE students
was put at over 250,000 (Scottish Executive, 2003d, p 28)[37].

This is not to say, however, that the Executive's strategy has been unproblematic.
An audit in summer 2003 revealed a high rate – around 40% – of college
enrolments dropping out or failing. There could be positive reasons for this,
for example individuals gaining a job or a university place. However, there
may be concern in the longer term, and some emphasis has been placed by key
figures on the difficulties the sector faces[38].

It is also possible to take first degrees in FE colleges – around 40% of all full-
time entrants to degree courses are in such institutions – which leads us on to
HE. Scotland has 21 HE institutions consisting of 14 universities (including

the Open University) and seven others. Funding is the responsibility of the Scottish Higher Education Funding Council, set up in 1993. A merger is proposed between the Further and the Higher Education Funding Councils to ensure coherence in the post-school sector and so to emphasise further the unity and centrality of lifelong learning. In the more traditional universities, students study for three years for an Ordinary degree and four for Honours.

Given the differences in timing between Scottish Highers and English A-levels, it is possible for Scottish pupils to enter university a year earlier than their English counterparts. Indeed there was a small, but telling, example of Scottish prickliness about education when, in summer 2003, plans were proposed in England and Wales for a revamp of the mechanisms for students being accepted at university. For complicated reasons, to institute the proposed changes would have knock-on effects for Scottish universities and this led an SNP spokesperson to denounce the proposals as "Anglo-centric" and as taking no account of "the Scottish system and Scottish schools"[39]. Potentially more problematic, however, is that policy divergence on university fees will lead to better-funded English institutions attracting academic staff from Scotland. In salary terms, therefore, there has arisen a perceived need for Scottish universities to remain competitive[40]. Recent financial demands by the university sector are touched upon towards the end of this chapter.

Such potential problems notwithstanding, by the beginning of this century some 50% of Scottish young people were pursuing degree courses, whether at university or in FE colleges. This exceeded the Executive's targets (and the proportion in England) and constituted a rise of 15% over five years[41]. Higher education, famously, was an area where Holyrood early on flexed its independent muscles. As in FE, from autumn 2000 tuition fees were abolished, although it is more accurate to say that up-front tuition fees were abolished as a graduate endowment scheme was also introduced. Nonetheless, the latter is more financially generous than the English system and it is complemented, again as in FE, with schemes aimed at encouraging students from low-income families to enter the sector, further evidence of a commitment to social inclusion and to equality of opportunity (Rees, 2002, p 106; for brief details of the schemes, Scottish Executive, 2003d, p 29). This is at least part of the reason for the 50% participation target being achieved and the further upsurge in applications to Scottish universities for 2003: 2.9% over the preceding year, double the increase in England[42]. We briefly return to the issue of student fees in Chapter Six.

The Executive clearly places considerable emphasis on HE. Its *Framework for Higher Education in Scotland* was published in March 2003. In the foreword, the Minister for Enterprise, Transport and Lifelong Learning stressed that, while Scotland had much to be proud of in this field, nonetheless "we live in a world where past success is no guarantee of future achievement in any sphere". In an interesting aside, he remarked that, while the contemporaneous English White Paper provided a context for discussions in Scotland, it did not determine them. The document itself again emphasised HE's role in lifelong learning, and thus its contribution to "personal fulfilment and enterprise; employability and adaptability; active citizenship and social inclusion". The Executive had shown its support for the sector by increasing its funding commitment in real terms every year since devolution. There were now some 0.25 million students in HE compared with around 0.12 million in 1986-87, with a noticeable rise in the numbers of those studying part-time. Scotland also came first in the OECD league table of graduation rates.

Significantly, however, the socioeconomic affiliations of undergraduates had stayed fairly steady, with partly skilled/unskilled family groups contributing only around 10% in 2001 – a qualification, therefore, on our earlier comment about HE and social inclusion. By coincidence, around the same proportion of the student body overall were non-EU citizens. These contributed some £70 million in fees, were estimated to spend £120 million off-campus, and so made a significant contribution to the economy. In conclusion, among the points the report highlighted were:

- a cap on expansion at around the 50% of Scottish young people in higher education, at least as far as Executive was concerned;
- a shift towards participation by disadvantaged groups;
- further targeting of overseas students;
- collaboration rather than competition within the sector in Scotland;
- and knowledge transfer, particularly between social science and policy makers[43].

## Scottish child welfare strategies

We have seen that for both New Labour and the Executive education embraces more than just children: it should be a lifelong experience. Likewise, concern about the young involves more than educational provision. In this section, we examine New Labour and Scottish attitudes to child welfare. The focus is less on the details of individual policies but rather on underlying aims and philosophy.

We should note from the outset that for the most part children exist within families, and strong family structures are central to New Labour's social welfare approach. Family policy, however, is notoriously difficult to define (Millar and Ridge, 2002, p 85). In the particular case of Scotland (see Wasoff and Hill, 2002), furthermore, many policy areas that impact strongly on family and child life are reserved to London.

Nonetheless, the Executive has sought to direct its policies in a child-centred way. We saw in Chapter Three the dimensions of child poverty and the Executive's determination to tackle the issue. Child poverty is seen not only as a social ill in itself. There is also the perception that early years matter and that disadvantage, once acquired, can be difficult to lose and thus establish a pattern for life and even for future generations. We have seen in this chapter that initiatives such as New Community Schools aim to integrate education and other forms of welfare provision, again in an attempt to provide a level playing field for all children. Similarly, early intervention and the provision of nursery places, with educational as well as care dimensions, clearly seek to equalise opportunity. Finally, we will find in the next chapter that children have been targeted as a group for particular attention as part of the Executive's strategy of health improvement, again on a catch-them-young basis.

Partly because of its original relationship to education, Scottish child welfare policy and practice has historically had differences with that of England (Stewart, 2001). In the post-war era, one of the most important innovations came with the 1964 Kilbrandon Report and the consequent 1968 Social Work (Scotland) Act. Essentially, this involved the creation of a system of children's hearings that separated out children from the adult justice system and promoted rehabilitation rather than retribution, and the requirement for local authorities to pursue children's welfare. As one group of commentators put it, the "positive promotion of welfare in the 1968 act was indeed revolutionary, and notably absent from parallel legislation in England and Wales" (Hill et al, 1998, p 96; also McGoldrick, 2001, p 88). In 1995 came the Children (Scotland) Act, which, as we have seen, also had an impact on subsequent educational legislation. This Act stressed children's rights and the corresponding duties and obligations of both parents and the state. It was in part prompted by the investigation into the Orkney child abuse case conducted in the early 1990s but also by the UK government's 1991 ratification of the UN Convention on the Rights of the Child (Hill et al, 1998, p 109; McGoldrick, 2001, pp 90-2; Waterhouse and McGhee, 2002, pp 144-5).

Turning to New Labour, Hendrick (2003), one of the foremost historians of English childhood and commentator on contemporary child policy, argues that its approach to child welfare has, in fact, referred less to child welfare as such, and more to children as "investments" or "the future" (p 205) – in other words, as human capital. The focus, therefore, is not on "the child as child, but on the child as adult in the making" (p 210). This has resulted, for instance, in the current concern with early childhood. In juvenile justice, there has been a shift towards retribution, in defiance of the UN Convention. Hendrick concedes that, since 1997, child well-being has in certain respects improved and that the importance of childhood has been officially acknowledged in an unprecedented way. Nonetheless, the government is also seeking to create a "passive child citizen" encumbered by responsibilities rather than rights. New Labour's attitude is thus both populist and subordinate to a human capital approach (Hendrick, 2003, p 243; on New Labour's *National childcare strategy*, see also Millar and Ridge, 2002, p 95ff). In the light of this critique and in the historical context of pre-existing Scottish child welfare practices, how can we view the situation since 1999? We start by examining key Executive documents, drawing out central themes some of which have already been variously encountered – human capital, child poverty and holistic welfare.

Late in 2001 came the remarkable 'For Scotland's children', produced by the Executive's Child Action Team, which in places reads like an updated version of *Pilgrim's progress*. In uncompromising fashion, this began by noting the disadvantages many children suffered: for example, the relatively high proportion entitled to free school meals and "some of the highest rates of relative child poverty in the developed world". Every child ought to have the same "starting point" on their "journey through life", but currently this was not the case. The family was the "principal guide" on this journey and some did indeed place their children on "a broad straight road". Other children, however, had to "claw their way out of a steep-sided valley, sometimes with those around them pulling them back down". Many current services, particularly those dealing with the most vulnerable, were near breaking point, although it was also felt that the macro-economic climate then prevailing would facilitate the implementation of improved and integrated services. The Executive was urged to "reaffirm its commitment to consider the impact of all legislation, policy and initiatives on children (and their families) through the publication of a child impact statement in relation to each measure"[44].

In its 2002 response to an enquiry into the need for a Children's Commissioner, the Executive affirmed its commitment to improving the quality of child life and to ending child poverty. The ultimate, often repeated, aim was a Scotland where "every child matters, where every child, regardless of its family background, has the best possible start in life". Children were at the "heart of the Executive's agenda". This was witnessed, for instance, by the establishment of a Cabinet Sub-Committee on Children's Services, one of whose central aims was nationwide integration of policy, funding and delivery of child welfare[45]. Also in 2002 came the recommendations of the Child Protection and Audit Review. This stressed that local authorities, in producing plans for integrated children's services, "should develop *positive childhood* initiatives". These should be underpinned by a "children's rights rather than a public service perspective" and thus "should promote *every* child's right to life, health, decency and development". The Executive itself should back this approach with a public campaign[46].

The section of the 2004-05 Budget statement on 'Education and Young People' stressed the need for close collaboration between government departments – for example when dealing with youth justice and the building of "safer communities" through tackling "persistent young offenders". Policies such as New Community Schools met children's needs in an "holistic way". Early intervention was necessary to "end routes into poverty and deprivation and provide routes out through education and support". The aim was thus to give all children, and especially those from disadvantaged or vulnerable backgrounds, the "best start in life"[47]. Finally, in autumn 2003 came the Report of the Child Health Support Group. This noted, inter alia, the aim of promoting "social justice through development of better integrated services for children". Such integrated services, which had not historically been the norm "but will become so for future generations", would result in real opportunities for health improvement. Integration had already been made possible by the 1995 Children (Scotland) Act and would be part of, for example, community-based child health services. These were an "essential element" in the drive against health inequalities as they allowed for the targeting of the most vulnerable in order to "close the opportunity gap"[48].

We might now make the following points:

1. The Executive has committed itself to a strategy that does not ignore children. As Wasoff and Hill (2002, p 178) put it, both action and rhetoric "have been characterised by more frequent and explicit commitments towards children than hitherto". We might compare this with Hendrick's remarks on the London government noted earlier in this chapter.

2. In Scotland as elsewhere, human capital arguments are used to justify child welfare policies.

3. While this and the previous point are not mutually exclusive, it is also possible to see such policies as attacking openly acknowledged problems of poverty and inequality; or, to put it another way, structural rather than individual causes of disadvantage. Interestingly, however, the Executive has resisted enlarging the scope of the free school meals programme, arguing that this is a clear case for a targeted benefit[49].

4. There is a repeated emphasis on the need for integration of services alongside an acknowledgement that in certain areas social services in particular are stretched to breaking point. This prompted, in late 2003, a recruitment drive costed at £11 million and justified, as one minister put it, by the introduction earlier in the year of "an ambitious child protection programme which will deliver national standards, a tough inspection system and a Children's Charter"[50]. The quest for integration, Wasoff and Hill (2002, p 179) argue, is being done "horizontally, that is, to improve cooperation among services and professionals dealing with children", so sharpening the division between services for children and those for adults. This is a salutary reminder of the problems of actually implementing joined-up government, where an integrative move in one field may have the unintended consequence of promoting division in another (school exclusions to promote school harmony but which go against concepts of social inclusion can also be seen in this light). Discussing a similar development in England, Millar and Ridge (2002, p 102) express doubt about the long-term viability of such a focus.

5. There is certainly a discourse based on human capital, but it is also possible to find a stress on children's rights. The very positive argument of the Child Protection and Audit Review seems especially noteworthy here as is the perceived relationship between the 1995 Children (Scotland) Act and devolved educational policy. Similarly, in Chapter Three we noted the recommendation that research on child deprivation build on "the views and experiences of children".

6. There is the question of autonomy and policy divergence. One devolved power that has been taken up is the promise of a Children's Commissioner, created by the Commissioner for Children and Young People (Scotland) Act passed in spring 2003. Similar posts have been created in Wales, Northern Ireland and England. More distinctively Scottish, however, is the system of

children's hearings. Writing in the late 1990s, Hill et al (1998, pp 100, 101) pointed out that the system had been controversial in Scotland itself while simultaneously arousing "sympathetic interest on an international scale". The system had remained virtually unaltered while juvenile justice in England and Wales was, by contrast, being "steered in a more punitive direction". A few years later, Waterhouse and McGhee (2002, p 147) were still able to make this claim while also observing that there had been no Scottish equivalent of the 1998 Crime and Disorder Act, a prime example for Hendrick (2003, p 226ff) of New Labour's shift towards retribution.

However, this is not to present Scotland as some liberal haven. The Executive's legislative programme announced in May 2003 promised to "crack down hard on anti-social behaviour", including through ongoing reform of the court and children's hearing systems. It was proposed, therefore, to introduce legislation allowing for, inter alia, "new Anti-Social Behaviour Orders for under-16s"; and electronic monitoring devices for children "as an alternative to secure accommodation"[51]. The Anti-Social Behaviour Bill duly revealed in autumn 2003 had, to say the least, a robust approach to juvenile offending. This was denounced by some opposition politicians as brutalising, stigmatising and alienating, but Executive Ministers are clearly committed to a hard-line strategy[52]. Hendrick's analysis, noted above, is clearly important here as is Baldwin's (2002, p 182) more general point that "New Labour policy on social care reveals a rhetoric of social justice, but a social control ethos as well".

## Conclusion

In his May 2003 parliamentary statement, the First Minister stressed the goal of "excellence in education for every child". The building programme would be increased and devolution to individual schools would continue alongside, raising professional standards and associated rewards. Two new Bills were to be introduced – "Powers for Ministers to Intervene" and "Additional Support for Learning". The former would compel local authorities to act on the recommendations of HM Inspectorate, the latter would be aimed at ensuring that each child's individual needs were met (a further example of education as social inclusion)[53]. As one newspaper put it, this indicated a decision to "take on" the educational establishment and local authorities by employing "hit squads" to take over failing schools. This was "in line with policies south of the border" and of itself a "profoundly Blairite idea". It had, apparently, been officially acknowledged that there would be opposition to such a move, but that this would have to be confronted[54].

However, the Executive was at pains to deny such an interpretation. The Education Minister stressed that "using private companies to rescue failing schools, a measure that has been widely used south of the Border" had in fact been ruled out. This, the report continued, confirmed Edinburgh's reluctance "to pursue the Blairite reform model for the public sector"[55]. Leaving aside for the moment the interpretative problems associated with the term Blairite, these reports further indicate what a sensitive subject state education is to the Scots. The details of the Education (Ministerial Powers of Intervention) Bill were announced in late 2003, and the Education Minister reiterated that hit squads would be not be used. Nonetheless, one teachers' leader described the proposals as a "gross insult" to his profession. Taking a more sanguine (or complacent?) view, a local authority spokesperson described the plans as "window dressing" on the grounds that "there are no failing schools in Scotland"; while a representative of the Scottish Parent Teacher Council described the whole exercise as "pointless"[56].

Increased responsibility, furthermore, was not simply to be confined to schools and local authorities. In summer 2003, the Education Minister, in a statement highlighting responsibilities as well as rights, stressed the need for a "new era" in which the parental role was to be stressed. Too many Scots had for far too long handed over children to the education system with the expectation of "a finished product (sic) some years later". Parents needed to be more active in engaging with their children's education and to be so would have a positive effect on, for instance, school discipline[57]. This sense of a new era was also present in a speech made by the First Minister late in 2003 where he called for a "decisive shift" away from limited choices for school pupils. Essentially, what he was suggesting was that more vocational courses be available in schools so that the less academically inclined did not have their options narrowed[58].

What these post-election episodes clearly illustrate is an ongoing Executive determination to reform education, not least for labour market reasons. However, they also illustrate the Executive's broadly consensual approach in a society where not only professional, but also popular, engagement with and support for state education are high. It is notable, for example, that the First Minister presented his November 2003 speech as seeking a

> child-focused education system capable of delivering an individual education in a universal system.

Modernisation, in other words, was to take place within a comprehensive framework. Whether this is achievable is another matter. As Paterson (2003, p 199) remarks, in a number of respects Scottish education faces a "paradox and a dilemma" at the beginning of the 21st century.

There also continues to be problems with parts of the education package. A report in August 2003 suggested that the "complex" New Community Schools scheme had often become "bogged down in bureaucracy and elaborate management structures". Confusion about aims was evident in some areas and the "cocktail of approaches" – for example, in health and drugs education – had "failed to make an impact". The supposed failure of the project, at a cost of £78 million, was thus seen as a blow to the Executive and its commitment to extend the scheme to all schools by 2007[59]. Later that year, further concerns were expressed about school exam pass rates, with Glasgow again a particular problem[60]. The same month, the Head of HM Inspectorate of Education reportedly claimed that "disadvantaged pupils have a poorer chance of success in the Scottish education system". He also called for greater parental participation and for schools to be responsive to individual pupil needs both, as we have already seen, also Executive aspirations[61].

In the HE sector, November 2003 saw claims that Scottish universities were seriously under-funded when compared with their equivalents in similarly sized European countries. In what appeared to be an attack on the First Minister's argument for more vocational school courses, a universities' spokesperson stressed the economic necessity of university graduates. This was followed up, at the precise time when the student fees issue was preoccupying Westminster, with the claim that Scottish higher education was seriously under-funded, to the tune of some £169 million, when compared with European competitor nations. The Executive made it clear, however, that there would be no easy answer to this issue[62].

Clearly, then, education and children have played a large part in Executive thought and action. Of course it would be wrong to see this as an exclusively Scottish phenomenon. Issues such as the enhancement of human capital and university funding are widely shared, not least with New Labour in London. Nonetheless, the Executive has seized the opportunities afforded by devolution. Put simply, there remains, albeit sometimes in a muddled way, a commitment to comprehensive schooling that clearly, increasingly and importantly distances Scotland from England. This commitment reflects a broader, historically grounded, support for this form of schooling. In higher education too there are distinctively Scottish characteristics, most famously in respect of student fees. And although the Executive has signalled its determination to modernise and reform education, it nonetheless seeks to do so not by confrontation but, where at all possible, by consensus, partnership and cooperation. Child welfare also has its own Scottish particularities although here, as elsewhere, issues common to the whole of the UK – for instance anti-social behaviour – can evoke similar responses. The broader implications of all this are dealt with in Chapter Six of this book.

## Notes

[1] www.scotland.gov.uk/who/dept_education.asp

[2] *The Guardian*, 4 May 1999, 'Scotland takes the Higher Road?'.

[3] www.scottishlabour.org.uk/ed.html

[4] www.scottishlabour.org.uk/ed.html

[5] *The Guardian*, 10 May 1999, 'Tony versus Donald'.

[6] www.scottishlabour.org.uk/ed.html

[7] *The Scotsman*, 28 June 2003, 'Private sector "will not bail out schools"'.

[8] www.scottishlabour.org.uk/ed.html

[9] for instance, www.scottishlabour.org.uk/health.html

[10] www.scottishlabour.org.uk/ed.html

[11] www.scottishlabour.org.uk/ed.html

[12] *Times Education Supplement*, 28 July 2000, 'Pace of reform won't slow'; 'Holyrood watchers hail rite of passage'.

[13] *Times Education Supplement*, 6 October 2000, 'Standards Act starts to filter into schools'; 17 November 2000, 'Act "needs to be promoted"'.

[14] www.scotland.gov.uk/library5/social.lili

[15] www.scotland.gov.uk/library5/education.awoo

[16] *The Guardian*, 7 October 2000, 'Scottish exam authority "riddled with ineptitude"'; 7 September, 2000, 'Galbraith dodges calls to resign over exam fiasco'.

[17] *The Guardian*, 23 February 1999, 'Aiming higher still'.

[18] *The Guardian*, 29 August 2000, 'Scottish system "stuck in a Victorian timewarp"'.

[19] www.bbc.co.uk, 5 November 2002, 'McConnell's schooling vision'.

[20] *Times Education Supplement*, 28 June 2002, 'Ideals and reality'.

[21] *The Scotsman*, 28 June 2003, 'Private sector "will not bail out schools"'.

[22] *The Scotsman*, 21 July 2003, 'New test system to wipe out school "cheats"'.

[23] *The Herald*, 25 September 2003, 'School league tables to be scrapped'.

[24] *The Scotsman*, 5 November 2003, 'MSPs lose battle on school league tables'.

[25] *The Guardian*, 9 October 2001, 'Brave hearts'.

[26] *The Scotsman*, 14 November 2003, 'Green light for £100m PPP schools in Highlands'.

[27] *The Guardian*, 11 June 2002, 'Scotland to fund schools research'.

[28] *The Guardian*, 28 October 2002, 'Report promises overhaul of Scottish education'.

[29] *The Guardian*, 25 June 2003, 'Scotland pledges £2m to cut class sizes'.

[30] *The Scotsman*, 27 August 2003, 'Pupil population falls by 6,500'.

[31] www.scotland.gov.uk/library3/education/PISA_2002

[32] For further detail of the role of specialist agencies, see www.scotland.gov.uk/library5/education/awoo. This document, 'A world of opportunity: a guide to education and training in Scotland', published in March 2003, as well as Scottish Executive 2003c and 2003d, are the main sources of what follows.

[33] www.scotland.gov.uk/stats/bulletins/00217

[34] www.scotland.gov.uk/stats/bulletins/00217

[35] *The Scotsman*, 31 July 2003, 'Awards to get simpler format'.

[36] www.scotland.gov.uk/library5/education/awoo

[37] also www.scotland.gov.uk/library5/education/awoo

[38] *The Scotsman*, 29 August 2003, 'Audit reveals colleges' increase in drop-out rates'.

[39] *The Scotsman*, 11 August 2003, 'University shake-up attacked'.

[40] *The Herald*, 22 September 2003 'English in top-up fees warning to Scots'.

[41] *The Scotsman*, 18 July 2003, 'More apply to Scottish universities'.

[42] As note 41.

[43] www.scotland.gov.uk/library5/lifelong/herp

[44] www.scotland.gov.uk/library3/education/fscr

[45] www.scotland.gov.uk/library5/health/ccs.pdf

[46] www.scotland.gov.uk/library5/education/iaar – emphasis in the original

[47] www.scotland.gov.uk/library5/finance/db05s

[48] www.scotland.gov.uk/library5/health/mwsc-03.asp

[49] *The Herald*, 5 June 2003, 'Outrage from Kane as MSPs reject free school meals for all'.

[50] www.bbc.co.uk, 21 October 2003, 'Move to cut social work shortfall'.

[51] www.scotland.gov.uk, 28 May 2003, 'Executive's Legislative Programme 2003-2004'.

[52] www.bbc.co.uk, 2 October 2003, 'Crime plans "stigmatise" children'; *The Scotsman*, 31 October 2003, 'McConnell bill to tag ten-year-olds'.

[53] www.scotland.gov.uk, 28 May 2003, 'Parliamentary Statement by the First Minister on the Executive's Programme for 2003-2004'.

[54] *The Herald*, 28 May 2003, 'Failing schools face takeover by McConnell's hit squads'.

[55] *The Scotsman*, 28 June 2003, 'Private sector "will not bail out schools"'.

[56] www.bbc.co.uk, 7 November 2003, 'Ministers to get new school powers'; *The Herald*, 7 November 2003, 'Promise to limit new school powers'.

[57] *The Scotsman*, 20 August 2003, 'Parents warned they must share responsibility for children's education'.

[58] *The Herald*, 3 November 2003, 'McConnell unveils plans for comprehensive education'.

[59] *The Scotsman*, 30 August 2003, '£78 million schools making no impact'.

[60] *The Herald*, 5 November 2003, 'Exams pass rate drops in key areas'.

[61] *The Scotsman*, 13 November 2003, 'Schools "fail to help children reach full potential"'.

[62] *The Herald*, 17 November 2003, 'Scottish universities want extra £100m to meet funding needs'; *The Scotsman*, 19 November 2003, '"No blank cheques" for universities'; www.bbc.co.uk, 9 December 2003, 'Cash plea from university chiefs'.

# FIVE

# Health policy

## Introduction

For over 50 years, the NHS has been part and parcel of what it means to be British. If you fall ill, the NHS is there. Its foundations – tax-based funding and care according to need – remain as valid today as ever. (Scottish Labour Party, 2001, p 19)

... as citizens we have failed to take real responsibility for our own health.

... in Scotland we still have some of the worst health statistics in Europe.

... improving our health service is not only about medical or social care.... It is also about improving standards of social care.... improving the quality of life.

We need reform to match investment – but we need reform to go with the grain of Scotland. I am as committed today (to its founding principles) as a generation of British people were to the NHS when it began in 1948. But we are building a health service for this new century and it must be a health service that takes those principles and applies them to the demands that we face today[1].

It is the duty of the Scottish Ministers to promote the improvement of the physical and mental health of the people of Scotland. The Scottish Ministers may do anything which they consider is likely to assist in discharging that duty.... (2003 National Health Service Reform [Scotland] Bill, part 2, section 7)

Scotland's economic performance currently lags behind the best international standards. With an ageing population projected for the coming decades, improved business growth and performance will depend in part on our ability to improve the health of the workforce, and to maintain and increase employment rates (Scottish Executive, 2003f, p 22).

... joint working in many areas may be desirable. In the care of the elderly it is essential.... We believe the old distinctions between, for example, a 'medical' and a 'social' bath, have no place in a modern care system[2].

The above extracts from a range of statements on health and healthcare bring out some of the key issues pursued in this chapter. These include the central priority afforded to health policy by the Executive and its determination to force through its plans for a healthier Scotland; the sense that such a strategy certainly has very real human and social dimensions, but is also seen as crucial to economic health; and a commitment to the NHS, albeit a reformed and modernised NHS. One recurring theme was articulated early on in the new Parliament's life. At the launch of the Scottish NHS Plan, the Health Minister pledged to "rebuild" Scotland's health system and to launch "the biggest health improvement drive ever seen". The then First Minister added to this by claiming that the plan afforded the chance to "address Scotland's needs with greater determination and focus than ever before", and that he and his colleagues were determined to "use our power and resources to make a real difference"[3]. The notion of rebuilding (on other occasions rewiring), and doing so in a specifically Scottish context, is important; hence, in part, the renaming of the health services in Scotland as NHSScotland. In part, it clearly relates to the New Labour concern with public service modernisation and reform. Rebuilding can also be construed, however, as a fundamental commitment to the NHS and a desire to compensate for the damage done under Conservative rule. The language of rebuilding is also employed by New Labour, but it may have an underlying difference of meaning north and south of the border. We explore this further in Chapter Six, especially, in our discussion of the devolved administrations as defenders of the welfare state.

We have already encountered, especially in Chapter Three, Scotland's poor health record, including the particular problems faced by Glasgow. News media in late summer 2003 reported that Glasgow was the "sickest city" in the UK and that Glaswegian males could expect to live around 10 years less than their counterparts in areas of southern England. An official from NHS Greater Glasgow commented that things were getting better – life expectancy was slightly up – but that:

> Poverty and deprivation are the main factors in the poor health record of Glasgow's people.

Ironically, this news came shortly after the announcement that UK men as a whole were now outliving their counterparts in much of the rest of Europe[4]. These reports were followed in autumn 2003 by further comparative analysis. Among its findings were that Scotland had not shared in the significant health improvements of the rest of the UK, particularly with respect to coronary heart disease, stroke, breast cancer and lung cancer; and that a child born in Scotland had a lower life expectancy than its counterparts in the rest of Europe[5]. This gloomy picture was further reinforced in spring 2004 when it was revealed that men in the Shettleston district of Glasgow had a life expectancy of around 14 years less than the national average; that this was, so it was claimed, comparable with countries such as Iraq; and that for men in the area, life expectancy had actually fallen, a phenomenon unknown since the end of the Second World War. Poverty and deprivation were stressed as causal factors, although media reports also made much of behavioural factors such as smoking and poor diet[6].

Academic analysis largely bears out these points. Hanlon et al (2003, pp 33, 38, 47, 49, 55), in a detailed survey, point to the following characteristics of Scottish health:

- there are significant health inequalities within Scotland itself, and again the geographical closeness between Glasgow and some of its more affluent, and healthier, neighbours is noted;
- Scottish life expectancy is low by European standards;
- although Scotland has seen an improvement in key areas such as heart disease and stroke, other nations have done even better, thereby maintaining Scotland's poor relative position; significantly in this context, they also remark that Scots are among Europe's most enthusiastic consumers of tobacco;
- Scotland has high rates of obesity and a poor record of dental health.

All this leads them to conclude, depressingly but accurately, that data show that recent improvements notwithstanding, "Scotland's health status and key determinants of health lag behind comparable countries in Northern and Western Europe". Within the UK, furthermore, Scotland has the worst health record and overall "projected trends suggest that Scotland is unlikely to change its relative position" (p 55).

The Executive is clear about its own role in health policy. However, it has increasingly stressed that individuals too have responsibilities and that, consequently, cultural changes are required. So, for example, campaigns have been mounted against tobacco and alcohol consumption and poor diet. The totality of this approach has the further implication that existing boundaries between, especially, social and healthcare – described by one former New Labour Health Minister as a Berlin Wall – are no longer acceptable. A famous attempt to realise such a strategy came with care for the elderly where Scotland has initiated distinctive policies from those in England. This episode, discussed later in this chapter, has raised the question of whether, as one commentator has put it, it constituted "Scotland's bid for distributive justice in later life", and as such was rather more in tune with the "social contract" of the late 1940s and a rejection of the "neo-liberalism" of New Labour in England (Blair, 2002, p 19 and passim). The implementation of free personal and nursing care thus provides an important case study in both the attempt to integrate health and social care and of policy divergence. The notion of distributive justice, moreover, highlights the possibility of Scotland as a defender of the founding principles of the NHS.

This chapter is divided as follows. First, we have an account of Scottish healthcare pre-1997. Second, we look at New Labour's approach to health policy. Then, third, we examine what the Executive has sought to do since devolution, and why. A discussion of free personal and nursing care for the elderly follows and we conclude with an assessment of the Scottish health service since 1999.

## Scottish healthcare to 1997

As with education, healthcare is a field in which Scotland has long taken pride in distinctiveness. Scottish medical education has traditionally been seen as of particularly high quality and its medical schools for many years exported doctors to other parts of the UK and beyond; and Scotland early on had its own elite professional bodies – the Royal Colleges of Glasgow and of Edinburgh. The country's geographical characteristics were acknowledged by the setting up in the first half of the 20th century of the Highlands and Islands Medical Service, sometimes seen as a prototype for the NHS. In passing, we should note that the remoteness of some Scottish rural communities appears to continue to affect health in those areas – in the phrase of Woods (2003, p 9), there is a "tyranny of distance". Again as with education, health matters were dealt with by a Scottish Office department. Difference – in terms of governance, geography, medical traditions and history – was recognised in the setting up of the NHS. In Scotland, this came with a separate (albeit virtually identical) Act from that for England and Wales, which nonetheless put control of the service in the hands of the Secretary of State for Scotland (Stewart, 2003). The Scottish medical profession was much more inclined to the new service than its English counterpart, something that Duprée (2000, pp 139-40) argues resonates up to the present day and to which we shall return. It would be wrong to suggest that the systems north and south of the border were radically different: the NHS in Scotland had only one close relative, and that was the health service in England and Wales, a service with which it shared a commonality of purpose and principle.

Nonetheless, there were differences. Before focusing on the period 1979-97, we can make three initial points.

1. The very fact of the NHS being governed separately always allowed for policy divergence. So, for instance, the 1974 reorganisation took a different (and less catastrophic) form in Scotland than in England and Wales. And, of course, the existence of a technically separate service made it a prime candidate for the remit of a Scottish Parliament.
2. The traditionally centralising tendencies of Scottish governance resulted, in the case of health, in the Scottish Office having a much tighter control over what went on in its localities than did the Ministry of Health, a characteristic that strengthened over time.
3. Differences notwithstanding, the Scottish health service was (and of course remains) essentially financed from London. Virtually from the outset, however, per capita spending on health was higher in Scotland than in England, another persistent characteristic. The Scottish Office became adept at bargaining with the Treasury and these higher levels became, as we saw in

Chapter Two, the baseline for the Barnett mechanism. Such higher levels of expenditure have been justified on the basis of rates of morbidity and mortality, and on the problems of providing universal healthcare to a widely dispersed population (see Chapter Four for similar arguments regarding education). It is worth noting here also that the Interim Report of the Wanless Committee in 2001 found more available hospital beds, more general practitioners per capita, and higher levels of prescribing in Scotland (and indeed in Wales and Northern Ireland) than in England (cited in Woods, 2002, p 27). These characteristics too are historically based (Stewart, 2003).

Against this general background, how did the Scottish NHS fare under Conservative rule at Westminster? There is no room here to go into detail (for this, see Webster, 2002, ch 3), but five important points stand out (for a brief account of the Scottish health services post-1974, see Turner, 1998, on which this section partly draws). First, Scotland was, like the rest of the UK, subject to Thatcherite zeal to bring the rigours of the market to the public services, including health. This was most notably the case with the 1990 National Health Service and Community Care Act and its attempt to create an internal market. Significantly, there was no separate piece of legislation here for Scotland.

Second, the majority of Scots did not willingly embrace the internal market. Greer (2003, p 200) suggests that in Scotland "advocates of the internal market had always been weaker and professional elites stronger", and that there was a general cultural antipathy to market mechanisms. Nor did the market work in the anticipated manner, although the latter was probably true more generally (Turner, 1998, pp 68, 70; Paton, 1999, p 55; Bruce and Forbes, 2001, passim;). Here we should also note the unwillingness of the Scottish NHS to go down the "managerialist" road so evident in England in the 1980s (Hunter and Williamson, 1991; McTavish, 2000), notwithstanding a much more rapid rise in the number of administrative personnel in the first half of the 1990s than was, proportionately, the case in England (Turner, 1998, p 60). These divergences are in large part attributable to Scottish governance's consensual and corporatist traditions, allied to a strong public sector ethos among both professional staff and the public. One small, but revealing, instance of this is that Scottish consultants were and are much less likely to carry out private work than their English colleagues. Greer (2003, p 197) thus makes an important point when he remarks that advocates of healthcare markets are found "where there are doctors and managers converted by their experience, a strong private sector, and right-wing think tanks – in England, but not in the rest of the UK". Also important in this context is that, just as in education, the private sector in healthcare was, and remains, much smaller in Scotland than in England (the issue of pay-beds, for example, was highly contentious in the latter while barely registering in the former).

Third, largely because of its higher levels of funding, Scotland's hospital service was much less prone to the ward closures and cancellation of operations that led to widespread publicity about yet another crisis in the health services, especially during the 1980s.

Fourth, a sense of particularity was further reinforced, for example, by *The Patient's Charter* of the early 1990s. This sought to establish a maximum waiting time for treatment of 24 months, when in fact the Scottish NHS had already instituted a maximum of 18 months (Turner, 1998, p 63).

Finally, and clearly leading on from the previous points, we need to revisit the relationship between healthcare and devolution noted in Chapter One. There we cited Nottingham's (2000, pp 175-6) comments on the Scottish Constitutional Convention and its argument for a "direct relationship between constitutional reform and good health policy". A Scottish Parliament would, so the case went, be better able to tailor health policies to specific Scottish needs, for example through a "broader vision of public health" that would allow "a far more effective attack on the many factors contributing to preventable ill health". The Conservative government's reforms of the 1990s, by contrast, were "prompted mainly by service pressures in England and in particular London". As Nottingham further remarks, Scotland's health record began to take on a "totemic political status", with all post-1979 changes seen as "alien impositions" with "no roots in Scottish experience or need". As such, Conservative health policy contributed to the party's crushing electoral rejection in 1997. The parallel here with education is striking.

By the mid-1990s, therefore, there was a strongly articulated feeling that Scottish health issues should be dealt with in a Scottish context and by Scottish mechanisms. The Conservative administration in London was ideologically unsympathetic to the majority of Scots and in healthcare was intent on imposing policies and practices out of keeping with those traditionally pursued in Scotland. Control of health policy would allow the Scots more adequately to address the widely acknowledged health problems from which Scotland suffered. Devolving healthcare would, moreover, and as with education, be relatively straightforward given that it already enjoyed a degree of autonomy. All this was, of course, to put an incredibly high level of expectation on what might realistically be achieved, at least in the short term. Before looking in more detail at the Executive's health strategy, however, we now look at how New Labour sees the nature and the future of the health services. The intention here is to pick out certain key issues as the backdrop to Scottish policy developments (for fuller analyses of New Labour and health, see Paton, 1999, 2002; North, 2001; Toynbee and Walker, 2001; Timmins, 2001; Webster, 2002; and, on finance, Glennerster, 2003).

## New Labour and health policy

Margaret Thatcher's claim that the NHS was safe in her government's hands notwithstanding, the health service was a major political issue throughout the UK during the 1980s and 1990s. In terms of its fundamental principles – funding from general taxation with most care free at the point of delivery and determined by need not personal income – there was at least as strong a sense of continuity as of change in health policy in this period (North, 2001, p 123). Nonetheless, after failing to respond adequately to Conservative initiatives in the 1980s, Labour, especially under Blair, came to realise that "the NHS constituted an electoral winning card" (Webster, 2002, p 209) and held "the key to the party's political rehabilitation" (p 208). We observed earlier the language of rebuilding (another example is the important 1995 policy document *Renewing the NHS: Labour's agenda for a healthier Britain*), and this was utilised to powerful effect during the 1997 election campaign with, as Webster (2002) puts it, much being made of the "evangelistic cry to 'save' or 'rebuild' the NHS in consistency with its 'historic principles'" (p 214; also, Paton, 2002, p 130). This was a deliberate reminder of the centrality of the socialised health service to post-war society and of Labour's role in its creation.

Nonetheless New Labour sought to present itself not simply as Old Labour rebranded but as a modernising political party. So while at pains to stress the historic principles of the NHS, it also began to accept that certain Conservative reforms and initiatives would remain. This acceptance took various forms: for example, the Blair governments continued the emphasis of their predecessors on the front-line role for primary care. They built on the 1997 NHS (Primary Care) Act by creating Primary Care Groups (later Trusts). These had a number of functions – including, in England, purchasing healthcare – but also moved towards a long-standing goal of NHS reformers, greater integration of the service and the breaking down of barriers between health and social care. Ultimately, therefore, Primary Care Trusts were to embrace not only GPs but also, from April 2003, social workers.

Rather more contentious was the acceptance of PFI, a means of bringing the private sector into areas such as hospital building. This was something that New Labour, as late as autumn 1996, had explicitly rejected. The conversion to PFI was largely determined by the decision to adhere to Conservative public spending plans, which consequently raised serious questions about how the NHS could indeed be rebuilt. To further contextualise this, during the John Major administration, health spending had grown, but at a historically low rate (Toynbee and Walker, 2001, p 72). As Timmins (2001, p 554) puts it, "if anything proved New Labour's new credentials the PFI did". Although services such as hospitals would still, in the last resort, be funded by public money, "the idea that Labour would allow them to be financed and run by the private sector would have been unthinkable even five years before". It is worth noting the scepticism of many commentators over the efficacy of PFI in a health service context. Paton (2002, p 137), for example, quite correctly describes it as "at heart a macroeconomically imposed constraint rather than an opportunity".

In the longer term, while Labour had attacked the internal market and indeed technically abolished it (although this was in fact rather more ambiguous than it at first appeared: as always, the devil was in the detail), nonetheless evidence of productivity gains appeared to suggest that these Conservative reforms had had some impact. Consequently, in 2002 the government, as Glennerster (2003, p 75) puts it, "proposed what was, essentially, a return to a modified form of internal market" whereby, from 2003-04, "all providers will be contracted to achieve a minimum volume of elective cases necessary to meet government waiting time targets". Failure to meet targets would result in a loss of income. Successful hospitals, on the other hand, would be accorded foundation status that allows for a certain degree of financial freedom of operation.

Building and expanding upon these brief observations, we can now make five points.

1. New Labour undoubtedly has seen health as an important electoral issue, both in 1997 and 2001, and one that Labour, given its strong association with the founding of the NHS, can exploit to its political benefit. There has been a rush of policy documents since 1997. North (2001) remarks that, in the first years of office, the government's "record in relation to health has been impressive, if only in terms of its productivity" (p 135) and that its health agenda is "ambitious, perhaps unrealistically so, and signifies a rethink of the state's role" (p 138). Paton (2002, p 141) marks his "report card" as "well-intentioned", with the government "trying hard against a difficult background of political economy". Unlike North, however, he sees health policy as "too defensive", despite large electoral majorities in 1997 and 2001. What unites these two commentators (and others) is the sense that New Labour is genuinely trying to do its best in difficult circumstances.

2. New Labour is indeed in some way committed to the NHS and, as it repeatedly claims, to providing the best in healthcare for the most part free at the point of delivery. Nonetheless, it has from the outset been pragmatic (see Chapter Four for a brief comment on this approach) as to how improvement and reform are to be achieved. As in other areas of political life, New Labour has no problems with the private sector – in England it has even, and famously, reached a concordat with private medicine – and is prepared to use it to further broader health policy goals. The then Health Service Minister Alan Milburn made it clear in January 2002, for instance, that private-sector finance was a significant part of his plans for the future and at the same time attacked the service for its outdated structures and ethos (Webster, 2002, p 229). There was to be a shift away from the so-called command and control version of NHS governance, so-called because this was a caricature of how the NHS, at least in England, had worked (see, for his acerbic comment, Webster, 2002, p 258). This was especially ironic given that health policy goals were, as in other areas of social welfare such as education, to have centrally determined rewards and punishments attached to them through the setting of targets and efficiency savings.

3. This was in turn part of a broader agenda of modernising and reforming the public sector through, not least, an attack on the forces of "conservatism". These include, as far as Blair is concerned, doctors and the rest of the "health establishment" (Toynbee and Walker, 2001, p 76). New Labour is thus both the defender of the historic principles of the NHS and an advocate of

reform and modernisation. Add to this a perceived need to inject a measure of stability into the service in 1997 after the upheavals of the earlier part of the decade – upheavals that had done little for staff morale – and it is apparent that New Labour's health policy is, to say the least, complex and potentially beset by internal contradictions. This is highlighted by the issue of foundation hospitals, the very idea of which immediately begs the question whether there can under such a system be equity of treatment and patient experience throughout the country. The response that the government is seeking to universalise the best is little more than a rhetorical flourish.

4. New Labour's adherence to Conservative spending plans was not a good start in government as far as the NHS was concerned. As Webster (2002, p 210) puts it, Labour went into the 1997 General Election with "the meanest spending package ever presented to the UK electorate since World War II". This was hardly consistent with rebuilding, renewing, or saving the NHS and there was a clear gap between rhetoric and public perceptions. In turn, this led to a dramatic shift in policy signalled by Blair, and then Brown, in 2000 – the relaunching of Labour's health policy. Famously, the fundamental move came when Blair agreed on television that spending had been tight in the NHS up to that point and that he was now proposing to bring it up to the EU average within five years. While the EU side of this commitment was at least for the time being quietly dropped, 2000 did see significant movement in health policy, most notably in Brown's Budget. As the Chancellor himself put it:

> In the years from now until 2004, NHS spending will grow by 6.1 per cent a year over and above inflation, by far the largest sustained increase in NHS funding in any period in its fifty-year history.

Put another way, when compared with 1999 by 2004 half as much again would be spent per household on health (Rawnsley, 2001, pp 339-40). In the same year *The NHS Plan* – described by Webster (2002, p 237) as a "further hasty compilation" – outlined what was expected in return for this investment, essentially hitting targets. The issue of matching European health funding re-emerged in 2002, when Blair, as one newspaper put it, "set off in pursuit of a new Holy Grail". The European average was 8.6% of GDP whereas that of the UK was 6.8%. Revealingly, however, Scottish spending was running at a much higher level, in fact around the European average. Put another way, in England and Wales per capita expenditure on health was £740, whereas in Scotland it was £904[7].

5. Finally, new funding, especially after the self-imposed limits of the early part of the Blair administration, was important not only for the NHS itself but also for New Labour's 2001 electoral prospects. As Paton (2002, p 138) points out, at the time of the General Election, the government's health plans were large and complex, revolving around the acknowledgement that

reforming the NHS was now a long-term project; hence the National Plan announced by Blair in spring 2000. Targets continued to be an integral part of achieving this 10-year programme and were to move towards, for example, the reduction of health inequalities and the number of deaths from illnesses, such as heart disease, where Britain has a poor record (Toynbee and Walker, 2001, p 82). There was to be greater integration in healthcare provision, a conscious counter to the Conservative notion of the internal market. And, as Webster (2002, p 236) puts it, there was also to be a "programme of major structural reform ... designed to shift the balance of power towards the front line staff most in touch with the needs of communities and individual patients" – another version of devolution. This was encapsulated in the title of the 2001 Department of Health document, *Shifting the balance of power within the NHS*. There is again the strong sense here of rebuilding and renewing the health services after the depredations of the Conservative era.

Whether or not New Labour's longer-term plans are achievable is another question. Paton (2002, pp 141-2), as noted, sees New Labour's health policy as both "well-intentioned" and "defensive", particularly in the face of unproven right-wing ideas; too closely involved with the private sector; and potentially struggling in an "international environment of low taxes". Webster (2002, p 252) agrees that the Blair government is committed to the NHS and higher spending on it, but is clearly sceptical about the attainment of European standards. Modernisation, he continues, is having, at best, mixed results and the "erratic course followed by the government is not calculated to inspire confidence". The direction of the relationship between the NHS and the private sector remains unclear and overall he sees a "real risk that the transformations now taking place ... will fail to yield the promised rewards and also constitute a more expensive way of providing the same inferior service". Against this background of Blairite ambition and scepticism on the part of some analysts, how has the NHS's sister service, NHSScotland, developed in recent years?

## Devolution and health policy

New Labour's victory in 1997 had an immediate impact on the Scottish health service. The minister responsible stated that some £10 million was to be saved by cutting down bureaucracy and six new PFI projects were announced, most notably the new Royal Infirmary in Edinburgh (Turner, 1998, p 68). Early in its lifetime, White Papers were published on the future of the health services of Scotland, England and Wales by the incoming government. Each stressed, for example, the need for cooperation rather than the competition of the internal market (although, as we have already noted, the purchaser/provider split was retained) and accountability. Here was a third way in health policy between the competitiveness of the Conservative era and the command and control model that supposedly preceded it. The overall strategy was to be evolutionary rather than revolutionary. This was, therefore, a rebuttal of the upheavals of the

1980s and 1990s on the one hand, while, on the other, an acceptance of some elements of Conservative reform (North, 2001, pp 129-30, 138; Webster, 2002, p 57).

The general tenor of each country's White Paper thus had a common underlying philosophy and commitment to the NHS as an institution as well as the recognition that change and reform were needed. Nonetheless, commentators have pointed to differences of style and policy. Sullivan (2002, p 60), for example, notes that, while the preamble to the English document focused on "modernisation", that for Scotland (and Wales) laid emphasis on restoration, yet another variant of rebuilding. The intention was thus to "restore the National Health Service as a public service working co-operatively for patients". He also points to what he sees as a more participative model of public involvement in the Scottish NHS. Turner (1998, p 69) observes an "implied ... more radical shift away" from Conservative philosophy, most notably in that general practitioners in Scotland, where fund holding was not nearly as widespread as in England, would have no powers to commission hospital care.

Woods (2002, pp 31-2) also picks up on this point, noting that, while all the White Papers announced an end to GP fund holding, a key element of the Conservative's 1989 reforms, nonetheless "very different approaches to its replacement emerged in Scotland from those in England". In the latter, the holding of secondary care budgets was "essentially extended to all GPs by the creation of Primary Care Groups" with, as we saw earlier, responsibilities for commissioning healthcare. These were eventually to transform themselves into Primary Care Trusts. In Scotland, Primary Care Trusts did not have this commissioning function, which remained with Health Boards. Woods contends that this "divergence in organisational structures based on the common idea of partnership" was more than just a "tartanisation" of Whitehall policy. Rather, it was an expression of policy differences among Labour ministers. To regard them as merely pragmatic or localised, he continues, "would fail to recognise deeper antagonism in Scotland to the Conservative's policies" and, something noted repeatedly in this volume, Scotland's devotion to communitarian values.

More could be said here about various differences that emerged after 1997, but more importantly we need to acknowledge the following broad points. First, differences pre-dating 1997 were clearly acknowledged and in some respects expanded upon with the advent of New Labour in the Westminster Parliament (that is, prior to the formation of the Scottish Parliament). These were in part a continuance of long-standing historical differences but were also an instance of Scotland's greater commitment to the public sector and a public-sector ethos. Second, health policy was to be the single largest power – in terms of staff (over 135,000) and budget – to be devolved to Edinburgh and expectations of what that body could achieve were to be high. In a survey carried out in 1997, in the wake of the referendum, some 65% of respondents thought that the NHS would be a lot/a little better with the advent of a Scottish Parliament (the respective figures for the economy and for education were 64% and 70%), at the very least a cautious optimism (McEwen, 2003, p 66).

Third, Jervis and Plowden (2001, p 4), commenting on post-devolution health policy and "policy villages", see the latter as characterised by "tight political and professional networks". There is thus the potential "for quicker and easier agreement over policy and strategy", while "health gain policies" could be realised more speedily because of Scotland's smaller size – in terms of population – and the relative ease of working across department boundaries. More generally, this also fits in with Scottish traditions of governance. This situation is reinforced by a political and social environment with widespread popular support for state provision of welfare services. So, for instance, we saw in Chapter Two that polling in 2002 revealed more Scots prepared to countenance tax increases to improve the health services than elsewhere in Great Britain.

Fourth, as Woods (2002, p 28) points out, given the weight of health policy in the responsibilities of devolved administrations the very success of devolution itself may be intimately tied up with this policy field. In turn, making a success of health policy is "commonly understood to require distinctive policies" geared to each constituent part of the UK. There is thus, given all these circumstances, considerable potential for Scotland continuing to pursue a different policy path from England and for the gap between the two countries' systems to widen further. What, then, has the Executive actually done?

## The Executive's health strategy

The first important development came with the relaunching of New Labour's health policy in 2000. We noted above that 2000 saw the injection of new monies by Blair and Brown, part of a longer-term plan to modernise the NHS and bring levels of spending up to EU levels. Like England, Scotland had its long-term plan – *Our national health: A plan for action* – announced some six months after its English counterpart. The timing of the Scottish plan emphasised, as one report put it, "Holyrood's ability to do things differently and at its own pace". The manner of announcement was also highlighted, the Scottish launch being a "more prosaic affair" than July's "joyous New Labour extravaganza" in England[8]. The plan itself appears to have been broadly welcomed by healthcare professionals. There was evidence of a "strong consensus" that "historical, cultural and epidemiological circumstances" meant that there should be "a specifically Scottish solution to Scottish health needs and problems". Alluding to cultural difference, for example, the chair of the Scottish council of the Royal College of General Practitioners claimed a "stronger feeling for the NHS in Scotland, both by the general public and by health professionals", with both "totally committed" to the institution and its principles[9]. These comments can be put in the context, observed earlier, of the limited penetration of GP fund holding in Scotland; the medical profession's more immediate acceptance of the NHS;

the much smaller market for private healthcare; and of the much repeated claim for Scottish solutions to Scottish problems.

The plan itself was, as the Health Minister put it in a now familiar expression, designed to "rebuild" the health service through the "biggest health improvement drive ever seen". Targets were being introduced: for example, by 2003 nobody would have to wait more than nine months for hospital care, with access to primary care within 48 hours. Others included halving, by 2010, deaths from heart disease among the under-75s and reducing by 20% the pregnancy rates for 13- to 15-year-olds. Unified Health Boards were to be introduced, thereby replacing trusts and health authorities, the aim being to cut bureaucracy and to improve local participation and accountability. There was to be no particular role for private hospitals. All this was aimed, according to the First Minister, at addressing Scottish needs even more systematically than previously. He was, he continued, "determined we will use our powers and resources to make a real difference"[10]. As a point of comparison, the Welsh plan announced shortly after was seen as a "further step away from Westminster control with the announcement of a radical NHS reforms package". This included the retention of community health councils (to be abolished in England), free prescriptions and dental checks to all aged under 25, and the bringing of "NHS strategic planning under direct control of the Welsh assembly"[11]. Also on Wales, Davies (2003, p 1) points to the scepticism of the ruling Labour Party on private finance initiatives in health.

A few months later, Scottish Labour's manifesto for the 2001 General Election reiterated that education remained the party's top priority, but nonetheless devoted considerable attention to health. The Scottish NHS that New Labour inherited in 1997 was "divided and fragmented, and staff were demoralised". Thanks, however, to Labour administrations in both London and Edinburgh, the health budget was to grow to £6.7 billion by 2003-04; a recruitment drive was to be launched for nurses and midwives; and initiatives were to be put in place to check growing health inequalities. Capital investment too was to grow, with an extended role for a "reformed" PFI. The latter, it was made clear, should not "be delivered at the expense of the pay and conditions of the staff employed in these schemes". On the other hand, the internal market had been abolished. In a measure aimed specifically at both Scotland's poor dental health record and the need to improve child health, free toothbrushes and toothpaste were to be provided for babies and toddlers in deprived areas: the target here was 60% of five-year-olds free from dental disease by 2010. Overall, the emphasis was on "rebuilding a National Health Service" to make it "once again the envy of the world" (Scottish Labour Party, 2001, pp 19-21).

Picking up on one particular aspect of what NHSScotland was to become, the Executive document, *Patient focus and public involvement* (Scottish Executive, 2001b), emphasised that the implementation of the National Plan required a "culture change". In a "modern healthcare service" it was "no longer good enough to simply do things to people". Such a service had to "do things with the people it serves" (p 2). This was to manifest itself not simply in the behaviour and attitude of staff – important as these were – but also in a clear and adequate flow of information to users and in public involvement with health service processes. Public involvement, previously seen as a "low priority", should now become a "day to day reality" and would act as a "catalyst for change" (p 10). As such, it would help achieve a major improvement in people's health while reinforcing public confidence in the NHS. A budget of £14 million over the next three years was to be set aside to achieve these aims. In a sideswipe at John Major's Conservative administration, it was remarked that the "UK-wide Patient's Charter was launched in 1991, and unsurprisingly no longer reflects the current position within NHSScotland" (Scottish Executive, 2001b, p 8, and passim).

Also picking up on these themes, and with a distinctly Scottish emphasis, was Labour's health and community care policy document produced in the run-up to the 2003 elections. This noted, for instance, the Executive's decision to utilise the findings of the Arbuthnott Review in respect of resource allocation within Scotland. The review sought to make the process "fairer" and to allocate "according to need", although as we shall see later in this chapter, this was not necessarily a view taken in Glasgow in summer 2003. There is an irony, too, in that the way in which funding is allocated to Scotland in the first place is not through a needs-based formula. In its own way, however, Arbuthnott is an interesting example of policy divergence and policy transfer in that the Welsh Assembly went down a different road while a later English review partially acknowledged its findings (Glennerster, 2003, p 66).

The policy document also noted the opportunity afforded by the creation of the Scottish Parliament for a "renewed stimulus and an improved vehicle for the delivery of health services designed to meet the specific needs of the people of Scotland" and how the national plan expressed that vision. Attention was drawn to the "particular priority" of health improvement; the various programmes associated with schools, some of which we encountered in Chapter Four and which once again highlight the Executive's organic approach to welfare; and the "bold, radical and distinctively Scottish step" of ring-fencing Scotland's share of tobacco tax to "support our biggest ever drive to improve the health of the nation and to close the health gap between rich and poor". As part of Labour's "comprehensive approach", smoking, alcohol consumption and diet were to be tackled. An important aspect of this was to further develop the four 'National Health Demonstration Projects', located in Glasgow, Lothian, Paisley, and the North East, which had the role of "national test beds for action". These would provide the model for the nation as a whole in health improvement by focusing on teenage sexual health, child health, coronary heart disease, and cancer.

Other key strategic aims were to raise the profile of public health while at the primary care level the importance of Local Health Care Cooperatives (LHCCs) was stressed. These cooperatives had been introduced in spring 1999 as groups of primary care providers brought together to encourage "effective teamwork" and hence more integrated, and cost-effective, primary care services.

These bodies too were central to a "vision of a local health service" attuned to patient needs and working in partnership with hospitals, social services and the voluntary sector. Overall, the aims were to provide "genuinely seamless health and social care services" focused on the needs of patients and their families and to tackle the "root causes of ill health and so bring about real improvements in the health and well-being of the Scottish people". Underpinning all this were the principles of "partnership, investment and reform"[12].

These aims were further articulated in the White Paper of early 2003, *Partnership for care*. As the very title suggests, this placed considerable stress on cooperative – and, by extension, integrated – healthcare. So, for example, the Executive's "model of a modern health service" emphasised "partnership, integration and redesign". One of the principal ends here was to do away with the fragmentation caused by the market, which had characterised much of the 1990s, and to "bridge the gap between primary care and secondary care and between health and social care" (Scottish Executive, 2003g, p 5). As the Health Minister put it in this document's foreword, such divisions were one of the "historic problems" of the health service. This was undoubtedly the case since, most notably, the tripartite division of healthcare services introduced in the late 1940s has, in various guises, continued to bedevil efficient healthcare provision.

The underlying approach to administration was a rejection of the "command and control management approach". Instead, power was to be devolved where possible to frontline staff while public participation was to be a key feature of the service of the future. So, for instance, at primary care level LHCCs had made "good progress in developing into responsive and inclusive organisations" (p 35) but this had to be further extended. It was intended, therefore, that these would develop into Community Health Partnerships (CHPs), among whose tasks would be ensuring professional and public involvement in primary care delivery, working closely with local authorities, and acting as a focal point for service integration. Nonetheless, since national standards were being set (to be monitored by NHS Quality Improvement Scotland), the Executive would, if necessary, intervene to ensure their achievement (and thereby give powers to ministers already available to their London counterparts). As we saw in Chapter Four of this book, this was a strategy the Executive was also prepared to adopt in education. Targets were to be backed by 'National Guarantees': if, for any patient, a guarantee was not met, they would have the right to treatment elsewhere, including in the private sector, the Golden Jubilee National Hospital at Clydebank, or, exceptionally, elsewhere in Europe.

To ensure clarity of purpose, each year NHSScotland was to focus on a maximum of 12 priorities. The achievement of targets, important as it was, was nonetheless not to be achieved through a "culture of blame" but rather through a "culture of improvement". The latter would recognise a "central new role for patients and staff" with whom the Executive was determined "to work in a renewed spirit of partnership" (p 63) – the repeated stress on a consensual approach is worth comparing with the approach to education encountered in Chapter Four of this book. Reform would also be encouraged by the merger of the Health Education Board for Scotland and the Public Health Institute of Scotland into one body, NHS Health Scotland. The document significantly commented upon the strong relationship between poverty and health inequality, Scotland's improving but still poor health record, and the need to focus on high-risk groups. Other prominent characteristics of the White Paper were its reference to health issues in related policy areas – for example, the National Priorities in Education – and the almost total absence of any mention of the private sector (Scottish Executive, 2003g, pp 8, 5, 35, 15, 65, 9).

Introducing the White Paper, the Health Minister stressed the Executive's commitment to improving the Scottish NHS, notably through an increase in expenditure over the lifetime of the 2003 Parliament, from £6.7 billion to £9.3 billion, an annual increase of 5.5% in real terms. He once again emphasised integration, decentralisation and partnership. The Executive's strategy had already been successful, he claimed, in bringing down waiting times and these were now to be subject to a specific guarantee, initially for heart disease but by the end of 2003 for all inpatient procedures. An impending health improvement plan would focus on four particular areas: very young children (another example of early intervention), teenagers, people at their workplace, and local communities. The proposed reforms were, he concluded, "comprehensive but pragmatic"[13]. Note again the very New Labour appeal to pragmatism.

The White Paper was backed up by the honestly entitled Executive publication, *Improving health in Scotland: The challenge* (Scottish Executive, 2003f). This stated bluntly, and as we have seen correctly, that Scotland faced "a tougher challenge to improve health than most other countries in the Western world" (p 3). The document's aim was to provide a framework for health improvement down to 2004, when the second phase of the programme would start. Health improvement was a "cross-cutting" (p 5) concern that would inform all aspects of Executive policy and action. The New Community Schools initiative was again cited as evidence of this organic social policy approach. In the broader context, the document, in a passage cited at the beginning of this chapter, commented upon the economic dimensions of Scottish health, especially given an ageing population. It was also recognised that health improvement required change "by both society and individuals"; that "strong cultural influences" on health had to be confronted; and that poverty was "a central feature of the problem" (Scottish Executive, 2003f, p 7). The mention of poverty is especially significant, if only because of its usual absence in New Labour (but not necessarily Scottish Executive) rhetoric.

## Health policy after the 2003 elections

We noted in Chapter One that health was a contentious issue in the 2003 elections. In their aftermath, the re-elected governing coalition's partnership statement stressed the continuance of a "radical agenda". This included specific targets and guarantees; for example, waiting times for inpatients were to be a maximum of nine months from the end of 2003, reduced to six months by the end of 2005; 18 weeks for coronary heart disease patients from 2004; and a maximum of 26 weeks for all outpatient appointments by the end of 2005. Cultural issues, such as excessive alcohol consumption, were to be tackled and as part of an investment in health promotion "we will systematically introduce free eye and dental checks for all before 2007" (a policy brought to the coalition by the Liberal Democrats). Executive support would be given to a Glasgow Centre for Population Health – an assault on the Glasgow effect – and there would be an end to postcode prescribing. The workforce would be enhanced, for example, by an increased programme to recruit, train and retain nurses, adding 12,000 by 2007. Once again, the private sector was notably absent in this section of the document[14]. Elaborating on these proposals, First Minister McConnell announced at the end of May the intention to introduce an NHS Reform Bill. This would, inter alia, "provide the final step needed to ensure that our health service delivers quality to all of its patients". Ministers would be empowered to intervene "as a last resort, to secure quality of care". These were new powers that McConnell hoped would never be needed, but would nonetheless be used without hesitation "in the interest of patient care". Concluding, he stated that the Executive would "match investment with reform. Not for its own sake. But to rebuild the health service of Scotland, to drive down waiting times, increase choice and drive up standards"[15].

The Bill was duly published in summer 2003. Defending the proposal for powers of ministerial intervention, the Health Minister repeated the Executive's aim of decentralising power, the main thrust of the Bill, and denied any inherent contradiction on this issue. The increased role for CHPs – NHS Boards were now required to see to the establishment of these where necessary – was cited as a specific instance of this commitment. As the minister put it, this would enhance the role of CHPs in service planning and delivery as well as their decision-making powers. This in turn would empower frontline staff and local communities, and give a voice to primary care in health policy formation. Stress was also placed on the proposals to slim down administrative structures and end the internal market through the final abolition of NHS Trusts, and the creation of unified NHS Boards. The latter would be required to cooperate in regional planning around issues such as specialist services. For *The Guardian*, with this Bill, "Scotland goes its own way on NHS reforms". As this report put it, as devolution became an established fact "the bill … places more clear blue water between the health services north and south of the border – by what it leaves out as well as what it contains". In particular, it was clear that foundation hospitals had no place in the Executive's plans[16].

Foundation hospitals were a controversial issue in 2003. One of the paradoxes of devolution was highlighted when Scottish Labour MPs, at the behest of a Minister of Health himself Scottish and representing a Scottish constituency, twice voted at Westminster in favour of introducing foundation hospitals in

England under the provisions of the Health and Social Care (Community Health and Standards) Bill. As one Labour opponent of government policy put it, Scottish MPs had "voted to bring in an element of privatisation into the English health service and they're not having it themselves". At the second vote, the majority of English Labour MPs voted against the government, which was thus saved by its Scottish supporters[17]. Nonetheless, the Executive's position remains clear. As a spokesperson put it, as the first Westminster vote was about to take place, Scotland was not going down the foundation hospitals route. They did not fit in with the Executive's "vision of creating a more integrated NHS" wherein the barriers between primary and secondary care had been broken down[18]. What we see here is both policy divergence and the much-repeated commitment to service integration.

Here we pause to make some preliminary observations on the Executive's health policy and actions. First, it implies a considerable financial investment. The proposals for universal, free eye and teeth checks, for example, were costed at a minimum of £37 million per annum. Nonetheless, the Finance Minister reiterated the Executive's support in September 2003 despite doubts cast on its efficacy, with professional bodies suggesting a more efficient use of resources through targeting. It was also pointed out that the Welsh Assembly had considered such a policy – again at the suggestion of the Liberal Democrats – but had rejected it in favour of a more focused approach[19]. The Executive's underspend of £500 million pounds has been dedicated to the recruitment of more public sector workers, including nurses[20]. However, on the broader finance front, the leader of the British Medical Association (BMA) in Scotland raised what is one of the historic questions in Scottish health policy: what have been the outcomes of high levels of expenditure? Calling for an independent investigation, Dr John Garner remarked that in 2001 the profession had welcomed newly increased funding, but, he added, "we have all been sadly disappointed; things have not changed". Dr Garner also claimed that although health policy fell within Holyrood's remit, "Westminster made things difficult if a decision was made that would have repercussions in England"[21].

Second, Dr Garner, in another article, elaborated on the last point by citing the case of negotiations over consultants' remuneration. This was a complex affair, but for our purposes the central point was his assertion that Executive officials constantly referred difficult decisions to London. Another BMA official also raised the matter of cultural difference by suggesting that part of the problem was that, in England, doctors carried out "private work, which is a much bigger issue in the south". We therefore find here, on the one hand, questions about the Executive's ability to pursue, in the last resort, a fully independent course of action; and, on the other, a reaffirmation of cultural difference. In his article, Dr Garner raised a further issue about devolution's impact on the Scottish NHS. He acknowledged that, since 1999, health policy had changed to accommodate both the demands of the health service itself and the needs of the Scottish people. However, it was impossible to ignore developments in other parts of the UK. So, for example, the creation of foundation hospitals in

England might have the effect not only of creating a two-tier system in that country, but might also attract, through the ability of such hospitals to vary pay and conditions, Scottish staff[22]. We can compare this with concerns encountered in the previous chapter of this book over the impact on Scottish university staffing of changes to English universities.

Third, the Executive has made clear its determination to encourage and implement a broadly based approach to healthcare. Responding to a report that obesity was costing the Scottish NHS as much as smoking, a spokesperson pointed out that this was precisely why bad diet and inactivity were under increased attack[23]. On Tayside, health officials put forward plans "to break the cycle of deprivation, disease and high death rates in the poorest areas of the region", initially by carrying out a survey of the population as to which issues they believed affected their health. Again, the juxtaposition of health and social problems is notable here[24]. Such an approach is clearly very positive.

## Problems?

Nonetheless, there have been areas of contention as well as problems and setbacks. It was revealed in summer 2003, for example, that while some waiting list targets had been met in some parts of the country, overall there had been a rise in the number of patients on waiting lists and in waiting times. Indeed, the situation had worsened since devolution, to the outrage of opposition parties and the Executive's embarrassment. An especially problematic area was Glasgow, with managers at NHS Greater Glasgow now being required to report monthly, "to show whether they will meet the nine-month waiting time target by the end of the year". Glasgow patients in particular faced the possibility of being treated at other NHS hospitals, either in Scotland itself or in England, or privately. All this took place in the context of record levels of health service expenditure. As yet another Scottish BMA official put it, it was significant that, "despite increased investment in waiting list initiatives and the purchase of the Jubilee Hospital in Clydebank, we are still on an uphill struggle to bring down waiting times for patients over the past year. We continue to have a problem with capacity in the NHS"[25].

The Glasgow effect had other dimensions. In early summer 2003, NHS Greater Glasgow was told it would receive some £11 million pounds less than anticipated from the Executive to fund new services. This was as a result of the Arbuthnott formula, which, although it took into account the city's poverty, had nonetheless led to a fall in income because of declining population. Glasgow's situation was further exacerbated by unanticipated extra demands on, in particular, the wages bill. Services facing a squeeze included mental health, child and maternal health, acute and primary care, and community services – rather a lot, in other words. A patients' representative remarked that it was "only right staff get a decent wage but patients expected new money would fund much-needed services". "Glasgow", he continued, "is a special case and needs a lot more money spent on it to really improve health provision"[26].

Later that summer, further budgetary problems were revealed. Dr Jean Turner MSP, who as we saw in Chapter One had successfully campaigned on a health service platform at the 2003 elections, dismissed claims that these problems would not impact on frontline services. People were, she commented, "already lying on trolleys in hospitals waiting for beds because there is apparently no more money for frontline services, so I fail to see how this latest shortfall will not impact further"[27]. Taken together with Glasgow's place as the UK's sickest city, we can see the magnitude of the problem facing its health authorities.

In other areas, too, there was at best a mixed message. While committed to tackling lifestyle issues, the Executive nonetheless backed away from proposals for a total ban on tobacco smoking in bars and restaurants[28]. This should be put in the context of the findings reported at the beginning of this chapter. In May 2003, a report by NHS Quality Improvement Scotland found that there was a uniform failure across the country to satisfy fully the criteria "aimed at providing patients with the safest and most effective treatment" – something of an indictment, although it should also be observed that the bodies under investigation were primarily the soon to be abolished NHS Trusts[29]. From the front line itself, the Royal College of Nursing Scotland highlighted problems in the Executive's attempts to integrate health and social care. The profession was, as one spokesperson stressed, "committed to ensuring patients receive seamless community care services" and such integration was, as another put it, part of the "extensive and radical changes" proposed by the Executive. However, bringing together workers from the health service and the local authority services meant that "you are dealing with two different cultures who speak different languages". The situation was, moreover, exacerbated by shortages of both nurses and, especially, social workers, with the result that in certain cases existing nursing staff were being used to cover social work tasks[30].

## A Scottish path?

The problems experienced by the Executive are shared, to a greater or lesser degree, by many healthcare systems, including England's. The demand for resources is potentially infinite; health inequalities between different parts of the country are hardly unique to Scotland; changing cultures of work and of personal behaviour is notoriously problematic; and integrating health and social care was never going to be easy. To put it another way, the Executive was unlikely to rebuild the Scottish NHS overnight (as in the rest of the UK a long-term plan seems appropriate), while it is undeniably the case that in crucial areas, such as waiting lists and the postcode lottery in drugs provision, severe problems remain. Again, as elsewhere, questions are being asked about the outcomes of increased investment. However, in the Scottish case, this has a particular edge given, over a long historical period, levels of expenditure significantly higher than, especially, those of England. It is in this broad context that we now turn to the issue of health policy divergence.

Shortly after the 2003 elections, *The Scotsman* remarked that the "gulf between the English and the Scottish arms of the NHS is set to grow". In an attempt to find out whether devolution had been a "force for good or bad" in health policy, a range of expert opinion had been solicited. This came largely, although not exclusively, from those in the field of cancer care, a major Scottish health concern. A health economist suggested that although both Scotland and England were run by Labour administrations, there were significant cultural differences between their health services. The Scottish ethos was "about collaboration", whereas in England it was "about competition". So, in the latter, people were sacked for not achieving targets; in the former they were not. "I sense", the health economist suggested, "that there is more of a drive to get things done in England". Picking up on Scotland's medical and public service traditions and the policy village effect, another respondent suggested that devolution had reinforced a common sense of purpose and of community and that government could be approached "directly and easily". Others found the Executive more attuned to the public and to its frontline health service workers than its UK counterpart; and, as one put it, there was "less aggro between managers and clinicians than there is in England". On the other hand, concerns were raised about funding and the need to avoid working in isolation from British and international research[31]. How do these perceptions fit a broader view of the Scottish NHS since devolution?

One extremely important distinction, and one that cannot be emphasised enough, between England and Scotland lies in an area already encountered: foundation hospitals. The Executive has been at pains to reject these, an approach often justified on the grounds of their inappropriateness to Scottish geography and population distribution. There is more to it than this, however, in that the thinking behind foundation hospitals – achieving a certain score, being able to act in a quasi-autonomous way from the rest of the health sector, not least in financial matters, and the implicit perpetuation of market mechanisms by another name – simply goes against a sense of a distinctive, and historically rooted, Scottish public-sector ethos. Indeed, the Executive has been lukewarm about almost any private-sector involvement in the actual administration and delivery of healthcare (as with education, private-sector involvement in construction projects is fairly widespread – although see the discussion later in this chapter). Again, this might be contrasted with the announcement by the UK government in autumn 2003 that, for the first time, private firms – some from outside the UK – were to run 24 NHS diagnostic and treatment centres[32].

Various commentators have elaborated upon such issues. An important early report came from Jervis and Plowden in summer 2001. They first asserted that the "core values and principles" underlying the NHS in England, Scotland and Wales were unlikely to be changed by devolution (although whether this remains the case in 2004 is another matter). Nonetheless, there was "scope for considerable variation in terms of policy, organisation and management" (p 4), and while little had immediately changed, in the 15 months preceding the report the pace of divergence had increased. A key example was the respective longer-term plans emanating from the White Papers of 2000 and 2001, which displayed "considerable differences of emphasis and priority". The plan for England was "widely perceived by clinicians, managers and politicians" to be concerned with "the administration of the NHS in England". In Scotland and Wales, by contrast, planning was aimed at improving health status. "It may be", the authors suggested, "that 'joined up' approaches to health are beginning to emerge faster in the smaller administrations" (p 11).

Jervis and Plowden also noted the rejection of a concordat with the private sector in Scotland and Wales; how these two smaller nations looked to each other's example, rather than that of England, for policy initiatives; and the more open and transparent Scottish and Welsh mode of governance. In summing up, they remarked upon, inter alia, the more rapid progress in Scotland and Wales from a "focus on health services to the broader issues of health and its wider determinants"; and the increasingly stark contrast in expenditure levels between, in particular, Scotland and England (thereby raising the possibility of an English backlash; see further Chapter Six of this book). Furthermore, devolution had affected the London government as there had been times when its "freedom of action" had been curtailed as a result of "the wishes of the devolved administrations". By the same token, however, English health proposals could still "influence heavily" perceptions in other parts of the UK. The timing of "English announcements and initiatives" could, therefore, "create constraints for devolved administrations" (Jervis and Plowden, 2001, p 30).

Woods, in an analysis published in 2002, suggested that, three years into devolution, "it appears that the forces of continuity – inherited policy, party political allegiance, the Barnett formula, a UK identity for the NHS, and a rapidly expanding health budget – remain dominant for all that some differences have emerged" (p 55). He also commented on the significance of the NHS for a shared sense of identity throughout the UK; and on the way in which the level of funding for the Scottish health service is controlled, in effect, by the Treasury. Like Jervis and Plowden, he further observed that in the early stages the devolved administrations had, through inheriting "partially implemented policy" and immediate health service problems, "little time and space left over for policy innovation" (p 36).

Nonetheless, Woods also points out that, over time, differences in health policy between the UK's various constituents began to emerge, his own qualifications notwithstanding. Again like Jervis and Plowden, he comments on the greater emphasis on a broad definition of health in the pronouncements of the Scottish and Welsh governments. There, ministers are "prominent in their support of public health initiatives" with debates at Holyrood, for example, on Scotland's poor health record "reflecting deep-seated anxieties about poverty and its impact on health" (p 47). He also raises the possibility that divergence in health policy "has its explanation in the innovation of English ministers" (p 49), an issue to which we return later in this chapter. Looking to the future, and in so doing raising some key questions about the direction of social welfare throughout the UK, he sees it as "entirely possible that parties with common origins and similar names in each country will develop distinctive identities and policies, less beholden to the UK leadership"( p 50). Woods also suggests that, in due course, one outcome of devolution will be that it will be "increasingly necessary to speak of the UK's national health services rather than of its NHS" (p 55). As he rightly points out, this might be seen as almost inevitable while also raising the question of the point at which diversity becomes "reinterpreted as inequality" (p 28).

Commenting on Woods' analysis, Sullivan (2002, p 65) argues that difference and divergence might be at least in part attributable to different versions of what constituted "the political philosophy of Labour" within England, Scotland and Wales. The different ends of the spectrum here were the collectivism of Wales on the one hand and the consumer orientation of Blairism on the other, with Scotland somewhere in the middle. This last comment is particularly interesting in the light of a slightly later analysis by Woods (2003, p 6), wherein he claims that, while expanding the role of the private and independent sectors in delivering publicly funded health services has become "a central tenet of Labour NHS policy in England", this has "not been replicated in Scotland". As such, it is a "prominent example of policy divergence".

Finally, Greer (2003) too has important points to make about policy divergence. He argues, first, that in organisational terms the Executive has sought to rebuild "the unitary NHS with strong planning and service integration", and that this is a "planning-oriented model" for the most part dominated by professionals and staff. This is a very different approach from that adopted in England, where "market-based service organisation and private participation" (p 198) dominate. On the other hand, of course, it is clearly in accord with the Scottish tradition of governance. Second, Greer suggests that Scotland has, to a lesser extent than Wales but to a greater extent than England, adopted a "new public health" strategy. This seeks to improve health and well-being by addressing socioeconomic conditions rather than focusing exclusively on medical treatment. As he quite rightly points out, advocates of the new public health face opposition from Scotland's well-entrenched and influential clinical elites. Nonetheless, it also has historical roots in a country that has "traditionally been stronger and more interventionist in public health" (p 205). Here we might quote a Scottish Labour policy document claiming that for "too long under the Tories, public health was sidelined within the NHS and within health policy. Labour is changing that". Targeted investment and the creation of the Public Health Institute for Scotland were given as examples of this change[33].

Third, Greer too points to different attitudes to the private-sector. Put at its most simple, the argument here is between advocates of "new public administration" who see public services as being supplied via contracts rather than necessarily directly (for example, through PFI); and, on the other, advocates of a "single NHS". Once again, Greer perceives a contrast between Scotland and England. The latter is the "most important site for PFI and its advocates", and the only part of the UK where the government "appears to see private sector involvement as an end, rather than a means". In Scotland, the government "pursues PFI for less ideological reasons, and it shows". As evidence of the rejection of widespread private-sector involvement, Greer cites the Executive's purchase of the former private hospital facility at Clydebank (now the Golden Jubilee Hospital). This not only increased NHS capacity but also "expressed a clear policy choice" (pp 208-10) since the Executive could, had it wanted to, simply come to a contractual arrangement with this institution.

Concluding, Greer finds "surprising policy divergence and even greater divergence in ... values" since devolution, for example in the contrast between the English emphasis on consumers and the Scottish emphasis on patients. He thus predicts that the health systems of the constituent parts of the UK "will look very different in a few years" and, like Woods, remarks that it is England that is the "likely diverger". This is because "England is the only country trying explicitly to reinvent its health services, and is certainly the only one that might reinvent the NHS out of existence". Greer suggests, rather gloomily but with due cause, that this "alone might strike people in Northern Ireland, Scotland and Wales as a reason for devolution" (Greer, 2003, p 213).

## Policy divergence and the integration of health and social care: the elderly

We return to a brief consideration of these points in the conclusion to this chapter and, in broader terms, in Chapter Six. In this section, we focus on care for the elderly, an area of both policy divergence and of an attempt to integrate social and health care.

Historically, Scotland tended to employ health resources more on institutional care, and less on community services. The elderly, for example, were more likely to end up in institutions than their English counterparts, and these institutions were much less likely to be found in the private sector (Taylor, 1998, pp 73, 74). Like many western societies, Scotland is also experiencing an ageing population, a situation exacerbated in this particular case by a low birth rate and population decline. This has profound labour market and welfare implications. An Executive enquiry of 2001, for instance, claimed that people over 65 years constituted some 15% of the population, and that this would rise by 2031 to 24%. Older people, it continued, "appropriately, are major users of health and social services", and in recent years their use of hospital emergency care in particular had substantially increased (Wood and Bain, 2001, p 5). Despite such investigations, some commentators argue that much more research needs to be done before an informed Scottish debate can take place on the implications of an ageing society (Wright, 2002, p 16).

Notwithstanding this last point, in early 2002 the Community Care and Health Act (Scotland) was passed. The Act brought in free personal and nursing care for the elderly, described by one set of analysts as "one of the most distinctive as well as one of the most controversial policies" introduced since devolution (Curtice and Petch, 2003, p 30). It is also clearly seen as a major achievement by the Executive. Introducing the May 2003 legislative programme, First

Minister McConnell suggested that "the first four years of our Parliament has been characterised by the improvements we delivered for our older citizens". The "burden of financial worry" had been removed from more than 75,000 pensioners "so that they will get the care and support they deserve". The Executive's commitment was reiterated in the coalition's post-election partnership statement[34]. However, the introduction of free nursing and personal care was, as a campaigning group for the elderly has pointed out, "a complex affair" (Age Concern Scotland, 2003, p 6). The intention here is not fully to describe or unravel all these complexities (for a good account, on which the following draws, see Simeon, 2003; also Blair, 2002; Age Concern Scotland, 2003; Glennerster, 2003), but rather to focus on key characteristics.

During the 1990s, health policy was, as Blair puts it, "dominated by the NHS and Community Care Act". This was "supposed to create greater partnerships between health and social care, but for many older people and their families it resulted in fragmentation and delay" (Blair, 2002, p 23). People were, furthermore, expected to make as much of their own provision for old age as possible rather than expect state support. The onus was thus on the individual and on families and much media coverage was given to the plight of old people who had to sell off their assets to pay for care. Individual and familial responsibility have not been abandoned by New Labour. With their stress on responsibilities as well as rights, the Blair administrations have continued to press "the need for people to make adequate provision for their old age" (Curtice and Petch, 2003, p 32).

Nonetheless, the incoming New Labour government set up the Sutherland Commission, a Royal Commission on Long-Term Care, which reported in 1999. The Majority Report concluded, in Glennerster's words, that, "on grounds of horizontal equity as well as efficiency", those needing "long-term intensive personal care should be treated in the same way as those needing long-term healthcare regardless of the public agency providing that care". There was in any event no clear boundary between health and social care and no justification for different funding principles. As Lord Sutherland himself later put it to a Scottish Parliament Committee, anyone who contracted an illness, even if this could be attributed to alcohol abuse or the consumption of tobacco, was given free medical treatment. On the other hand, someone with dementia was means-tested. The Commission thus concluded, "the principles that apply to the NHS, tax-funded services, based on need, free at the point of use, should also apply to long-term nursing and personal care". What constituted personal care was considered in some detail and included help with bathing and dressing. The Commission also suggested that the cost of providing such care would be relatively modest (Glennerster, 2003, pp 98-100; Lord Sutherland, quoted in Simeon, 2003, p 218).

The Majority Report's proposals were soon rejected by both London and Edinburgh, with a time-lag of some four months between the announcements of the former and of the latter. Rejection was justified on the grounds of cost. Both administrations thus adhered to the Minority Report, which suggested that the Majority Report had underestimated the required expenditure and that in any case free care would lead to an increase in demand, so in turn disproportionately benefiting middle-class applicants. Benefits such as personal care should thus be targeted, not universal, although the London government also claimed to be making "unprecedented" investment in services for older people (Baldwin, 2002, p 172; Glennerster, 2003, p 100; Simeon, 2003, p 218).

In Scotland, however, the matter did not rest there. In late 2000 (that is, just after the Executive had rejected free personal care), the then First Minister, Henry McLeish, announced a policy reversal. After various further investigations and political manoeuvrings – the junior coalition partner, the Liberal Democrats, threatened a revolt if free personal care was not properly introduced – the Act was passed, with free personal and nursing care being available from July 2002. As McLeish, now no longer First Minister, remarked:

> Politics can be a tough business – but at the end of the day the satisfaction is that devolution is making a difference[35].

Equally importantly, organisations such as Age Concern Scotland mobilised a strong campaign in support of the Majority Report, and their arguments found an echo in other voluntary and professional bodies. As the director of Age Concern Scotland put it in early 2002, free personal and nursing care had been decided upon by Holyrood, was "an historic decision", and so a positive outcome of devolution. And as she also pointed out, the extent of this free care was relatively modest, and was free only at the point of delivery – "those who are old have paid and continue to pay taxes" (Blair, 2002, p 27; Age Concern Scotland, 2003, p 6). An information leaflet delineated what personal care might involve under the broad headings of personal hygiene; continence management; food and diet; problems of immobility; counselling and support; simple treatments; and personal assistance[36].

What themes emerge from this episode, and what do they tell us about social welfare in post-devolution Scotland? As with the process itself, this is a complex question. First, and obviously enough, we find here a clear case of policy divergence, with personal care for the elderly being provided on a universal basis in Scotland, and on a selective basis in England. Both the process itself and the outcome reveal, suggests Bauld (2001, pp 36-7), "a clear example of devolution in practice" and so raise questions of "disparity" with other parts of the UK. And, as Simeon (2003, p 220) puts it, a public perception has arisen that "Scottish pensioners are now better off than their peers in England, Wales and Northern Ireland" – as evidence of this, see the comments of the member of the House of Lords cited in Chapter Two of this book. Looking at the process as a whole, Woods (2002, p 44) remarks that it clearly illustrates "the dilemmas facing health (and other public) policy making in the devolved administrations". It arose from a "UK government enquiry; its proposals fall predominantly within the competence of the devolved administrations, but the resources available to them are the Barnett consequences of policy decisions taken in Whitehall".

Second, the measure was clearly intended to facilitate the integration of health and social care. This has not, however, been straightforward. We noted earlier issues raised by the Royal College of Nursing – as Baldwin (2002, p 176) remarks more broadly, collaboration between healthcare workers and social care workers can be particularly difficult as the former tend to utilise a medical model of clients' needs whereas the latter adhere more to a social model. Age Concern Scotland found that the Executive's policy had been widely welcomed by the elderly and that it had not been inundated by complaints about implementation. Nonetheless, there remained a "lack of clarity" about what actually constituted free personal care, and consequently what services would, and would not, be provided. There was some evidence that local authorities were interpreting central guidance differently and these bodies were also expressing concern about levels of funding. In turn, there was a fear that "in order to limit expenditure the emphasis will move from providing care at home to residential care". This was, Age Concern Scotland (2003, pp 21-2) suggested, "contrary to the ethos of community care and individual choice". If such a move were to transpire, there would be a clear gap between intentions and outcomes.

Third, free personal care has been popular with the Scottish public. As Curtice and Petch (2003, pp 46-7) point out, on "this issue at least devolution has resulted in public policy being more in line with the public's preferences than would otherwise have been the case". However, as their investigations revealed, such a move would have been popular in England as well. At least in this particular case, therefore, divergence is not about differences between popular attitudes in Scotland and England, but rather about how governments view welfare provision and their relationship with their electorates. On policy for the elderly, devolution is thus definitely working in the sense that the Executive is responding positively to public opinion. We can observe here too the policy villages effect in the ability of bodies such as Age Concern Scotland to access influential Executive members with relative ease.

Fourth, overtly political factors came into play. Initially, the Executive adopted the same policy as London. It then, however, undertook a policy reversal, partly because of public pressure but also because of pressure from the other main parties. It is also possible that this reversal owed something to the desire of an incoming First Minister (McLeish) to assert Scottish distinctiveness and to show, in his own words, that devolution was "making a difference". We might also observe in passing that the prediction of Woods noted above – that political parties outside England might go their own way on some issues – applies not only in this instance to Scottish Labour, but also to the Scottish Conservative Party.

Fifth, the UK government was unhappy with Edinburgh's new policy. It was notable that one of the authors of the Minority Report of the Sutherland Committee and Labour peer, Lord Lipsey, launched an attack on the Executive's policy reversal as a "populist wheeze" with detrimental long-term implications (quoted in Blair, 2002, p 25; also Simeon, 2003, p 220). There was, moreover, a very public dispute between the Executive and the Department of Work and Pensions over Attendance Allowances. The former asked for a transfer of funds to cover the cost of these benefits but was refused, so adding to the cost of the implementation of free care. This refusal, purportedly originating with Chancellor Brown, was seized upon by the SNP. A spokesperson claimed that New Labour was determined to stop Scotland "going its own way, even on devolved matters". London's attitude can be seen as a point of constitutional principle, as resistance to a policy with which it fundamentally disagreed, or, most likely, a combination of the two. Implementation was delayed for several months, although the anticipated second U-turn did not materialise[37].

Finally, the whole episode raises fundamental issues about the direction of the Scottish welfare state. In a much-quoted article, Player and Pollock (2001, p 252) argue that, as a result of the London government's stance, long-term care of the elderly in England will "continue to be predicated on publicly unaccountable private provision where shareholders take priority". What this means is that the "neoliberal ideologies of New Labour's 'Third Way' are in full swing and the poor, the old and vulnerable will bear the consequences of this severing of the 1948 social contract". What might this tell us about the situation in Scotland? Simeon suggests that, in going its own way over care for the elderly, Scotland was "expanding the welfare state". Policy variations, she further claims, may reveal "a conflict over the appropriate boundaries of social citizenship, with the devolved administrations defining it more broadly than London". Simeon (2003, pp 231-2) quite rightly points out that "free personal care was defended as the fulfilment of the NHS principle of universal access from cradle to grave, free at the point of delivery. It was not defended in the name of a uniquely Scottish need". This would thus put devolved administrations in the position of defenders of the welfare state against the retrenchment of London.

Curtice and Petch (2003, p 40) comment that the whole issue was "in many respects an argument about the fundamental principles of the welfare state in Britain" – universalism versus selectivity. Blair, meanwhile, detects a "sustained drive … to facilitate distributive social justice for older people in Scotland" (Blair, 2002, p 34). Parry (2002, p 318) argues that this episode, like that of student fees, illustrates the possibility of "conceptual challenges to the Blair/Brown orthodoxy" on means testing and on limiting unnecessary middle-class benefits from the welfare state. All this, of course, should be put in the context of the political manoeuvring that took place and Scottish Labour's initial rejection of the Majority Report. Nonetheless, policy is created in Scotland in different political and social circumstances from those in England. Given also the sense in which England has been seen as a diverger not just on this issue but also in other health policy areas, then the idea of devolved administrations expanding or even defending the welfare state takes on particular significance.

---

## Conclusion

Any discussion of the Scottish health service must always take account of its close familial relationship with other UK health services. Policy debates in Scotland do not take place in isolation from similar debates in England, Wales and Northern Ireland, and the problems faced by each have much in common. Given, moreover, Labour's current dominance in London, Edinburgh and Cardiff, it is unsurprising that all three administrations emphasise public service reform and modernisation. The Scottish Executive is just as prepared to set health service targets as its London counterpart and is prepared to take on powers for ministers to intervene in what are deemed to be failing institutions, notwithstanding equally New Labour rhetoric about devolving powers to the front line. The parallels with the Executive's approach to education are striking.

Even allowing for the health policy autonomy of the devolved administrations, it is also important to bear in mind that funding comes, in essence, from the Treasury. This is thrown into sharp relief by the Executive's current refusal to use its limited tax-raising powers, evidence of public backing for such a move notwithstanding. And, while fully agreeing with Greer's observation on the lesser ideological commitment to PFI in Scotland, the fact remains that it is still used by the Executive to improve health facilities. On the other hand, the nature of Treasury funding does remind us that in very broad terms the NHS in all of its constituent parts of the UK remains, for the present at least, funded by general taxation and by and large free at the point of delivery. And in an even wider context, all governments are faced with issues such as cost and equity as well as the role of cultural and lifestyle factors in shaping individual and collective health outcomes. Nonetheless, just as there are common patterns, so too are there distinctive characteristics of Scottish health policy. These are outlined briefly here, with the underlying basis of such differences being more fully dealt with in Chapter Six.

First, health policy, with education, has been at the heart of devolution. This largely derived from pre-existing and historically rooted relative autonomy. Second, differences from, in particular, England can be explained not just in administrative and legal terms, but also by political and, in the broad sense of the expression, cultural attitudes. These embrace the continuation of a more consensual form of health service governance and distaste for private-sector and market mechanisms. Such differences derive from a more generally pro-public-sector ethos among public and professionals alike, and thereby, most notably, a rejection of foundation hospitals. Third, there is the issue of Scotland's stunningly poor health outcomes. Here, the Executive has been at its most committed in seeing welfare as an organic whole, for instance, in the health functions of New Community Schools; as involving factors such as poverty, deprivation and inequality; and, perhaps most significantly of all, in openly acknowledging the importance of lifestyle issues. Among the biggest problems the Executive thus faces are, at a macro level, the national as well as local impact of the Glasgow effect; and, at the micro level, individual behaviour in areas such as diet. The latter is recognition that while Scotland has spent, and continues to spend, highly on healthcare, this alone will not, if the historical record is anything to go by, improve the country's health record. This is an area where the 'Scottish solutions to Scottish problems' approach is fully merited.

What all this suggests is the actuality of, and further potential for, policy divergence. The most obvious and spectacular example of this came with care for the elderly, but probably more important are areas such as foundation hospitals, public health, and participation and partnership. The approaches here have been shaped partly by historical, partly by cultural, and partly by political considerations – the universalist approach to care for the elderly, evidence for some of distributive social justice, is especially notable. And, as we have remarked, certain commentators see the possibility of a further widening of the gap between Scottish health policy and that of, especially, England. Greer's comments on the distinction between Scotland's aspiration to rebuild "the unitary NHS with strong planning and service integration" compared with England's market – and private participation – based approach is especially striking here. What we now need to do, however, is explore more fully why this should be so, and this forms an important part of our next, and concluding, chapter.

## Notes

[1] www.scottishlabour.org.uk, 11 February 2003, 'First Minister, Jack McConnell: Building a health service for this new century: speech at Ninewells Hospital in Dundee'.

[2] www.scotland.gov.uk/library3/health/ltcare_speech.pdf, 'Statement on Older People',

[3] *The Guardian*, 14 December 2000, 'Plan to "rebuild" NHS in Scotland'.

[4] *The Herald*, 22 August 2003, 'Lowest life expectancy marks Glasgow as sickest city in UK'; www.bbc.co.uk, 22 August 2003, 'Glaswegians "live shorter lives"'; and www.bbc.co.uk, 9 July 2003, 'British men outlive many in Europe'.

[5] *The Scotsman*, 26 September 2003, 'Scotland's health fails to improve in line with rest of UK'.

[6] *The Observer*, 14 March 2004, 'You'll be lucky to live to 60 here. But it's not the third world … it's Glasgow's East End'.

[7] *Scotland on Sunday*, 24 February 2002, 'The big health gamble'.

[8] *The Guardian*, 14 December 2000, 'Diagnosis good for Scottish NHS plan'.

[9] *The Guardian*, 12 December 2000, 'Why Scotland wants its own NHS plan'.

[10] *The Guardian*, 14 December 2000, 'Plan to "rebuild" NHS in Scotland', 'Diagnosis good for Scottish NHS plan', and 'Scotland's NHS plan – the main points'; www.scottishlabour.org.uk/health.html.

[11] *The Guardian*, 2 February 2001, 'Welsh NHS plan to widen access to free prescriptions'.

[12] www.scottishlabour.org.uk/health.html

[13] www.scottishlabour.org.uk, 27 February 2003, 'Health Minister, Malcolm Chisholm: "Partnership for Care"'.

[14] www.scotland.gov.uk/library5/pfbs.pdf

[15] www.scotland.gov.uk, 28 May 2003, 'Parliamentary Statement by the First Minister on the Executive's Programme for 2003-2004'.

[16] *The Scotsman*, 28 June 2003, 'Chisholm defends NHS plan'; *The Guardian*, 27 June 2003, 'Scotland goes its own way on NHS reforms'.

[17] *The Scotsman*, 9 July 2003, 'Fury over "lobby-fodder" Scots MPs'; 20 November 2003, 'Scots save Blair from humiliation'.

[18] *The Scotsman*, 8 July 2003, '"Obsessional" reform fails to improve NHS'.

[19] *The Scotsman*, 23 June 2003, 'Free eye tests "just a waste of resources"'; 17 July, '£37m bill for eye and dental check ups'; www.bbc.co.uk, 11 September 2003, 'Kerr promises free check-ups'.

[20] *The Scotsman*, 1 August 2003, '£500m to boost frontline services'.

[21] *The Scotsman*, 4 July 2003, 'Doctor asks: Where has NHS cash gone?'.

[22] *The Scotsman*, 30 June 2003, 'Medics fear foundation hospitals could produce a two-tier NHS'; 26 June 2003, 'Department of Health "sabotaged" GP (sic) deal'.

[23] www.bbc.co.uk, 11 June 2003, 'Scots obesity bill "tops £170m"'.

[24] *The Scotsman*, 31 July 2003, 'Health chiefs to tackle poverty and death rates'.

[25] *The Herald*, 29 August 2003, 'Record hospital waiting lists'; *The Scotsman*, 29 August 2003, 'Record investment fails to improve NHS waiting times'.

[26] *The Scotsman*, 18 June 2003, 'Cash squeeze forces cuts on health trusts'.

[27] *The Herald*, 20 August 2003, 'Services promise as health board deficit hits £27m'.

[28] *The Scotsman*, 30 August 2003, 'Executive shies away from ban on smoking in restaurants'.

[29] *The Scotsman*, 28 May 2003, 'NHS trusts fail to meet standards'.

[30] *The Scotsman*, 16 August 2003, 'Red tape hitting patient care, say nurses'.

[31] *The Scotsman*, 14 May 2003, 'Cancer care and devolution'.

[32] www.bbc.co.uk, 12 September 2003, 'Firms to run 24 NHS centres'.

[33] www.scottishlabour.org.uk/health.html

[34] www.scotland.gov.uk, 28 May 2003, 'Parliamentary Statement by the First Minister on the Executive's Programme for 2003-2004'; www.scotland.gov.uk/library5/pfbs.pdf.

[35] www.bbc.co.uk, 6 February 2002, 'Free personal care plan gets go-ahead'.

[36] www.scotland.gov.uk/library5/health.fpncl-00.asp

[37] *The Observer*, 14 October 2001, 'London blocks £23m care cash for Scots'; Woods, 2002, p 45; Simeon, 2003, pp 219, 225.

# SIX

# Scottish social welfare after devolution: autonomy and divergence?

## Introduction

In his speech to the Labour Party conference in autumn 2003, First Minister McConnell acknowledged that, "under Tony Blair's leadership", there was now increased investment in public services. Such resources, nonetheless, were to be employed in Scotland to meet the specific needs of the Scottish people. The Executive's "reforming agenda" would thus be different from that pursued elsewhere in the UK. So, for example, McConnell reaffirmed his faith in comprehensive education, although he also asserted that parents demanded and deserved "diversity". Explicitly Scottish policies indicated that "devolution is working", notwithstanding that the administrations in Edinburgh, London and Cardiff shared "values and objectives". Emphasising the need for reform, this was nonetheless "not an end in itself". Rather, it was the means of "improving public services, tackling inequalities, creating choice, saving lives, delivering real opportunities, and supporting growth in the economy"[1]. This statement captures many of the complexities, ambiguities, and even potential contradictions, in Executive welfare strategy. We saw in Chapter Five of this book, for example, that there are at the very least differences of emphasis in healthcare policy between London, Edinburgh, and, for that matter, Cardiff, and this clearly brings in to question notions of shared values and objectives.

In this chapter, we sum up and analyse Scottish social welfare after devolution. We do so by, first, placing Scotland in its UK context. We then identify more obviously Scottish characteristics of the Executive's role and strategy. The next section asks whether, as is often claimed by its supporters, devolution has made a positive difference. Next we move on to what – if anything – is distinctive about the Scottish approach to social welfare; and, if so, how this has come about. In conclusion, we ask who is diverging from what, and what this might mean, now and in the future.

## Scotland in the UK

In this section, we consider five points that remind us of the explicitly UK context within which the Executive operates, although each will, to varying degrees, be subsequently qualified. First, when New Labour enacted devolution it always intended that this would take place within a framework whereby the Westminster Parliament retained sovereignty. This was clearly understood and agreed to by the parties that, since devolution, have formed the governing coalition – there was to be no divorce from the UK. The episode encountered in the previous chapter of this book where the Executive, in pursuing its policy for care for the elderly, ran into problems with the Department of Work and Pensions and the Treasury can, as we noted, be seen as an example of London asserting its constitutional position. It is extremely unlikely that there will be any fundamental change in this constitutional arrangement in the foreseeable future, at least through conscious political choice in London.

Second, Westminster sovereignty most obviously manifests itself in spheres embracing or impacting on welfare policy through the reserving of particular powers to London, notably social security and macro-economic policy. As we noted in Chapter One, the former especially was not in some way historically inevitable; it therefore constituted a policy choice. As to macro-economic policy, there is no possibility that the Treasury, or Chancellor Brown, will devolve any significant powers. These are important constraints on the Executive's actions in the field of welfare and an obstacle to a truly holistic policy approach. We opened Chapter Three, for instance, with an Executive statement that asserted its commitment to tackling child poverty while simultaneously acknowledging that important means of tackling this problem were outside its remit. To put it another way, areas of welfare that are of huge significance to the people of Scotland have indeed been devolved to Edinburgh. Nonetheless, the Executive has little control over the economic context in which these operate and indeed through which they are ultimately paid for; nor over other equally crucial components of the welfare state, including cash benefits.

Third, as McConnell's statement rightly implies, the ultimate source of funding for Scottish welfare resides in London. Incremental change delivered by Barnett derives from negotiations between UK functional departments and the Treasury. The Executive itself is not directly involved in these negotiations (and nor was its predecessor) and thus has no direct bargaining power. As we saw in Chapter Two, it is unlikely that the much-criticised Barnett formula will be changed, at least in the short to medium term. Given the volume of public money that Barnett brings to Scotland when compared in particular with England, it would certainly not be in the immediate political interests of the existing coalition to challenge this historically based arrangement. And while nothing can be ruled out forever, there seems to be no indication that the Executive will deploy its (marginal) tax powers in the near future. This means that at present, and in general terms, the Executive is spending money that it has no part in raising.

Fourth, New Labourism is not a political phenomenon confined to England. Again, as the First Minister's statement amply illustrates, the notions of reform, modernisation, and diversity underpin much Executive rhetoric as does the need, for instance, to create a knowledge economy for a globalised marketplace. And as we saw especially in Chapters Four and Five, Scottish Labour, as the dominant party in the governing coalition, has not been slow to set priorities and targets and to have their attainment measured by performance indicators. Those chapters also revealed that, again in New Labour-ish mode, Scottish Ministers have frequently talked of devolving powers to frontline staff while making it clear that, if the previously noted performance indicators are not reached, direct intervention will follow. Whether the rhetoric commonly employed in both Scotland and England conceals more fundamental political and philosophical differences is another matter (and is discussed later in this chapter). However, in broad terms, it seems unlikely that at least in some way New Labourism has not impacted on Scottish political thought and action. It is also worth bearing in mind that leading members of the UK cabinet are both signed up to the New Labour project and members of the Scottish Labour Party, the same party as McConnell and the majority of his ministers.

Finally, and leading on from the previous point, even in those welfare areas where the Executive does have significant powers, there is certainly a case for what McConnell calls shared "values and objectives" with parallel services elsewhere in the UK. To this we might add administrative structures and delivery. Taking these points together, we find, for instance, that in broad terms an NHS hospital patient in England has much the same service as an NHS hospital patient in Scotland. Both receive care free at the point of delivery, funded out of general taxation collected by the Treasury, and in an institution over which public authorities have complete, or considerable levels of control. Even devolved welfare services, therefore, belong to the same family as those in other parts of the UK, as cousins if not as siblings.

## Welfare autonomy

The preceding points are self-evidently important and cannot be discounted from any analysis of Scottish social welfare after devolution. However, devolution has nonetheless created, or, more accurately, perpetuated, a rather different welfare landscape north of the border.

First, as a contextual point and as the preceding statement suggests, Scotland prior to devolution had relative autonomy in key welfare areas, and indeed had done so since the Union of 1707. While this should not be overstated, there did develop distinctive welfare traditions, practices and philosophies. These were, in turn, important constituents of Scottish self-identity (as was noted in Chapter Four, the role of education was especially significant here). This goes a long way to explaining the hostile reaction of the 1980s and 1990s when the Conservative administrations sought to impose change from London. Such impositions were, to the majority of Scots, alien, insensitive to Scottish traditions, and the work of a party to which they did not owe political allegiance. Moreover, Old Labour – associated with the classic post-war welfare state – was not perceived to have failed in Scotland to the extent it appeared to have done in England, and there was no direct equivalent of the quasi-Thatcherite Middle England so dear to the New Labour heart. So, our earlier point notwithstanding,

New Labour gained less purchase north of the border (and, for that matter, west of Offa's Dyke). Resistance to Conservative welfare reform, defence of the welfare state, and support for devolution became organically intertwined. In broad terms, pre-existing differences have widened since 1999 (we discuss this later in this chapter's section on who is diverging from whom).

Second, it is certainly the case that the Executive has no control over important areas of welfare policy. But it does have control over others (most notably education and health) and indeed social welfare constitutes the bulk of its remit. In a very real sense, devolution is about welfare. As we saw in Chapter Five of this book, it has been quite correctly remarked that, for instance, success in health policy is crucial to the success of devolution itself. This welfare focus is further sharpened by the nature of devolved Scotland's politics. The elections of 1999 and 2003 have both resulted in a centre-left coalition government and a centre-left opposition, both of which operate alongside a plethora of minority parties, often themselves with radical social policy agendas. On the funding issue, the Executive inherited both Barnett and rates of welfare expenditure that were, and long had been, high when compared with, especially, England. The Executive has consistently defended this situation both on account of Scotland's particular problems and her continuing participation in the UK. And while it is true that the Executive spends money it has not itself raised, it does have a degree of discretion over how this money is actually allocated. It thus may be that all this allows for more flexible and creative welfare thinking.

Third, there are important administrative and sociological factors that again mark out Scotland from England, in particular. Part of the devolution arrangements, for instance, was an emphasis on consensual government. This built on a tradition of governance that embraced corporatism, consensualism and centralisation and had adherents across the political spectrum (although as we saw especially in Chapter Four, it also had its critics for whom the words 'cosy' and 'complacent' were more appropriate). A recent instance of this approach, also encountered in Chapter Four, was the settlement with teachers in the wake of the McCrone Inquiry. It is worth recalling too that the Scottish Parliament is unicameral. When taken alongside Scotland's relatively small population – and hence tightly knit political and administrative classes – and the associated policy villages effect, this means that decisions can be taken and implemented quickly, possibly too quickly on occasions. The announcement of the abolition of school league tables without apparently taking into account the implications of the 2002 Freedom of Information Act is one instance of over-zealousness. In passing, this reminds us that both Parliament and Executive are still young bodies whose members have had to learn quickly, and much energy was devoted to this during the first Parliament. So, for example, Labour MSPs with backgrounds in local government, in many areas a virtual Labour monopoly, have had to adapt to coalition with the Liberal Democrats – much is made of their partnership, another instance of a more consensual approach. Policy creation and implementation are potentially much easier for devolved administrations in small countries so creating greater opportunities (albeit not always realised) for the much-vaunted aim of holistic welfare. Equally, the Executive would claim that its policy processes are more accountable, more transparent, and more sensitive to popular opinion. As we saw in the previous chapter, free care for the elderly can be seen in such a light.

Fourth, this last example brings us to actual policy divergence. Most publicity has been attached to student fees and care for the elderly, and the Executive's strategy in these two areas has had an important impact on those concerned, their families, and more broadly on the quest for social inclusion. In late 2003, First Minister McConnell reiterated his opposition to student fees at a time when these were the topic of considerable debate in the London Parliament prior to their introduction in England[2]. Probably even more important in the longer term, however, are Executive attitudes towards issues such as comprehensive education and foundation hospitals. Regarding the former, while there are undoubtedly ambiguities, the point made in Chapter Four remains fundamentally valid: the overwhelming majority of Scottish people experience comprehensive education and want the same for their children. This popular perception is shared by the Executive, the majority of whom, of course, were also educated in the state system. As to foundation hospitals, these have been ruled out as a policy option by the current Executive as categorically as it is possible to do so while in England they continue to be at the heart of the Blair government's NHS policy.

## Has devolution made a difference?

For the Executive, the answer to this question is unequivocally 'yes', with the important rider that it has only just begun. The last point, as we saw in Chapter One, was a central theme in the 2003 elections. Initiatives such as New Community Schools, childcare programmes and policies for the elderly (which include not only free care but also, for example, support for central heating costs) are felt by ministers to be particularly noteworthy. Similarly, if rather more intangibly, the creation of a more socially inclusive Scotland is likewise seen as a positive achievement by Executive members. This is, of course, and again as noted in Chapter One, intrinsic evaluation.

It is also, however, a reasonable enough assessment in its own terms. The Scottish Parliament has only been in existence for a short time and operates under particular constraints. There has been a perceived need to rebuild the public services after a long period of neglect, a neglect that should not be underestimated. The social problems from which Scotland suffers were, moreover, unlikely to evaporate overnight. Given all this, the Executive has done reasonably well since 1999 and its strategy can be deemed a qualified success. To focus for a moment on health, we have seen that levels of expenditure have been, and continue to be, higher than for, especially, England. Similarly, Scotland also has more available hospital beds, more general practitioners per capita, and higher levels of prescribing. Despite all this, the Scottish health record was and is poor.

While the Executive continues to justify high expenditure, partly on historical grounds, it has also (and it is this that is particularly to its credit) realised that money devoted to the hospital and curative services is not of itself enough. Initiatives have therefore been taken to address lifestyle and cultural issues such as diet and excessive alcohol and tobacco consumption. As if to remind us of the need for such an approach, it was revealed in late 2003 that rates of obesity for Scottish children were among the highest in Europe and showing no signs of improvement[3]. There has thus been, as we saw in Chapter Five, a renewed emphasis on public health and preventive measures, broadly defined. Such a strategy also fits in with the declared aim of a more holistic approach to welfare provision as witnessed by, for instance, the health role of the New Community schools. Interestingly, it is also an approach increasingly favoured by many other small units of political organisation throughout the world[4].

On the other hand, it cannot realistically be argued that Executive strategy and policies have been flawless or that all targets have been hit. On some occasions, this has resulted from the sort of unintended consequences that so characterise social welfare history. We saw in Chapter Four, for example, that Scotland's attempt at placing children at the centre of all policies was in effect sharpening the division between services for children and those for adults. An integrated approach to social welfare has also – unsurprisingly given the history of attempts to implement such an approach – proved problematic. Again, in Chapter Four, we observed that the New Community Schools scheme has been criticised for failing to make an impact and in being, at least for some, unclear in its aims. Such criticisms have, however, been recognised by Executive members who respond that more investment, more community planning, and more clearly defined strategic outcomes are required, while reiterating the scheme's central role in promoting social inclusion. Nonetheless, it undeniably has problems.

In more conventionally educational terms, reports in late 2003 showed that almost 50% of 14-year-olds failed the national writing test, thereby reinforcing concerns identified earlier in the year in Higher English results. In fact, the results were both an improvement on previous years while simultaneously struggling to reach declared targets[5]. Around the same time, the Executive revealed that children from state schools were much less likely to go to university than those privately educated – hardly, it must be said, much of a revelation. Given the small size of Scotland's private education sector, the more significant findings showed that there were wide variations among state-educated children according to where they lived. Some 50% of school leavers in East Renfrewshire entered higher education, compared with 20% in neighbouring Glasgow[6]. This again illustrates both the Glasgow effect and, as with the preceding point, the distance the Executive still has to travel to achieve both educational and social inclusion aims.

Returning to health, there are worries about, for instance, waiting lists. Evidence in late 2003 suggested that the situation was deteriorating, not improving, notwithstanding the volume of resources devoted to the Scottish health services. This was disputed by the Executive and pounced upon by its opponents[7]. However, the former's objections should also be viewed alongside an independent report carried out for an Edinburgh think tank that claimed that Scotland was using its health resources inefficiently. Among the consequences of this would be even longer waiting times; and that the privately run diagnostic and treatment centres to be introduced in England (see Chapter Five) would further highlight the Scottish situation when English waiting lists fell. All this took place, moreover, in a health system that spent proportionately 20% more than its southern counterpart[8]. Around the same time, it also transpired that hospitals in the West of Scotland had had to cancel operations and turn away patients because of bed shortages[9]. These are serious concerns given the Executive's commitment to reducing waiting lists and to the health service in general.

An analysis published in late 2003 by the Joseph Rowntree Foundation/ New Policy Institute clearly illustrates the overall mixed message. The report acknowledged that, in Britain as a whole, progress had been made in reducing poverty over the lifetime of New Labour in government. The country was now beginning to move away from the bottom of the European poverty league. On the other hand, when particular indicators were closely examined, it was found that, for example, there still remained concerns about the impact of a low-wage economy on poverty and in the fact that "the best that can be said is that there is no sign whatsoever of health inequalities starting to fall" (Palmer et al, 2003, p 14). Focusing on Scotland, it was more "typical of Britain as a whole than any of the English regions, having uniquely the same proportions of rich and poor as Britain as a whole". Scotland, moreover, was around average on many indicators of poverty and social exclusion "but *much* worse on particular subjects" (p 15; emphasis in the original). Especially, and unsurprisingly given what we have already encountered, the poorest outcomes were in health. The number of premature deaths, particularly among men, was significantly higher than elsewhere in Great Britain. Male premature deaths were 20% worse than the worst English region and 60% worse than the best. Within Scotland, for under-65s the death rate was twice as high in deprived than in non-deprived districts – a further reminder of the point encountered in Chapters Three and Five, Scotland's own health inequalities. Among five-year-olds, dental health was the worst in Britain. All this bears out the validity of Executive initiatives on health, inequality, and personal lifestyle, for instance, that we came across in Chapter Five on children's teeth. On a brighter and more socially inclusive note, school exclusions in Scotland (and in Wales) were significantly lower than in England (see also Palmer et al, 2003, p 21).

As suggested earlier in this chapter, complex and deeply embedded social problems were not going to disappear overnight. Nonetheless, in health especially the situation is at best static, with as yet little real progress having been made. For some critics, this proves not only that the current and preceding governing coalitions have failed, but also that devolution itself has not improved aspects of Scottish society, and may even have made them worse. Once again, however, we need to put this in context.

First, the Executive has made a concerted effort to create the proper means of evaluating and measuring disadvantage, for example through the Indices of Deprivation and the Annual Reports on Social Justice discussed in Chapter Three. This is an attempt to address a problem to which many commentators pointed, the relative inadequacy of Scottish data. If it is agreed that solving problems first requires an understanding of their dimensions, then such initiatives are highly positive.

Second, the preceding analysis from the Joseph Rowntree Foundation/New Policy Institute confirms earlier analyses from the same body encountered in Chapter Three. Put simply, in general terms Scotland is not that different from the rest of, in this case, Great Britain in terms of indicators of poverty and exclusion. But where it is different, and health is again central here, it is spectacularly different. Leaving aside any other considerations, this of itself might be a justification for Scottish solutions to Scottish problems.

Third, ministers have made it clear that tackling Scotland's social problems is a central component of attaining social justice and that this will be a major project for the second Parliament. In particular, the aim is to reach the most deprived 10-15% of the population on whom Executive social policy has as yet had little impact – those, to put it another way, who have not yet been fully embraced by social inclusion. It is not entirely disingenuous to portray any of this as a long-term project. Another lesson from welfare history is that too often short-term fixes are put in place when what is needed to achieve desired outcomes is longer-term planning and implementation. Indeed, given the broad consensus on these issues and the policy villages effect, such a strategy might be more readily realised in a small country like Scotland than in England.

Fourth, we again have to recognise, as we have seen that the Executive itself does, that, because of the reserved powers, tackling poverty and inequality is hardly a matter entirely in its own hands. As we have had cause to mention on a number of occasions, the Treasury retains tight control over the UK economy as a whole and increasingly engages with broader domestic policies. Scotland's historic status as a low-wage economy is a factor that cannot be directly addressed by the Executive. Such constraints, however, might be an argument for further devolution rather than its rejection – hence, for instance, the proposals encountered in Chapter Two for fiscal autonomy.

## A distinctively Scottish approach?

All this leads to a question implicit throughout this volume – is there a distinctively Scottish approach to social welfare? We start on a note of caution. In our discussion of free care for the elderly, we observed that, although this was enacted in Scotland but not in England, nonetheless popular opinion on the subject was much the same in both countries. The difference, therefore, was at the level of government. Unsurprisingly, attitudes to welfare are often highly similar throughout the UK and the welfare state itself is frequently identified as a key component of British identity. As we saw in Chapter One, Prime Minister Blair himself has played on this electorally in Scotland. And as we also saw in the same chapter, commentators such as Paterson have claimed that the continuing attachment of many Scots to Britain can be explained through adherence to British values precisely in areas such as welfare. To all this we should add the points made about the relationship between Scotland and the UK earlier in this chapter.

Nonetheless, Scotland does, at least in some spheres, operate its own welfare system and, more crucially, go its own way. The former certainly could be explained simply in terms of administrative convenience, although when looked at from an historical perspective this is not, ultimately, a plausible argument. And in any event, Scotland's pursuit of its own path is certainly not explicable in such simple terms, and we now need to engage more fully with the underlying reasons as to why this should be so.

We start with the observation that there has been a long-standing resistance to private-sector mechanisms and involvement in key welfare areas. This resistance has come in part from public-sector workers and welfare professionals. Of course, it can be quite reasonably pointed out that such groups have a vested interest in the state sector, although this does not explain why, for example, NHS doctors in Scotland spend much less time on private work than NHS doctors in England. However, the historically rooted belief that the state, rather than the market, should be responsible for welfare provision and delivery is widely shared throughout Scottish society, the point about commonality of attitudes throughout the UK notwithstanding. It manifests itself, for instance, in low levels of participation in private health and education; and in the policy stances on foundation hospitals and comprehensive education. There is an evident scepticism about the appropriateness, and indeed the ability, of the market to resolve Scotland's social problems. To all this we might add the Scottish tradition of governance with, most notably, its stress on most notably consensus. In short, we have a public-sector, collectivist ethos and culture in Scotland that markedly distinguishes it from New Labour aspirations and policies and, perhaps, from the currently dominant value system in England. It is notable here that one recent commentator, analysing differences between Scandinavian and English health policy, has remarked on the much less positive view of the state held in England and the sharper distinction between state and society (Vallgarda, 2001, p 392). This is a point also worth bearing in mind when we discuss, later in this chapter, who is diverging from whom.

Scottish distinctiveness, however, still needs further explanation. A useful place to start is with Lindsay Paterson's contribution to our understanding of Scottish society. In Chapter One, we encountered his contention that pre-devolution Scottish governance was characterised by social democratic unionism; that historically civic republicanism had been an important constituent of Scottish political thought; and that he found a contrast between Blairite individualism and Scottish social democratic communitarism, a phenomenon again with deep historic roots. We might note here in passing that, as we saw in Chapter Five, Woods too uses the term 'communitarianism' when discussing Scottish attitudes to health policy, while Sullivan discerns different ideological emphases in England, Scotland and Wales. In Chapter Three, we similarly came across Paterson's assertion that the new Parliament had the capacity to promote social cohesion and a role to play in articulating a sense of common identity, while in Chapter Four we encountered the argument of Reynolds that historically the non-English parts of the UK had pursued education policies as much concerned with equality of outcomes as with equality of opportunity.

While terms such as communitarian, social democratic and social cohesion are far from unproblematic, Paterson is nonetheless clearly making an important series of observations. His analysis suggests, inter alia, that over a long period there has emerged a particularly Scottish way of looking at the world that variously embraces its relationship with England, its mode of governance, and, crucially, its emphasis on the collectivity as much as the individual. This in turn has shaped attitudes, past and present, towards social welfare. While it would once again be easy to overstate this form of Scottish distinctiveness, by the same token there is strong evidence in Paterson's support.

So, for example, we have seen throughout this volume a repeated emphasis on the need for social inclusion and social justice, a discourse different from that usually utilised by New Labour in England. One small, but perhaps telling, instance of this came with First Minister McConnell's announcement in late 2003 that the failure to produce an identity card would not, in Scotland, disqualify applicants for welfare. Part of the rationale for the introduction of such cards – a UK government-level decision – is precisely to disbar those seen as not entitled to services such as health[10]. Put simply, should this scheme be introduced Scotland will be adopting a more socially inclusive approach than England precisely in the social welfare sphere. Social inclusion, then, is clearly important to the Executive and we have recently noted that its members see a more inclusive Scotland as already in the process of coming into being.

Social justice too has been repeatedly stressed as an Executive aim, and is exemplified by the creation of a designated cabinet post (the title has changed, its fundamental aims have not) and by the publication of reports monitoring progress to this end. While frequently portrayed as being constituted by such imprecise terms as fairness, in fact the often highly explicit nature of this discourse is worth stressing. Associated with the pursuit of social inclusion and social justice is the stated need to tackle poverty and reduce inequality, again a rather different emphasis from south of the border. In Chapter Three, for instance, we encountered an official document asserting the intimate relationship between wealth creation and wealth redistribution. As we have also observed, independent commentators such as the Child Poverty Action Group (CPAG) and Blamey et al have drawn attention to the Executive's more positive engagement, both rhetorically and in its policies, with poverty and inequality. Likewise, Greer's assertion in the last chapter that Scotland was embracing the new public health more enthusiastically than England involves, as we saw, a greater commitment to socioeconomic and cultural as well as medical approaches to ill health.

Community has likewise been emphasised, being clearly meant as an integrative concept on a number of levels, from the Minister for Communities with her role of bringing together and coordinating welfare services and promoting social justice to a broader sense of what Paterson describes as social cohesion. Community in its fullest sense is thus what is achieved through social inclusion and social justice, including the reduction of inequalities. To pick up on Reynolds's point cited earlier in this chapter, throughout devolved Scottish social welfare policy there is a concern, not always clearly articulated but nonetheless present, with equality of outcomes as well as equality of opportunity. We might remind ourselves here of the sort of Scotland First Minister McConnell, in a speech cited in Chapter One, claimed to be seeking to build. A central characteristic of this society was one where "social justice for any one of us only comes through social justice for all". As such, it is in clear and deliberate contrast to the fragmentation and alienation of the unfettered market economy and individualism. The achievement of such a society might prove easier in a country like Scotland if for no other reason than its relatively small population size: it is often remarked that Scandinavian social democracy flourishes in large part because those countries do not contain particularly large numbers of people, and are relatively homogeneous.

Given such a set of aims and underlying beliefs, the claim that devolution can and should make a difference becomes all the more plausible. Such a difference, in the first instance, is to the Scottish people, but it also implies the creation of differences within the UK as a whole. There is thus a strong case for identifying a distinctive set of Scottish attitudes to welfare that derive not simply from political or socioeconomic circumstances but also from deep cultural values and beliefs; and which may be actually realised as a result, in part, of sociological and demographic characteristics as well as of political and social will.

## Who is diverging from whom?

Leading directly on from the preceding points, it is therefore unsurprising that policy divergence has taken place, and seems likely to continue to do so. But who is diverging from whom? In Chapter Five, we found Player and Pollock suggesting that the London government's stance on care for the elderly constituted a breach of the 1948 social contract – the founding ethos, that is, of the British welfare state with its purported emphasis on universalism and social consensus ('purported', since the reality was rather more complicated; see Stewart, 1999). By this account, Scotland must therefore be adhering to this part of the social contract. Over the same episode, we saw Simeon arguing that Scotland's stance could even be construed as expanding the welfare state, fulfilling the original promise of the NHS by universalising care, and, potentially, offering a broader version of social citizenship. Other analysts too pointed to the universalist (and so more inclusive) Scottish approach, a marked contrast with targeting in England. More generally, we also noted, for instance, Greer's sense of divergence over health both in policy and in values – the Scottish stance on foundation hospitals again stands out here. In education, meanwhile, we can see very real differences between Scotland and England over comprehensives and league tables, not to mention student fees.

As we observed in Chapter Five of this book, this raises the rather tricky question of who is diverging from whom. Devolved administrations, of which that in Scotland has the most wide-ranging powers, are following different paths in many of the policy areas that fall within their remit, and will almost certainly continue to do so in the future, although the shadow of Treasury financial control and engagement with welfare issues undoubtedly looms large. However, a perfectly good argument can be made that it is England that is diverging and not the other constituent parts of the UK, at least if we take the so-called classic welfare state as our starting point. To put it another way, a powerful case can be made for bodies such as the Scottish Executive as defenders of the welfare state.

Let us take, for instance, Scottish aspirations for a unitary NHS that is also concerned with socioeconomic and cultural, as well as strictly medical, determinants of health and actively seeks to break down the barriers between health and social care. Add to this a state education system that continues to emphasise equality of opportunity and of outcomes, and approaches to issues such as care for the elderly that stress universal rather than selective benefits. Underpin such concerns and approaches with a cultural, administrative, and political climate and tradition that favour and largely deliver public rather than private provision of welfare. All this is much more attuned to the ethos and aspirations of the post-war welfare state than to what the Conservatives sought to do after 1979 and, even more significantly, to important aspects of New Labour's welfare strategy since 1997. Might it even be the case that Scotland is moving more towards a social democratic welfare regime while England further pursues the Anglo-American model? At least in expenditure terms, this is already the situation, although a brake on a full realisation of such a regime is the current refusal to utilise tax-raising powers for both welfare and redistributive reasons. But, as we have seen, there is at least a sense that utilising tax-raising powers is not entirely off the political agenda, if only in the longer term.

If we accept that a Scottish path is being pursued, a path that might continue to diverge from its English counterpart, what implications does this have for the future? Will social policy divergence lead, in a famous phrase, to the break up of Britain? In the short term this seems improbable, but a number of questions will not go away, and answers will have to be found sooner rather than later. First, to what degree will the current London government be prepared to accept further policy divergence, whether in the first instance generated by itself or by the devolved administrations? If, in the last resort, the Treasury holds the purse strings, when will it decide to call a halt to initiatives such as free personal care for the elderly?

Second, it seems unlikely that the issues of the Barnett formula and higher expenditure levels can be fudged forever, however unlikely abolition or serious amendment might be in the short term. The Joseph Rowntree Foundation/ New Policy Institute study of 2003 cited earlier in this chapter showed what was already widely believed or known: that some English regions are, on certain social indicators, worse off than Scotland. As we saw in Chapter Two, there are political factors that might dampen down overt criticism of current financial arrangements, but equally these may be undermined or qualified by events or further revelations of apparent Scottish advantage. So, for example, an Executive report produced in late 2003 appeared to show that Scotland was being subsidised by England to the tune of some £8 billion. Scotland retained its budget deficit and per capita expenditure on public services was now over £1,000 per year more than in England. In effect, as one newspaper put it, "wealth generated and raised in taxes in the prosperous south is being used in increasing quantities to pay the benefits, health-care costs and education of the Scots"[11]. Resentment at such subsidies and deficits may be further heightened for English Labour MPs by the support of Scottish Labour MPs on policies such as student fees and foundation hospitals at the Westminster Parliament, while the Labour-dominated Scottish Executive follows a consciously different path on these issues.

Third, the previous two points also raise the matter of equity across the UK as a whole. Put simply, why should Scottish pensioners and students, for example, be better off than their southern counterparts? As with all these questions, a perfectly good explanation can be produced on socioeconomic and, indeed, constitutional grounds – it was, after all, precisely in areas such as these that devolved powers were granted to find Scottish solutions to Scottish problems. And, in any event, the case could be argued as a matter of principle rather than privilege. Why should English pensioners and students not receive the same treatment as their Scottish equivalents? However, if New Labour's current welfare agenda continues to be pursued at Westminster, or indeed if in a third term it goes even further down the modernising and reforming (and privatising?) path, again this is an issue that will need to be addressed.

Finally, what will happen when the political complexion of the governments in Edinburgh and/or London changes? At the former, this seems unlikely in the foreseeable future, partly because of the very nature of Scottish politics, partly because of the system created by devolution. It seems equally likely that New Labour will be returned to Westminster for a third time in the forthcoming UK General Election. But once again, this is not a situation destined to last for ever and the implications for Scottish welfare of a right-wing administration in London facing a centre-left administration in Edinburgh are potentially profound, most obviously because at a UK level the Conservative Party has never been much of a fan of either large-scale state welfare or, for that matter, devolution.

In conclusion, then, devolution has raised, and will continue to raise, fundamental questions about the nature and extent of social welfare, not only in Scotland, but also throughout the UK as a whole. More than this, and certainly an unintended consequence of the devolution settlement, welfare issues could quite conceivably become matters of crucial concern, not simply in their own right, but also in shaping the very nature and future of the political entity currently known as the United Kingdom.

## Notes

[1] *The Herald*, 30 September 2003, 'Labour Conference: McConnell promises reforms'.

[2] *The Scotsman*, 2 December 2003, 'First Minister rules out top-up fees'.

[3] *The Scotsman*, 1 December 2003, 'Fat or fit – the stark choice that faces our ever-growing children'.

[4] I owe this point to Dr Pat Day, University of Bath.

[5] *The Scotsman*, 10 December 2003, 'Almost half of 14-year-olds failed national writing tests'.

[6] *The Scotsman*, 11 December 2003, 'State schools losing out on university entrance'.

[7] *The Scotsman*, 28 November 2003, 'Patients have to wait longer'.

[8] *The Scotsman*, 4 November 2003, 'NHS lists growing with poor use of resources'.

[9] www.bbc.co.uk, 12 November 2003, 'NHS winter plans under microscope'; *The Scotsman*, 13 November 2003, 'Bed shortage cancels operations'.

[10] *The Guardian*, 14 November 2003, 'Blunkett's plan for ID cards faces Celtic dilemma'.

[11] *The Scotsman*, 11 December 2003, 'Scotland's subsidy at record levels'.

# References

## Online resources for newspapers, journals and other media

| | |
|---|---|
| BBC | www.bbc.co.uk |
| *The Guardian* and *The Observer* | www.guardian.co.uk |
| *The Herald* | www.theherald.co.uk |
| *The Independent* | www.independent.co.uk |
| *The Scotsman* | www.scotsman.co.uk (links to *Scotland on Sunday*) |
| *Times Education Supplement* | www.tes.co.uk (links to Scottish material) |

## Useful websites

| | |
|---|---|
| Age Concern Scotland | www.ageconcernscotland.org.uk |
| Catalyst Forum | www.catalystforum.org.uk |
| Child Poverty Action Group | www.cpag.org.uk |
| The Constitution Unit (University College, London) | www.ucl.ac.uk/constitution-unit |
| ESRC Devolution and Constitutional Change Programme | www.devolution.ac.uk |
| Hansard | www.parliament.the-stationery-office.co.uk |
| Institute for Public Policy Research | www.ippr.org.uk |
| Joseph Rowntree Foundation | www.jrf.org.uk |
| Public Health Institute of Scotland | www.phis.org.uk |
| Scottish Centre for Research on Social Justice | www.scrsj.ac.uk |
| Scottish Council Foundation | www.scottishpolicynet.org.uk |
| Scottish Executive | www.scotland.gov.uk |
| Scottish Labour Party | www.scottishlabour.org.uk |
| Scottish Parliament | www.scottish.parliament.uk |
| The Treasury | www.hm-treasury.gov.uk |

## Bibliographical references

Age Concern Scotland (2003) *'Free for all?':Age Concern Scotland's report into free personal and nursing care*, Edinburgh: Age Concern Scotland.

Anderson, R. (1999) 'The history of Scottish education, pre-1980', in T.G.K. Bryce and W.M. Humes (eds) *Scottish education*, Edinburgh: Edinburgh University Press, pp 215-24.

Atkinson, R. and Savage, S.P. (2001) 'Introduction: New Labour and "Blairism"', in S.P. Savage and R. Atkinson (eds) *Public policy under Blair*, Basingstoke: Palgrave, pp 3-15.

Bailey, N., Flint, J., Goodlad, R., Shucksmith, M., Fitzpatrick, S. and Pryce, G. (2003) *Measuring deprivation in Scotland: Developing a long-term strategy: Interim report*, Glasgow: Scottish Centre for Social Justice.

Baldwin, M. (2002) 'New Labour and social care: continuity or change?', in M. Powell (ed) *Evaluating New Labour's welfare reforms*, Bristol: The Policy Press, pp 167-88.

Barnett, Lord (2000) 'The Barnett Formula: how a temporary expedient became permanent', *New Economy*, vol 7, no 2, pp 69-71.

Bauld, L. (2001) 'Scotland makes it happen', *Community Care*, 18-24 October, pp 36-7.

Bell, D. and Christie, A. (2001) 'Finance – the Barnett Formula: nobody's child?', in A. Trench (ed) *The state of the nations*, London: Constitution Unit, University College London, pp 135-51.

Bell, D. and Christie, A. (2002) 'A new fiscal settlement for Scotland?', *Scottish Affairs*, no 41, pp 121-40.

Blair, S.E.E. (2002) 'Free personal care for older people: is this Scotland's bid for distributive justice in later life?', *Scottish Affairs*, no 39, pp 19-38.

Blamey, A., Hanlon, P., Judge, K. and Muirie, J. (eds) (2002) *Health inequalities in the new Scotland*, Glasgow: Health Promotion Policy Unit/Public Health Institute of Scotland.

Bloomer, K. (2001) *Learning to change: Scottish education in the early 21st century*, Edinburgh: Scottish Council Foundation.

Bradshaw, J. (2001) 'Child poverty under Labour', in G. Fimister (ed) *An end in sight?: Tackling child poverty in the UK*, London: CPAG, pp 9-27.

Brewer, M., Goodman, A. and Shephard, A. (2003) *How has child poverty changed under the Labour government? An update*, London: Institute for Fiscal Studies, Briefing Note 32.

Bromley, C. and Curtice, J. (2003) 'Devolution: scorecard and prospects', in C. Bromley, J. Curtice, K. Hinds and A. Park (eds) *Devolution – Scottish answers to Scottish questions?*, Edinburgh: Edinburgh University Press, pp 7-29.

Brown, U., Scott, G., Mooney, G. and Duncan, B. (eds) (2002) *Poverty in Scotland 2002: People, places and policies*, London: CPAG/Scottish Poverty Information Unit.

Bruce, A. and Forbes, T. (2001) 'From competition to collaboration in the delivery of health care: implementing change in Scotland', *Scottish Affairs*, no 34, pp 107-24.

Campbell, C., Gillborn, D., Lunt, I., Sammons, P., Vincent, C., Warren, S., Whitty, G. and Robertson, P. (2001) *Developments in inclusive schooling*, Edinburgh: Scottish Executive Education Department.

Clasen, J. (2002) 'Modern social democracy and European welfare state reform', *Social Policy and Society*, vol 1, no 1, pp 67-76.

CPAG (Child Poverty Action Group) Scotland (2002) *Press Release 4th November 2002: Government report card – 'trying hard but must do better'*, Glasgow: CPAG Scotland.

Crawford, F. (2001) 'Social capital – a short discussion paper' (www.phis.org.uk).

Croxford, L. (2002) 'The effects of poverty on early education – findings from the Early Intervention Programme in Scotland', in U. Brown, G. Scott, G. Mooney and B. Duncan (eds) *Poverty in Scotland 2002*, pp 144-50.

Curtice, L. and Petch, A. (2003) 'Does the community care?', in C. Bromley, J. Curtice, K. Hinds and A. Park (eds) *Devolution – Scottish answers to Scottish questions?*, pp 30-48.

Darby, J., Muscatelli, A. and Roy, G. (2002) 'Fiscal federalism and fiscal autonomy: lessons for the UK from other industrialised countries', *Scottish Affairs*, no 41, pp 26-55.

Davies, S. (2003) *Inside the laboratory: The new politics of public services in Wales*, London: Catalyst Forum.

Denver, D. (2003) *Elections and voters in Britain*, Basingstoke: Palgrave.

Digby, A. (1989) *British welfare policy*, London: Faber.

Driver, S. and Martell, L. (2002) *Blair's Britain*, Oxford: Polity Press.

Duprée, M. (2000) 'Towards a history of the NHS in Glasgow and the west of Scotland', in C. Nottingham (ed) *The NHS in Scotland: The legacy of the past and the prospect of the future*, Aldershot: Ashgate, pp 138-49.

Esping-Andersen, G. (1990) *The three worlds of welfare capitalism*, Cambridge: Polity Press.

Esping-Andersen, G. (1999) *Social foundations of postindustrial economies*, Oxford: Oxford University Press.

Esping-Andersen, G., Gallie, D., Hemerijck, A. and Myles, J. (2002) *Why we need a new welfare state*, Oxford: Oxford University Press.

Finlay, R. (1994) 'Scotland in the twentieth century: in defence of oligarchy?', *Scottish Historical Review*, vol 73, pp 103-12.

Finlay, R. (2001) 'Does history matter? Political scientists, Welsh and Scottish devolution', *Twentieth Century British History*, vol 12, no 2, pp 243-50.

Giddens, A. (2000) *The third way and its critics*, Cambridge: Polity Press.

Glennerster, H. (2001) *United Kingdom education 1997-2001*, CASEpaper 50, London: Centre for Analysis of Social Exclusion (CASE), London School of Economics.

Glennerster, H. (2003) *Understanding the finance of welfare: What welfare costs and how to pay for it*, Bristol: The Policy Press.

Goudie, A. (2002) 'GERS and fiscal autonomy', *Scottish Affairs*, no 41, pp 56-85.

Greer, S. (2003) 'Policy divergence: will it change something in Greenock?', in R. Hazell (ed) *The state of the nations 2003: The third year of devolution in the United Kingdom*, London: Constitution Unit, University College London, pp 195-214.

Hanlon, P., Walsh, D. and Whyte, B. (2003) 'The health of Scotland', in K. Woods and D. Carter (eds) *Scotland's health and health services*, London: The Stationery Office, pp 31-61.

Harvie, C. (1998) *No gods and precious few heroes: Twentieth century Scotland* (3rd edn), Edinburgh: Edinburgh University Press.

Harvie, C. (2001) 'Scotland after 1978: from referendum to millennium', in R.A. Houston and W.W.J. Knox (eds) *The new Penguin history of Scotland: From the earliest times to the present day*, London: Penguin, pp 494-531.

Harvie, C. (2002) *Scotland: A short history*, Oxford: Oxford University Press.

Hassan, G. (ed) (1999) *A guide to the Scottish Parliament: The shape of things to come*, Edinburgh: HMSO.

Heald, D. and McLeod, A. (2002a) 'Beyond Barnett? Financing devolution', in J. Adams and P. Robinson (eds) *Devolution in practice: Public policy divergences within the UK*, London: IPPR, pp 147-75.

Heald, D. and McLeod, A. (2002b) 'Fiscal autonomy under devolution: introduction to symposium', *Scottish Affairs*, no 41, pp 5-25.

Hendrick, H. (2003) *Child welfare: Historical dimensions, contemporary debate*, Bristol: The Policy Press.

Hill, M., Murray, K. and Tisdall, K. (1998) 'Children and their families', in J. English (ed) *Social services in Scotland*, Edinburgh: Mercat Press, pp 91-117.

HM Treasury (2002) *Funding the Scottish parliament, national assembly for Wales and Northern Ireland assembly: A statement of funding policy* (3rd edn), London: HMSO.

Holman, B. (1998) *Faith in the poor*, Oxford: Lion.

House of Commons Library (1998) *The Barnett formula*, Research Paper 98/8, London: House of Commons Library.

House of Commons Library (2001) *The Barnett formula*, Research Paper 01/108, London: House of Commons Library.

Houston, R.A. and Knox, W.W.J. (2001) 'Introduction: Scots and their histories', in R.A. Houston and W.W.J. Knox (eds) *The new Penguin history of Scotland: From the earliest times to the present*, London: Penguin, pp xxiii-lviii.

Humes, W. (1999) 'Policy making in Scottish education' in T.G.K. Bryce and W. Humes (eds) *Scottish education*, Edinburgh: Edinburgh University Press, pp 73-82.

Humes, W. and Bryce, T. (1999) 'The future of Scottish education', in T.G.K Bryce and W. Humes (eds) *Scottish education*, Edinburgh: Edinburgh University Press, pp 1005-16.

Hunter, D. and Williamson, P. (1991) 'General management in the NHS: comparisons and contrasts between Scotland and England', *Health Services Management*, vol 87, no 4, pp 166-70.

Hutchison, I.G.C. (2001) *Scottish politics in the twentieth century*, Basingstoke: Palgrave.

Innes, S. (1999) *Children, families and learning: A new agenda for education*, Edinburgh: Scottish Council Foundation.

Jervis, P. and Plowden, W. (2001) *Devolution and health: Second annual report*, London: Constitution Unit, University College London.

Johnson, P. (2001) 'New Labour: a distinctive vision of welfare policy?', in S. White (ed) *New Labour: The progressive future?*, Basingstoke: Palgrave, pp 63-76.

Kearns, A. and Parkes, A. (2003) 'Housing, neighbourhoods and communities', in C. Bromley, J. Curtice, K. Hinds and A. Park (eds) *Devolution – Scottish answers to Scottish questions?*, Edinburgh: Edinburgh University Press, pp 49-74.

Kellas, J.G. (1989) *The Scottish political system* (4th edn), Cambridge: Cambridge University Press.

Kendall, I. and Holloway, D. (2001) 'Education policy', in S.P. Savage and R. Atkinson (eds) *Public policy under Blair*, Basingstoke: Palgrave, pp 154-73.

Kenway, P., Fuller, S., Rahman, M., Street, C. and Palmer, G. (2002) *Monitoring poverty and social exclusion in Scotland*, York: Joseph Rowntree Foundation/ New Policy Institute.

Lee, C.H. (1995) *Scotland and the United Kingdom: The economy and the union in the twentieth century*, Manchester: Manchester University Press.

Levitt, I. (1983) 'Scottish poverty: the historical background', in G. Brown and R. Cook (eds) *Scotland: The real divide*, Edinburgh: Mainstream, pp 66-75.

Lister, R. (2001) 'New Labour: a study in ambiguity from a position of ambivalence', *Critical Social Policy*, vol 21, no 4, pp 425-47.

Littlewood, P. (1998) 'Education', in J. English (ed) *Social services in Scotland* (4th edn), Edinburgh: Mercat Press, pp 141-62.

Lowe, R. (1999) *The welfare state in Britain since 1945* (2nd edn), Basingstoke: Macmillan.

Lynch, P. (2001) *Scottish government and politics: An introduction*, Edinburgh: Edinburgh University Press.

McCormick, J. and Leicester, G. (1998) *Three nations: Social exclusion in Scotland*, Edinburgh: Social Council Foundation.

McCrone, D. (1999) 'Culture, nationalism, and Scottish education: homogeneity and diversity', in T.G.K. Bryce and W. Humes (eds) *Scottish education*, Edinburgh: Edinburgh University Press, pp 235-43.

McCrone, G. (1999) 'Financing Scottish government', in B. Jamieson (ed) *An illustrated guide to the Scottish economy*, London: Duckworth, pp 139-54.

McEwen, N. (2003) 'Is devolution at risk? Examining attitudes towards the Scottish Parliament in the light of the 2003 election', *Scottish Affairs*, no 44, pp 54-73.

McGoldrick, R. (2001) 'Child care provision', in M. Chakrabarti (ed) *Social welfare: Scottish perspective*, Aldershot: Ashgate, pp 86-100.

McLean, I. (2000) 'Getting and spending: can (or should) the Barnett Formula survive?', *New Economy*, vol 7, no 2, pp 76-80.

McTavish, D. (2000) 'The NHS – is Scotland different? A case study of the management of health care in the hospital service in the west of Scotland 1947-1987', *Scottish Medical Journal*, vol 45, pp 155-8.

Meston, M.C., Sellar, W.D.H. and Cooper, Lord (1991) *The Scottish legal tradition*, Edinburgh: Saltire Society/Stair Society.

Midwinter, A. (1999) 'The politics of needs assessment: the Treasury Select Committee and the Barnett formula', *Public Money and Management*, April-June, pp 51-4.

Midwinter, A. (2000) 'The Barnett Formula: why replacing it would be a mistake', *New Economy*, vol 7, no 2, pp 72-5.

Midwinter, A. (2002a) 'Territorial resource allocation in the UK: a rejoinder on needs assessment', *Regional Studies*, vol 36, no 5, pp 563-77.

Midwinter, A. (2002b) 'The limits to fiscal autonomy under the devolution settlement', *Scottish Affairs*, no 41, pp 102-20.

Millar, J. and Ridge, T. (2002) 'Parents, families and New Labour: developing family policy?', in M. Powell (ed) *Evaluating New Labour's welfare reforms*, Bristol: The Policy Press, pp 85-106.

Mitchell, J. and the Scottish Monitoring Team (2001) 'Scotland: maturing devolution', in A. Trench (ed) *The state of the nations 2001*, London: Constitution Unit, University College London, pp 45-76.

Mitchell, J. and the Scottish Monitoring Team (2003) 'Third year, third First Minister', in R. Hazell (ed) *The state of the nations 2003: The third year of devolution in the United Kingdom*, London: Constitution Unit, University College London, pp 119-39.

Mitchell, R. and Dorling, D. (2002) 'Poverty, inequality and social inclusion in the New Scotland', in G. Hassan and C. Warhurst (eds) *Tomorrow's Scotland*, London: Lawrence and Wishart, pp 168-87.

Mooney, G. and Johnstone, C. (2000) 'Scotland divided: poverty, inequality and the Scottish parliament', *Critical Social Policy*, vol 20, no 2, pp 155-82.

Morgan, K. (2001) 'The new territorial politics: rivalry and justice in post-devolution Britain', *Regional Studies*, vol 35, no 4, pp 343-8.

Munn, P. (2000) 'Can schools make Scotland a more inclusive society?', *Scottish Affairs*, no 33, pp 116-31.

Muschamp, Y., Jamieson, I. and Lauder, H. (1999) 'Education, education, education', in M. Powell (ed) *New Labour, new welfare state?*, Bristol: The Policy Press, pp 101-21.

Naidoo, R. and Muschamp, Y. (2002) 'A decent education for all?', in M. Powell (ed) *Evaluating New Labour's welfare reforms*, Bristol: The Policy Press, pp 145-65.

North, N. (2001) 'Health policy', in S.P. Savage and R. Atkinson (eds) *Public policy under Blair*, Basingstoke: Palgrave, pp 123-38.

Nottingham, C. (2000) 'The politics of health in Scotland after devolution', in C. Nottingham (ed) *The NHS in Scotland: The legacy of the past and the prospect of the future*, Aldershot: Ashgate, pp 173-90.

O'Connor, A. (2001) *Poverty knowledge: Social science, social policy, and the poor in twentieth-century US history*, Princeton, NJ: Princeton University Press.

Palmer, G., North, J., Carr, J. and Kenway, P. (2003) *Monitoring poverty and social exclusion 2003*, York: Joseph Rowntree Foundation/New Policy Institute.

Parry, R. (1997) 'The Scottish Parliament and social policy', *Scottish Affairs*, no 20, pp 34-46.

Parry, R. (1998) 'The view from Scotland', in H. Jones and S. MacGregor (eds) *Social issues and party politics*, London: Routledge, pp 194-213.

Parry, R. (2002) 'Delivery structure and policy development in post-devolution Scotland', *Social Policy and Society*, vol 1, no 4, pp 315-24.

Parry, R. (2003) 'Invest and reform: spending review 2002 and its control regime', in C. Bochel, N. Ellison and M. Powell (eds) *Social Policy Review 15*, Bristol: The Policy Press, pp 31-48.

Paterson, L. (1994) *The autonomy of modern Scotland*, Edinburgh: Edinburgh University Press.

Paterson, L. (1997) 'Scottish autonomy and the future of the welfare state', *Scottish Affairs*, no 19, pp 55-73.

Paterson, L. (1998) *Education, democracy and the Scottish parliament*, Glasgow: Scottish Local Government Information Unit.

Paterson, L. (2000a) 'Social inclusion and the Scottish parliament', *Scottish Affairs*, no 30, pp 68-77.

Paterson, L. (2000b) 'Scottish democracy and Scottish utopias: the first year of the Scottish parliament', *Scottish Affairs*, no 33, pp 45-61.

Paterson, L. (2000c) *Education and the Scottish parliament*, Edinburgh: Dunedin Academic Press.

Paterson, L. (2000d) *Crisis in the classroom: The exam debacle and the way forward for Scottish education*, Edinburgh: Mainstream.

Paterson, L. (2002) 'Scottish social democracy and Blairism: difference, diversity and community', in G. Hassan and C. Warhurst (eds) *Tomorrow's Scotland*, London: Lawrence and Wishart, pp 116-29.

Paterson, L. (2003) *Scottish education in the twentieth century*, Edinburgh: Edinburgh University Press.

Paterson, L., Brown, A., Curtice, J., Hinds, K., McCrone, D., Park, A., Sprotson, K. and Sturridge, P. (2001) *New Scotland, new politics?*, Edinburgh: Polygon.

Paton, C. (1999) 'New Labour's health policy: the new healthcare state', in M. Powell (ed) *New Labour, new welfare state?*, Bristol: The Policy Press, pp 51-75.

Paton, C. (2002) 'Cheques and checks: New Labour's record on the NHS', in M. Powell (ed) *Evaluating New Labour's welfare reforms*, Bristol: The Policy Press, pp 127-43.

Peat, J. and Boyle, S. (1999a) 'Scotland in overview', in B. Jamieson (ed) *An illustrated guide to the Scottish economy*, London: Duckworth, pp 8-37.

Peat, J. and Boyle, S. (1999b) 'The regions', in B. Jamieson (ed) *An illustrated guide to the Scottish economy*, London: Duckworth, pp 54-71.

Pickard, W. (1999) 'The history of Scottish education, 1980 to the present day', in T.G.K. Bryce and W. Humes (eds) *Scottish education*, Edinburgh: Edinburgh University Press, pp 225-34.

Pirrie, A. and Lowden, K. (2002) 'What is education for?', *Research in Education*, vol 71, pp 4-5.

Pittock, M. (2001) *Scottish nationality*, Basingstoke: Palgrave.

Player, S. and Pollock, A. (2001) 'Long-term care: from public responsibility to private good', *Critical Social Policy*, vol 21, no 2, pp 231-55.

Powell, M. (2002a) 'Introduction', in M. Powell (ed) *Evaluating New Labour's welfare reforms*, Bristol: The Policy Press, pp 1-17.

Powell, M. (2002b) 'New Labour and social justice', in M. Powell (ed) *Evaluating New Labour's welfare reforms*, Bristol: The Policy Press, pp 19-37.

Powell, M. (2002c) 'Conclusion', in M. Powell (ed) *Evaluating New Labour's welfare reforms*, Bristol: The Policy Press, pp 231-49.

Rawnsley, A. (2001) *Servants of the people: The inside story of New Labour* (rev edn), London: Penguin.

Rees, G. (2002) 'Devolution and the restructuring of post-16 education and training in the UK', in J. Adams and P. Robinson (eds) *Devolution in practice: Public policy divergences within the UK*, London: IPPR, pp 104-14.

Reynolds, D. (2002) 'Developing differently: educational policy in England, Wales, Scotland and Northern Ireland', in J. Adams and P. Robinson (eds) *Devolution in practice: Public policy divergences within the UK*, London: IPPR, pp 93-103.

Sammons, P., Power, S., Robertson, P., Elliot, K., Campbell, C. and Whitty, G. (2002) *National evaluation of the New Community Schools pilot programme in Scotland: Phase 1 (1999-2002): Interim findings and emerging issues for policy and practice*, Edinburgh: Scottish Executive Education Department.

Scott, P. (2000) 'Review: Scottish education', *Scottish Affairs*, no 31, pp 128-32.

*Scottish Affairs* (2002) 'Special issue: fiscal autonomy', no 41.

Scottish Executive (2000a) *A Scotland where everyone matters: Annual report 2000: Summary*, Edinburgh: Scottish Executive.

Scottish Executive (2000b) *Improving our schools: A consultation paper on national priorities for schools education in Scotland*, Edinburgh: Scottish Executive.

Scottish Executive (2001a) *Poverty and social exclusion in rural Scotland: A report by the rural poverty and inclusion working group*, Edinburgh: Scottish Executive.

Scottish Executive (2001b) *Patient focus and public involvement*, Edinburgh: Scottish Executive.

Scottish Executive (2002a) *Social justice: A Scotland where everyone matters: Annual report 2002*, Edinburgh: Scottish Executive.

Scottish Executive (2002b) *National priorities in education newsletter: Issue 1, April 2002*, Edinburgh: Scottish Executive.

Scottish Executive (2002c) *Statistical bulletin: Education series: Examination results in Scottish schools 2000-2002*, Edinburgh: Scottish Executive.

Scottish Executive (2003a) *Government expenditure and revenue in Scotland 2000-2001*, Edinburgh: Scottish Executive.

Scottish Executive (2003b) *Educating for excellence: Choice and opportunity: The Executive's response to the national debate*, Edinburgh: Scottish Executive.

Scottish Executive (2003c) *Factsheet: Education*, Edinburgh: Scottish Executive.

Scottish Executive (2003d) *Education and training in Scotland: National dossier 2003: Summary*, Edinburgh: Scottish Executive.

Scottish Executive (2003e) *Life through learning, learning through life: The lifelong learning strategy for Scotland – Summary*, Edinburgh: Scottish Executive.

Scottish Executive (2003f) *Improving health in Scotland: The challenge*, Edinburgh: Scottish Executive.

Scottish Executive (2003g) *Partnership for care: Scotland's health White Paper*, Edinburgh: Scottish Executive.

Scottish Executive: Central Research Unit (1999) *Experiences of social exclusion in Scotland*, Edinburgh: Scottish Executive.

Scottish Labour Party (2001) *Ambitions for Scotland*, Glasgow: Scottish Labour Party.

Scottish Labour Party (2003) *Four years, forty real achievements*, Glasgow: Scottish Labour Party.

Scottish Parliament Information Centre (2000) *The Barnett formula*, Edinburgh: HMSO.

Scottish Poverty Information Unit (1998) *Poverty data, anti-poverty strategy and Scottish devolution*, Glasgow: Scottish Poverty Information Unit.

SCRSJ (Scottish Centre for Research on Social Justice) (2002) *First annual report: October 2002*, Glasgow: SCRSJ.

SCRSJ (2003) *SCRSJNews*, issue 1.

Shaw, M., Dorling, D., Gordon, D. and Davey Smith, G. (1999) *The widening gap: Health inequalities and policy in Britain,* Bristol: The Policy Press.

Shepard, A. (2003) *Inequality under the Labour Government*, Briefing Note 33, London: Institute for Fiscal Studies.

Simeon, R. (2003) 'Free personal care: policy divergence and social citizenship', in R. Hazell (ed) *The state of the nations 2003: The third year of devolution in the United Kingdom*, London: Constitution Unit, University College London, pp 215-35.

Stewart, J. (1995) 'Children, parents and the state: the Children Act 1908', *Children and Society*, vol 9, no 1, pp 90-9.

Stewart, J. (1999) 'The twentieth century: an overview', in R. Page and R. Silburn (eds) *British social welfare in the twentieth century*, London: Macmillan, pp 15-32.

Stewart, J. (2001) '"The most precious asset of a nation is its children": the Clyde Committee on homeless children in Scotland', *Scottish Economic and Social History*, vol 21, no 1, pp 43-66.

Stewart, J. (2003) 'The National Health Service in Scotland, 1947-1974. Scottish or British?', *Historical Research*, vol 76, no 193, pp 389-410.

Strategy Action Team (1999) *All together: Local action to tackle poverty*, Edinburgh: Scottish Executive.

Sullivan, M. (2002) 'Health policy: differentiation and devolution', in J. Adams and P. Robinson (eds) *Devolution in practice: Public policy divergences within the UK*, London: IPPR, pp 60-6.

Taylor, R. (1998) 'Community care and the personal social services', in J. English (ed) *Social services in Scotland*, Edinburgh: The Mercat Press, pp 72-90.

Timmins, N. (2001) *The five giants: A biography of the welfare state* (rev edn), London: HarperCollins.

Toynbee, P. and Walker, D. (2001) *Did things get better?*, London: Penguin.

Turner, T. (1998) 'Health services', in J. English (ed) *Social services in Scotland*, Edinburgh: Mercat Press, pp 40-71.

Vallgarda, S. (2001) 'Strategies for improving the health of the nations in England, Denmark, Norway and Sweden', *European Journal of Public Health*, vol 11, no 4, pp 386-92.

Wasoff, F. and Hill, M. (2002) 'Family policy in Scotland', *Social Policy and Society*, vol 1, no 3, pp 171-82.

Waterhouse, L. and McGhee, J. (2002) 'Social work in Scotland: after devolution', in M. Payne and S.M. Shardlow (eds) *Social work in the British Isles*, London: Jessica Kingsley, pp 131-55.

Watt, J. (1999) 'Pre-five education', in T.G.K. Bryce and W. Humes (eds) *Scottish Education*, Edinburgh: Edinburgh University Press, pp 307-15.

Webster, C. (2002) *The National Health Service: A political history* (2nd edn), Oxford: Oxford University Press.

Wickham-Jones, M. (2003) 'From reformism to resignation and remedialism? Labour's trajectory through British politics', *Journal of Policy History*, vol 15, no 1, pp 26-45.

Wilkinson, R. (1996) *Unhealthy societies: The afflictions of inequality*, London: Routledge.

Wood, R. and Bain, M. (2001) *The health and well-being of older people in Scotland: Insights from national data: Executive summary*, Edinburgh: Information and Statistics Division, Common Services Agency for NHS Scotland.

Woods, K.J. (2002) 'Health policy and the NHS in the UK 1997-2002', in J. Adams and P. Robinson (eds) *Devolution in practice: Public policy divergences within the UK*, London: IPPR, pp 25-59.

Woods, K.J. (2003) 'Scotland's changing health system', in K.J. Woods and D. Carter (eds) *Scotland's health and health services*, London: The Stationery Office, pp 1-29.

Wright, R.E. (2002) 'Can Scotland afford to grow old?', *Scottish Affairs*, no 39, pp 15-18.

# Index